About the Author

In twenty years of writing about the motion picture and its fabulous personalities, Jack Spears has earned an admirable reputation as a skilled and dedicated film historian. His books and magazine articles on film grew out of a lifelong fascination with movies. His first book, *Hollywood: The Golden Era,* drew rave reviews.

Spears makes his home in Tulsa, Oklahoma, where he is a knowledgeable and experienced medical-society administrator. A former Trustee of the American Association of Medical Society Executives, he has received several awards for public relations and civic activities. Spears was instrumental in promoting Tulsa's new medical school and a mass immunization project that wiped out poliomyelitis in the area.

A graduate of the University of Arkansas, Spears's honors thesis explored the work of young Hollywood directors. He is a collector of old silent films—his special field of expertise—and has a huge library of motion-picture books, periodicals, stills, and memorabilia. Spears believes the study of motion-picture history should be serious and compassionate, evoke memories for older readers, and stimulate an intelligent interest in the cinema in young persons.

Also by JACK SPEARS:

HOLLYWOOD: THE GOLDEN ERA

THE CIVIL WAR
ON THE SCREEN
AND OTHER ESSAYS

"THE BIRTH OF A NATION is like writing history in lightning."
—*Woodrow Wilson*

Jack Spears

South Brunswick and New York: A. S. Barnes and Company
London: Thomas Yoseloff Ltd

A. S. Barnes and Co., Inc.
Cranbury, New Jersey 08512

Thomas Yoseloff Ltd
Magdalen House
136-148 Tooley Street
London SE1 2TT, England

Library of Congress Cataloging in Publication Data

Spears, Jack, 1919-
    The Civil War on the screen, and other essays.

    Filmography: p.
    Bibliography: p.
    CONTENTS: The Civil War on the screen.—Nazimova.
—Edwin S. Porter.—Louis Wolheim.
    1. Moving-pictures—United States—Addresses,
essays, lectures,   I.   Title.
PN1993.5.U6S58   791.43'0973   75-5176
ISBN 0-498-01728-1

PRINTED IN THE UNITED STATES OF AMERICA

Contents

Acknowledgments

SO many people have contributed to the production of this book, in one way or another, that it is impossible to thank all of them. However, I would be amiss if I did not express my gratitude to the following: H. Lyman Broening, Edward Delaney Dunn, George J. Folsey, Charles J. Van Enger, S. E. Hunkin, Lew Ayres, Paul Ivano, the late Arthur C. Miller, Anthony Slide, Geoffrey N. Donaldson, Samuel E. Peeples, Charles Smith, Samuel Gill, the late Henri Diamant-Berger, Don Malkames, Lewis Milestone, Kenneth H. Lawrence, Charles Ford, Walter H. Stainton, and the Cornell University Archives.

The articles on Edwin S. Porter and Louis Wolheim appeared in their original form in *Films In Review*, and I am indebted to Charles Phillips Reilly, editor, for permission to use this material.

Most of all, I wish to thank two fine gentlemen, not only for their personal friendship and encouragement over a period of many years, but also for the significant contribution that each has made to motion picture history—Henry Hart, editor of *Films In Review* from 1950 to 1972, and Robert Florey, film director and scholar of the cinema who has so generously shared his recollections of the golden era of Hollywood.

THE CIVIL WAR
ON THE SCREEN
AND OTHER ESSAYS

1

The Civil War on the Screen

THERE is an old Hollywood axiom that motion pictures about the American Civil War never succeed.

The exceptions that prove the rule are D. W. Griffith's monumental *The Birth of a Nation* (1915), generally conceded to be the most significant film in screen history, and the enormously popular *Gone With the Wind* (1939), a colossal blockbuster that has racked up a near-record domestic gross of $74 million (with no end in sight as it is periodically reissued to abundant box-office returns). Although no reliable figures are available, Griffith's earlier film may have grossed as much as $50 million. A third paradox is Buster Keaton's classic silent comedy, *The General* (1926), frequently included on any list of the ten best motion pictures of all time.

Aside from these three historic films, the theory seems to have validity. By and large, Civil War pictures do not make money and have limited appeal to moviegoers. In one way or another, such pretentious films as *The Red Badge of Courage* (1951) and *Friendly Persuasion* (1956) have failed, although there is much of merit in each. With rare exceptions, the biographical dramas about Abraham Lincoln have met an indifferent audience response. Dozens of other Civil War pictures produced over the past sixty years have sunk into obscurity, many with substantial financial losses. Those that have succeeded best are such

escapist entertainments as John Ford's *The Horse Soldiers* (1959) and the action-filled *Shenandoah* (1965), with James Stewart.

The reasons for the failure of most movies about the Civil War are difficult to establish. The basic elements for success are all present: star-crossed lovers in romantic settings, stirring battles re-created on an epic scale, personal and philosophical conflict, heroism and sacrifice, colorful uniforms and gowns, action, comedy, suspense, and the dramatic final retributions of victory and defeat. Yet, the ingredients seldom jell as they did in *Gone With the Wind,* and the majority of Civil War pictures are artificial and cliché ridden, put together in predictable patterns of mediocrity. They are expensive to produce, requiring elaborate sets and costumes, huge casts, and complex battle sequences difficult to photograph. Seldom do these films communicate any of the enormous power of the most important and tragic period in American history.

The Civil War drama was a staple of motion picture content in the formative years between 1908 and 1917, cresting in *The Birth of a Nation.* Despite the impact of the Griffith masterpiece, it vanished from the screen after the outbreak of World War I, lost in a deluge of topical propaganda films stressing unity in the nation, and then surfaced infrequently during the twenties and thirties. The tremendous success of *Gone With the Wind* in 1939 surprisingly failed to rekindle Hollywood's interest in Civil War themes, although the number of such pictures, never great, grew somewhat after the mid-fifties. Many of these were disguised Westerns with the conflict of Blue and Gray played against the dusty backgrounds of the Great Plains or lawless gun towns.

The Civil War film had its period of greatest popularity in the early silents, soon after the motion picture had made a precarious transition from peepshow to nickelodeon. With many theaters changing bills daily, the demand for films was enormous, and pioneer producers made and remade a handful of basic plots in Civil War settings. The grim struggle of 1861-65 was less than a half-century old, remembered with both nostalgia and bitterness by those who had lived through it. In contrast, the brief Spanish-American War of 1898, perhaps too recent in memory, lacked the charisma of the War Between the States and was not a popular screen subject. Beginning about 1908, studios turned with increasing frequency to patriotic melodramas and crinoline romances of the North and South, mostly one- and two-reelers, to meet the insatiable appetite of the expanding motion-picture industry.

The major companies producing Civil War films in the ten years preceding World War I were Kalem (which made literally dozens), Selig, Universal, Champion, and to a lesser degree Vitagraph and Lubin. Edison and Thanhouser had little interest in this type of picture, and Biograph, dominated by D. W. Griffith, whose heritage was deeply rooted in the Civil War, surprisingly turned out less than a dozen films on the subject. After 1912, the emergence of Thomas H. Ince as an inventive producer led to a spate of Civil War dramas, many featuring the promising Charles Ray, for such Ince companies as the New York Motion Picture Company, Broncho, Bison, and Triangle. Other studios, including the budding Famous Players and Lasky, virtually ignored Civil War vehicles.

EARLY CIVIL WAR-FILM THEMES

One of the most familiar themes of early Civil War films was the conflict within a family—most often a proud Southern family—when a favorite son disgraced himself by enlisting in the enemy forces. Brother is seen fighting brother, a father sits in life-and-death judgment upon a son captured in battle, a sister betrays her brother as a spy, and a bewildered mother is emotionally destroyed by the issues that have separated her family. Inevitably, there was a sweetheart's love sacrificed (at least temporarily) by the hero's painful choice.

In D. W. Griffith's *In Old Kentucky* (1909), Henry B. Walthall angrily stalks out of the family plantation to join the rebels when he can no longer stomach the Northern sympathies of his father (Verner Clarges). Walthall was also a Southerner who remained faithful to the Union in Essanay's *The Sting of Victory* (1916). After the war he returns home, but finds neither his family nor his sweetheart will forgive him for his defection. A Confederate partisan's son in Champion's *The Copperhead* (1911) is disowned when he enlists in the Union Army. In Lubin's *The Battle of Shiloh* (1913), a Tennessee mother tells her son, a United States cavalry officer, that she will never forgive him if he deserts the South, but he returns to his command. Josephine Crowell played a Northern mother who had lost two sons in the war in Majestic's *A Question of Courage* (1914). She forces a third son (Elmer Clifton) to desert the army by threats of suicide. In Thanhouser's *The Flag of His Country* (1910), a Southern wife leaves her husband when he enlists in the federal forces.

Pathé's *In the Days of War* (1913) told of a Union officer (Paul Panzer) who finds himself in a deadly knife fight with his Confederate brother-in-law (Crane Wilbur) on a Civil War battlefield. Both are wounded, but are reconciled in a military hospital as the war ends. In I.M.P.'s (Independent Motion Picture Company, later Universal) *Dixie* (1910), a son promises his mother not to fight for the Confederacy, but after her death he forgets his vow and becomes a war hero. In Bison's *Sundered Ties* (1912), a border-state family divides over secession, and a senseless murder of a beloved son follows. Vitagraph's *The Carpenter, Or the Stranger in Gray* (1913) centered around a mysterious carpenter, symbolic of Christ, who brought peace to a family torn between divided loyalties to the North and the South.

Countless Civil War films pitted brother against

brother. Essanay's *He Fought for the U.S.A.* (1911) was about a Southern boy who joined the Union Army and later saved the life of his Confederate brother in a skirmish. Vitagraph's *A Southern Soldier's Sacrifice* (1911) had a similar theme, except that the young rebel lost his own life for helping his brother escape from a Union prison camp. In Kalem's *The Soldier Brothers of Susanna* (1912), a Northern trooper (Guy Coombs) is faced with the dilemma of exposing both brother and sister as Confederate agents. He turns traitor and allows them to escape with vital

military plans. Selig's shocking *Brother Against Brother* (1909), on the other hand, portrayed the intense hatred of two alienated brothers, one a Unionist and the other a secessionist, who remorselessly try to kill each other in a savage grudge fight and then later on a Civil War battlefield. In Kay-Bee's *The Great Sacrifice* (1913), two brothers fight on opposite sides. After the surrender at Appomattox, the Southern brother returns home to find that his wife, believing him dead, has married the other brother.

Even more dramatic was the situation of a father

Louise Glaum, not yet the vamp who lured men to destruction, was the heroine of *The Boomerang* (1913), a Civil War drama that turned on a tragedy of a young soldier killing his own father.

called upon to condemn a son fighting for the enemy forces. In Reliance's *A Man's Duty* (1912), Wallace Reid was a Union guerrilla brought before his father, a Confederate colonel, who sentences him to death. Fortunately, a reprieve from General Robert E. Lee, obtained by the boy's brother, arrives in time to save him. Champion's *With Sheridan at Murfreesboro* (1911) turned the circumstances around when a Union soldier who had captured his Confederate father permits him to escape. The son is sentenced to be shot as a traitor, but is spared when his father returns to take his place before the firing squad. Kalem's *A Southern Boy of '61*, released in 1911, was about a son who comes faces to face with his father on the battlefield, but cannot bring himself to kill him. In contrast, Broncho's *The Boomerang* (1913) had Charles Ray as a vengeful Union soldier who deliberately shoots down his father, a Southern officer who had deserted the boy and his mother years before. Bison's *Son of a Rebel Chief* (1916) described how a Virginia lad (Marc Fenton) enlists in the Union Army and unknowingly kills his father (William V. Mong) in battle. In Edison's three-reel epic of 1914, *The Southerners*, a Confederate general (Bigelow Cooper) orders heavy artillery trained on Union attackers led by his son (Allen Crolius). The youth survives and is reconciled with his father when peace comes.

Most often the element of conflict in Civil War films was expressed by lovers torn apart by differing loyalties. The hero was frequently a dashing Union officer and the girl a Southern beauty fierce in her pride of the Confederacy. Inevitably, the tide of battle would sweep him back into her arms, and the heroine would find some way of saving his life while remaining loyal to her cause. There were infinite variations of this theme, with love always triumphing over a succession of unbelievable adversities.

Perhaps the best known of such pictures was Metro's *Barbara Frietchie* (1915), in which Mary Miles Minter played a spirited Southern belle who falls in love with a visiting Northerner. He joins the Union Army when war breaks out and returns to her home leading an occupation force. Their love finally overcomes her bitterness, but she is mortally wounded while trying to save him from Confederate raiders, and both die. Based on a John

Anna Q. Nilsson and Mary Miles Minter in a scene from the 1915 version of *Barbara Frietchie*. Miss Minter was only thirteen when she played a spirited Southern belle who fell in love with a Yankee captain.

Greenleaf Whittier poem then known to every schoolchild—"Shoot if you must this old gray head, but spare your country's flag!"—and a popular Broadway play by Clyde Fitch, *Barbara Frietchie* had intense dramatic power, particularly in the scene where Miss Minter angrily rips the Union flag to shreds as Northern soldiers invade her home. Although not her first film, it was the picture that brought the actress, an imitator of Mary Pickford, to public attention. (Her career ended in 1922 when she was linked with the unsolved murder of William Desmond Taylor; Miss Minter could not survive the scandal of being revealed as one of Taylor's paramours.) Guy Coombs was the hero, and a good cast included Anna Q. Nilsson and the distinguished Broadway character actress, Mrs. Thomas W. Whiffen. Herbert Blaché directed.

Several other versions of *Barbara Frietchie* reached the screen under the same title, beginning with Vitagraph's seven-minute adaptation of 1908 and a Champion one-reeler three years later (in which the heroine is merely inspired by Barbara Frietchie's bravery to make a similar sacrifice). In 1924, Thomas H. Ince remade *Barbara Frietchie* with Edmund Lowe and Florence Vidor in the leads. This time a happy ending was substituted in which the despairing lovers survive and are reunited after the war. Slow moving and sac-

William Desmond Taylor and J. Barney Sherry stand before a Confederate firing squad in this scene from Thomas H. Ince's *A True Believer* (1912). Taylor subsequently became a leading director for Mary Pickford and other stars, but he was the victim of a sensational murder case in 1922 that was never solved.

Florence Vidor and Edmund Lowe were the lovers in Thomas H. Ince's *Barbara Frietchie* (1924). Unlike most screen versions of John Greenleaf Whittier's famous poem, it had a happy ending.

charine, it failed where the Minter version had succeeded nine years earlier. Much of the fault lay in the confused direction of Lambert Hillyer, best known for a long series of William S. Hart Westerns.

Sometimes love blinded the heroine to her duty. In Kalem's *Rivals* (1915), Anna Q. Nilsson was a Southern girl who betrays the Confederacy by helping her Yankee sweetheart (Guy Coombs) bring guns and ammunition to the beleaguered Union troops. In Essanay's *Vain Justice* (1915), Lillian Drew was a Virginia belle sent to kill the federal officer (Richard C. Travers) who executed her brother, but instead she falls in love with him and saves his life. Dorothy Gish played a Confed-

erate scullery maid in Majestic's *The Tavern of Tragedy* (1914), directed by Donald Crisp. She is seduced by a Yankee spy (Fred A. Turner), keeps her father from murdering him, steals rebel military plans, and finally escapes to the North with her sweetheart, presumably to live happily ever after.

The eternal triangle set in the chaos of the Civil War was a frequent theme of early films—the heroine who was loved by both a Unionist and a Confederate, with their rivalry often ending tragically on the battlefield. In Vitagraph's *A Rose of the South* (1916), Antonio Moreno was a dashing Southern officer known as "The Flying Colonel." His competitor for the hand of pretty Peggy Hy-

Bessie Eyton and Thomas Santschi were the lovers torn apart by the Civil War whom Abraham Lincoln (Sam D. Drane) brought together in *The Crisis* (1916).

land was a Union Captain (Gordon Gray). Despite a lifelong friendship, the two men kill each other in combat, faithful to the principles that brought them to opposing sides. Herbert Brenon, later the renowned director of *Peter Pan* and *Beau Geste*, both directed and starred in *The Dividing Line*. In this I.M.P. drama of 1910, he portrayed a Confederate soldier who lost his life in saving a Union rival for a beautiful Southern girl. In Champion's *The War and the Widow* (1911), a young widow living between the lines is alternately courted by a Union and than a Confederate officer. Unable to make up her mind between them, she helps each to escape in turn when they are captured by the enemy.

Lubin's *Between Two Fires* (1914) was about a Pennsylvania girl who loved a rebel, a scout for General Lee's invasion forces. Another suitor, a Union officer, shoots him when he comes to visit her one evening. The Southerner loses his memory from the force of the bullet and no longer cares for the girl, whereupon his vengeful rival enlists him in the Union Army! At the Battle of Gettysburg the hero's memory returns when he sees the Confederate flag, and he rejoins his comrades. Because

of his blue uniform, the youth is mistaken for a spy, and General Lee orders him shot. His sweetheart arrives in time to explain everything and to save her lover's life. Few plots were so complex or unbelievable. Broncho's *The Pride of the South* (1913) had a Kentucky girl disinherited when she married her Union sweetheart, while in Vitagraph's *A Dixie Mother* (1910), Norma Talmadge, playing her first important role, was not forgiven by her Southern family for eloping with a Northerner until years after the war.

The rivals for the heroine were not always on opposite sides. In Kay-Bee's *The Favorite Son* (1913), Francis Ford and Charles Ray were two Union brothers who competed for the affections of Grace Cunard. A year later Ray appeared as the black sheep of two Southern brothers who loved the same girl in Broncho's *A Military Judas*. To pay off gambling debts, he sells military secrets to a Yankee spy. The good brother is suspected, but Ray finally exonerates him and commits suicide in disgrace. The rival good-and-bad brothers was a plot device for many other films, including Kalem's *The Rally Round the Flag* (1909), I.M.P.'s *The Brothers' Feud* (1910), Pathé's *The Rival Brothers' Patriotism* (1911), and D. W. Griffith's *The Informer* (1912), in which Henry B. Walthall and Walter Miller were two Confederate brothers in love with Mary Pickford. Allan Dwan's *The Powder Flash of Death* (1913) was more than a triangle—Pauline Bush, the Dixie heroine, had *three* suitors: a Yankee (Wallace Reid), a rebel (Marshall Neilan), and an indecisive fellow (J. D. Kirkland), described by a title as "jes' plain neutral!" Reid got the girl, but not until the war ended. In Bison's *Soldiers Three* (1913), a Southern belle with three suitors promised to marry the one who earned the highest rank in the Confederate Army. Years later she learns her husband got his commission by deceit.

In Lubin's *Fitzhugh's Ride* (1914), Louise Huff was loved by two Confederate swains—one a chivalrous hero, the other an unscrupulous ne'er-do-well. After they go off to war in the same cavalry unit, the worthless boy intercepts the girl's love letters to his rival (Edgar Jones). Thinking her sweetheart has forgotten her when he does not write, the heroine agrees to marry the scalawag suitor while he is home on leave. Jones learns the truth

Norma Talmadge (kneeling), later one of Hollywood's brightest stars, was only thirteen when she played her first important role in Vitagraph's *The Dixie Mother* (1910). Florence Turner was the anguished Southern wife whose plantation was overrun by Yankee soldiers. Note the white actor in blackface playing an old slave.

Charles Ray prepares to commit suicide in *A Military Judas* (1914) after he betrays the South for money to pay gambling debts.

An enemy agent tempts Charles Ray (right), a Confederate lieutenant, to sell military secrets to pay his gambling debts in Ince's *A Military Judas* (1914).

and reaches the church in time, galloping down the aisle to swoop Miss Huff from under the nose of the villain. The make-believe romance of the film led to a real wedding for Edgar Jones and Louise Huff. They were married January 27, 1914 in the same little church in Norristown, Pennsylvania that had been used as a set for the interrupted wedding scene. The Rev. George W. Barnes, who played the role of the parson in the picture, performed the ceremony.

The triangle was occasionally inverted, like in Kalem's *The Romance of a Dixie Belle* (1911), in which two young women, classmates at a girls' school, fall in love with the same Union officer. When the Civil War breaks out, he marries the Northern girl, while the heartbroken Southern lass returns home. Later, the fortunes of war bring him to her plantation. Despite her love for him, she will not betray the Confederacy and forces him at gunpoint to give up the stolen military plans he is carrying to the north. Wallace Reid was a Virginia soldier in Allan Dwan's *Women and War* (1913), who is loved by two sisters. He becomes engaged to the elder. When he is blinded in combat, the boy comes to realize that he really loves the younger sister, who nurses him back to health. *Their One Love*, a Thanhouser tearjerker of 1915, was about two sisters who love the same soldier.

Jean Hathaway receives the advances of an older Southern officer in this scene from Ince's *The Heritage of Eve* (1913).

He is killed at Gettysburg, and his wallet, containing a letter that reveals he loved both sisters equally, is returned to them. They live out their lives together as lonely old maids, each happy in her memories.

Sometimes the Civil War brought an inadvertent family tragedy that separated the lovers even more decisively. In Broncho's *The Sharpshooter* (1913), Charles Ray was the wastrel son of a wealthy Northerner. He is parted from his Dixie sweetheart by the war, and becomes a sharpshooter in the Union Army. In the climactic battle that follows, Ray kills a twelve-year-old Confederate drummer boy who is the brother of his lover. Although she ultimately forgives him, he dies in battle before they can marry. Kalem's *A Wartime Escape* (1911) also concerned a Southern girl alienated from her Northern admirer by conflicting loyalties. He wounds her brother in battle, but carries him to safety, and, after the war, persuades the girl to forgive and forget. Much the same plot was used in Broncho's *The Sinews of War* (1913), when a Union officer (Joseph King) won back his Georgia sweetheart by saving the life of her brother (Charles Ray).

Another popular plot device centered around the Civil War soldier who abandoned his post to return home to see a wife, a sweetheart, an ailing child, or a dying mother. Broncho's *Silent Heroes* (1913), produced under the supervision of Thomas H. Ince, was about a Southern officer (Robert Edeson) who resigned his command on the eve of a great battle to visit his critically ill mother, and is thought a coward. After her death, he vindicates himself by leading his troops in a desperate attack on a Union stronghold. In another Broncho film of 1913, *A Child of War*, a sentry accidentally wounds his own daughter. He deserts his post to take the child to his wife and is subsequently sentenced to death. Mutual's *The Soul of Honor* (1914), directed by James Kirkwood, had a Confederate dispatch rider (Henry B. Walthall) delay important orders to spend a night with his wife (Blanche Sweet). An important battle is lost because of his dereliction. The soldier's father forces his son to commit suicide, and saves the family honor by making it appear the boy had been killed by Northern guerrillas.

In Vitagraph's *Ransomed* (1910), Leo Delaney

The heroine of Thomas H. Ince's *The Sharpshooter* (1913) says good-bye to her brothers, not knowing her Union sweetheart will inadvertently kill the drummer boy. Joseph King is the older Confederate officer.

Another Ince film that revolved around a young drummer boy in the Civil War was *The Drummer of the 8th* (1912).

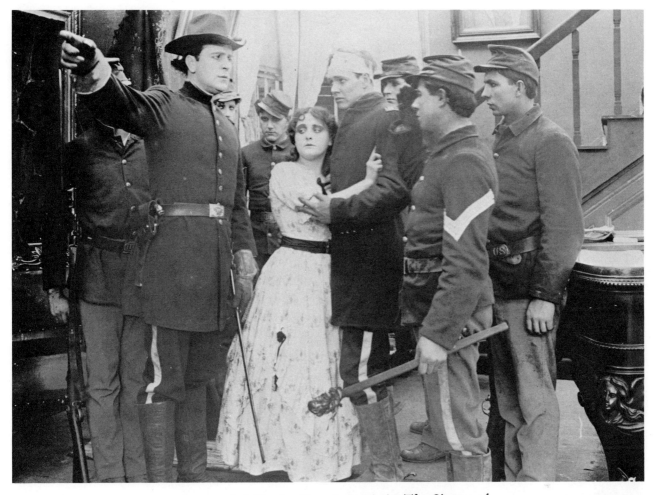

A wounded Charles Ray (center) in *The Sinews of War* (1913) is reluctant to leave the arms of Margaret Bracken. Joseph King is the Union officer.

was a Confederate captain who promised his crippled son (Kenneth Casey) that he would return home to celebrate the boy's fifth birthday. He gets leave, and there is a happy reunion with his wife (Clara Kimball Young) and the lad, but the officer is captured by the Union Army when he tries to rejoin his unit. Delaney is mistaken for a spy and sentenced to death, but is saved by a plea from the little boy, who offers his birthday present—a much-loved toy—to the Northern general as a ransom. *Service Under Johnston and Lee*, produced by Champion in 1911, had a similar theme. General Lee pardons a deserter when he learns the man left his post to search for a lost son. Again, it is the lad who pleads for his father's life.

Cowardice was a recurrent theme of early Civil

War motion pictures. D. W. Griffith's *The Honor of His Family* (1910) was about a Confederate officer (James Kirkwood) who kills his son (Henry B. Walthall) when he discovers him fleeing from the enemy in panic. To save the family from disgrace, he carries the son's body back to the battlefield and places it among the fallen Southern heroes. (In Broncho's *A Wartime Mother's Sacrifice*, it was an anguished mother who took her son's corpse back to the battlefield after he committed suicide in remorse over his cowardly desertion.) In 1911, Griffith did an even more elaborate Civil War drama for Biograph, *The House With Closed Shutters*, on the theme of cowardice concealed by a proud Southern family. Henry B. Walthall was the Confederate agent who deserts

In *The Lost Dispatch* (1911), Joseph King is court-martialed from the Confederate Army.

In *On Secret Service,* a Union officer caught by the Confederates is revealed to be a woman (Anna Little). Richard Stanton (center), later a Fox director, was the hero of this Thomas H. Ince production of 1912.

in fear and returns home drunk. In an unbeliev-able twist to the plot, his sister (Dorothy West) disguises herself as the brother and completes his mission behind the Union lines. She is caught and executed, and is buried under his name. The cra-ven brother is shown twenty-five years later in "the house with closed shutters," where he has been hidden by his family to keep his disgrace secret. The theme of a woman disguised as a heroic soldier was used in numerous films, including Kalem's *The Little Soldier of '64* (1911) and The *Drummer Girl of Vicksburg* (1912), Rex's *The*

Defender of the Name (1912), and Vitagraph's *The Wages of War* (1911).

Kalem's *The Colonel's Son* (1911) was about the weak scion of a Confederate officer who joins the Union Army and is captured in battle. The father sentences him to death, but deceives the boy into thinking the execution is a sham so he will not display cowardice before the firing squad. In Universal's *The Field of Honor* (1917), Allen Holubar, who also directed, was a Confederate officer shot by his own men when he loses his nerve in the face of an enemy charge. Later, he

Another girl in uniform was Dot Farley, shown here with Leo Maloney in Ince's *The Little Turncoat* (1912). In later years, Miss Farley played the plump, bellig-erant mother-in-law in Edgar Kennedy comedies.

commits suicide rather than tell his son of his disgrace. Less grim pictures saw the coward redeem
himself. A rebel soldier in Kalem's *A Spartan
Mother* (1912) flees in terror when the fighting
begins and takes refuge in his home nearby. His
mother gives him a Confederate flag and sends him
back to his unit, where his bravery helps turn the
tide of battle for the South. In Champion's *The
Redemption of a Coward* (1911), a craven soldier
deserts in fear, but regains his courage when he
sees Union troopers mistreating a Southern family.
Ray Myers was a Confederate deserter in Bison's
The Coward's Atonement (1913), who is shamed
by his sweetheart (Ethel Grandin) into returning
to the fighting.

The most important of silent pictures about
cowardice and regeneration in the Civil War was
Thomas H. Ince's *The Coward* (1915). Remembered as the film that made a star of Charles Ray,
it builds upon the psychological factors that moti-
vate a young man to desert from the Confederate
Army. Ray played a sensitive youth whose domineering father (Frank Keenan) forces him to enlist at gunpoint. In a sudden and not altogether
plausible climax, the son becomes a hero when he
steals Union plans and smuggles them through the
enemy lines. He is killed while performing other

Having overheard the Union plans below, Charles
Ray hides on the roof of a house in *The Coward*
(1915).

brave acts, dying in the arms of his self-righteous
father. Although rich in Civil War detail, *The
Coward* is an intensely personal study of a confused
boy who cannot understand the meaning of war.
In one of his famous "soul struggles" that he did
so well, Ray gave a superb performance. It stood
out in sharp contrast to the heavy-handed dra-
matics of Frank Keenan as the father, who seemed
unable to adapt his stage training to the more intimate style of motion-picture acting. The perceptive
direction, erroneously credited to Ince in many
sources, was actually the work of Reginald H.
Barker. (A truncated version of *The Coward*, running about fifteen minutes, was turned out by
Pathé in 1911. Kay-Bee's *Blood Will Tell* of 1912
had an identical story, except that the hero was
inadvertently shot to death by his father as he
arrived at Confederate headquarters with the stolen
plans.)

Perhaps the most unique of early Civil War
films was *A Southern Cinderella* (1913), produced
by Thomas H. Ince, in which the famous fairy
tale was transformed into a charming romance of
the Blue and Gray. In this case, Cinderella was the
daughter of a rich Southern planter who marries a
haughty Yankee widow with an arrogant but mar-
riageable daughter. He goes off to fight in the Civil
War, leaving his daughter to suffer the slights of
her stepmother and stepsister. Cinderella is de-

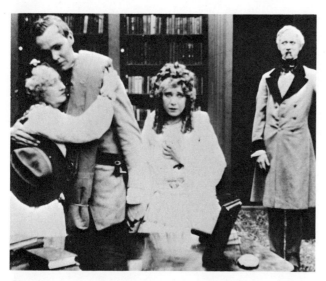

Charles Ray (left) was the sensitive youth in Thomas
H. Ince's *The Coward* (1915) who is forced to fight
in the Civil War by a domineering father, Frank
Keenan (right). Gertrude Claire was the mother, and
Margaret Gibson played the girl who loved Ray.

An understanding mother (Gertrude Claire) reaches
out to a son (Charles Ray) who does not want to fight
in the Civil War in this scene from *The Coward*
(1915). Note the ornate wallpaper and drapes.

The Cinderella story in a Civil War setting was featured in Ince's *A Southern Cinderella* (1913). Here,
the wicked stepsister listens to Prince Charming, a
Union Officer, courting Cinderella.

prived of her room in the manor house and banished to the slave quarters. Her fairy godmother is an enormous black mammy who finds ingenious ways to protect Cinderella and to harass the cruel stepmother. Prince Charming turns up in the person of a handsome Northern officer whose troops are raiding the area. Cinderella bests her stepsister in winning his attentions, but her romance is blighted when her father, leading a company of Confederate cavalrymen, arrives to attack Prince Charming and his men. Word of peace at Appomattox is received, and the old Southerner finally approves of his daughter's marriage to Prince Charming, Yankee though he be. The cute idea for the plot originated with Ince himself, and the picture was well directed by Burton King. For some reason, the advertising for the film did not dwell on the parody of the fairy tale, and it was described as "a massive war production."

A battle scene from Ince's *A Southern Cinderella* (1913).

Another classic transplanted to the Civil War was Anna Sewell's *Black Beauty*, the basis for the plot of Edison's *Your Obedient Servant* (1917). The faithful horse was separated from his Southern master (Pat O'Malley) when the fighting broke out, but was reunited with him after a long series of tribulations. Peggy Adams was the girl, and Edward H. Griffith directed. The film lacked

the charm of the original novel and its settings of Victorian England. (Another Civil War melodrama with a horse as the hero was Solax's *The Equine Spy*, released in 1912. Don, the Wonder Horse, a trained circus star, saved the Confederates by stealing Yankee plans and leading enemy troops away from a rebel supply train.)

Although a New Englander by birth, Thomas H. Ince was a Civil War buff with a great sympathy for the Southern cause. He produced numerous films devoted to this period of American history, and in 1913 brought out an expensive five-reel special, *The Battle of Gettysburg*, which re-created the famous struggle with considerable accuracy. It was to be the most famous of Civil War pictures until the release of Griffith's *The Birth of a Nation* two years later. The emphasis was upon action and spectacle, and Ince, always the master showman, had no hesitation in billing it as "the greatest motion picture in the world!" Exhibitors were charged special terms for this attraction, and it played several weeks in New York and Chicago at advanced admissions. *The Battle of Gettysburg* is one of the few films that Ince personally directed, although two of his regular staff directors, Raymond B. West and Charles Giblyn, were credited as assistants and worked closely with Ince in its production. Heading the large cast were Enid Bennett, Charles K. French, Herschel Mayall, Enid Markey, Ann Little, J. Barney Sherry, and two future directors, Frank Borzage and Walter Edwards. Some of Ince's other Civil War dramas of 1912-14 bore such titles as: *When Lee Surrendered*; *The Toll of War*; *For the Cause*; *When Lincoln Paid*; *With Lee in Virginia*; *The Drummer of the Eighth*; *The Pride of the South*; *The War Correspondent*; *Silent Heroes*; *A Slave's Devotion*; *The Sinews of War*; *In the Fall of '64*; *The Lost Dispatch*; *Bread Cast Upon Waters*; *The Soul of the South*; and *Heart Throbs*.

Ince's *The Battle of Gettysburg* was forced to compete with another large-scale Civil War drama that was released the same week, Kalem's *Shenandoah*, based on Bronston Howard's stage success. It opened with the bombardment of Fort Sumter, followed the Confederate hero (Henry Hallam) through his capture and an exciting escape from a Union prison camp, and finally moved into the Shenandoah Valley for the climactic battle. The

A tense moment in Kay-Bee's *For the Cause* (1912) as Harold Lockwood (left) says good-bye to Ann Little before leaving to serve the Confederate Army. Ray Myers (center) was his rival. Frank Opperman is at right.

In *Bread Cast Upon Waters* (1913), Charles Ray was a wounded Union soldier saved by a Southern family he once befriended. Here, the ladies of the house disguise him with a liberal application of burned cork.

historic twenty-mile ride of General Philip H. Sheridan from Winchester to Cedar Creek to rally the federal troops and save the day for the North—immortalized by Thomas Buchanan Read's famous poem—made exciting film fare. *Shenandoah*, expertly directed by Kenean Buel, contained many spectacular panoramas of battle (foreshadowing *The Birth of a Nation*) shot by cameraman George Hollister from a nearby mountainside. Several hundred extras took part in a realistic rout of the Confederates of General Jubal Early following a heavy bombardment. Alice Hollister was the heroine, Hal Clements the villain, and Robert G. Vignola, soon to become a leading director, was impressive as Sheridan. *Shenandoah* originally ran four-and-a-half reels, but was pared down to three because Kalem President Frank Marion did not think audiences would sit through such a long picture! (Depending on many variables, a full reel ran about twelve minutes.)

General Phil Sheridan's desperate ride was also enacted in many other films, including Vitagraph's *Sheridan's Ride* (1908), Selig's *In the Shenandoah Valley* (1908), Champion's *With Sheridan at Murfreesboro* (1911), and D. W. Griffith's *Abraham Lincoln* (1930). Bison's *Sheridan's Ride* of 1912 appears to have been shortened by ten minutes and released by Universal in 1916 as *After the Battle*. William Clifford, as Sheridan, had some romantic interludes with Victoria Forde (one of Tom Mix's wives).

D. W. GRIFFITH—HIS BIOGRAPH-CIVIL WAR FILMS

Although the fighting had ended nearly ten years earlier when D. W. Griffith was born on January 23, 1875, the Civil War was bred into his heart. It became a great saga of glory for the impressionable Kentucky youth, and years later he would reverently re-create it on film as *The Birth of a Nation*. As a boy, Griffith listened spellbound to nostalgic accounts of brave deeds told by old soldiers for whom time had dulled some of the tragedy and suffering of the War Between the States. The most important of these spinners of tales was a father whom Griffith much admired, Colonel Jacob Griffith, a country politician and un-

successful farmer whose booming voice earned him the sobriquet of "Roaring Jake."

For a half-century after the first success of *The Birth of a Nation* in 1915, Griffith's father would be painted as a Civil War hero, a genteel man of means, a plantation owner, and a major strength to Kentucky in the trying days of Reconstruction. Much of this fiction came from the Griffith studio publicity department, and it was not until years later that the true facts were pieced together. An inept physician with little training for his profession, Jake Griffith had served in the Mexican War and searched for gold in California before settling down in Oldham County, Kentucky. Except for several terms in the state legislature, most of his time was spent drinking home-made whiskey from the barrel on the porch of his 520-acre farm—scarcely a plantation—that steadily deteriorated from his indolence. He died in 1882, not from his war wounds as often reported, but from an unwise mixture of pickles and raw liquor.

That portion of the Jake Griffith legend portraying him as a hero of the Confederacy had some basis in fact. He went off to the Civil War in October 1861 as a cavalry sergeant and took part in the bloody battle of Shiloh. Later, he was wounded in the fighting in the Sesquatchie Valley of Tennessee, and was promoted to captain. By 1863 he had been made a colonel and led the First Kentucky Cavalry in the futile Confederate rearguard action at Missionary Ridge, Chattanooga. He surrendered in Georgia while, so he said, trying to lead Confederacy President Jefferson Davis to safety. In later years, Jake Griffith's favorite story, constantly embellished in repeated tellings, was how he led a desperate charge, although wounded in the hip from a Union minié ball, while riding in a buggy. His son insisted it was true, although there is no documentation of the incident in any histories of Kentucky or the Civil War.

D. W. Griffith later wrote in his fragment of autobiography that *The Birth of a Nation* "owes more to my father than it does to me," and said the Civil War stories told of and by Roaring Jake "were burned right into my memory."[1] To these tunes of glory he would add the miserable, poverty-

---

[1]. D. W. Griffith, *The Man Who Invented Hollywood* (Louisville, Kentucky: Touchstone Publishing Company, 1972), p. 26.

stricken days of Reconstruction, which still lingered in his youth, to the broad canvas that became *The Birth of a Nation*. As with many great works of art, it was an intensely personal expression of a heritage both proud and bitter.

Beginning in 1896, Griffith worked as an actor in a series of stock companies and traveling productions, appearing in support of such stage luminaries as Ada Gray, Melbourne MacDowell, and Nance O'Neill. His ambition was to be a playwright, although his only produced effort, "The Fool and the Girl" (1907), starring Fannie Ward, was a failure. To support himself and his wife (actress Linda Arvidson) while writing plays in New York, Griffith began to act in motion pictures, first for Edison and then at Biograph. He occasionally sold a plot outline to a studio, for which he was paid $15 to $25. In 1908, he was given an opportunity to direct at Biograph, and his innovative use of the camera, emphasis upon significant story content, and development of a more sophisticated style of motion-picure acting quickly established him as the embryo screen's foremost director.

Only a handful of Griffith's films at Biograph utilized Civil War settings. Such pictures were relatively expensive to produce, requiring outdoor locations, elaborate costumes and large casts, and at first Griffith concentrated upon contemporary dramas and comedies that could be made cheaply at the brownstone studio at 11 East 14th Street. The growing quality of the Griffith films soon improved Biograph's shaky finances, making possible more important and costly projects. Location shooting at Fort Lee and Coytesville in New Jersey, at Fishkill and Cuddebackville in New York, and eventually in southern California, became quite common.

Griffith's first Civil War drama was *The Guerrilla,* released in November 1908. It was about a drunken Confederate renegade who forces his attention upon a Southern belle left unprotected at her plantation. A faithful slave goes for help, and the girl's lover, a Union soldier, manages to break through the enemy lines and rescue her. *The Guerrilla* had an exciting chase filmed at Coytesville, and a good cast included Arthur Johnson, Dorothy West, Harry Myers, Herbert Yost, Harry Salter, and Mack Sennett. Griffith did only one Civil War vehicle the following year, *In Old Kentucky*

(1909), which was entirely photographed at the Caudebec Inn, a popular summer resort in the Orange Mountains of New York. It used the familiar theme of two brothers fighting on opposite sides. Henry B. Walthall was the son who threw in his lot with the Confederacy, while Owen Moore remained faithful to the Union. Moore captures Walthall, whose mother helps him to escape. The picture had a touching ending in which Walthall, in the tatters of his Gray uniform and carrying a blood-stained Confederate flag, is welcomed home by his mother (Kate Bruce) and sweetheart (Mary Pickford) as the family celebrates the North's victory. The scene had some slight similarities to Walthall's famous homecoming in *The Birth of a Nation.*

In 1910, Griffith brought out four more Civil War dramas for Biograph. *The. Honor of His Family*, released in January, had the shocking premise of a Confederate officer who kills his cowardly son. Walthall, James Kirkwood, and W. Chrystie Miller had the leads. The battle scenes were again made at Coytesville and required a second cameraman (Arthur Marvin) to assist the faithful G. W. "Billy" Bitzer. In May, back from several months in California, Griffith did *In the Border States, or A Little Heroine of the Civil War.* It also had a good chase, this time shot at Delaware Water Gap, New Jersey, and featured the hackneyed theme of a Union girl who fell in love with a Confederate soldier. *The House With Closed Shutters*, described earlier, came out in August. Griffith filmed the exteriors at the Biograph studio in two days, and the following week did three days of exteriors at Coytesville. Trade critics thought the picture depressing.

In late September 1910 Griffith began *The Fugitive*, which was not released until November. Owen Moore, Lily Cahill, Lucy Cotton, Edward Dillon, Edwin August, and Joseph Graybill headed the cast. It had a maudlin story of a Confederate mother who shelters a hunted Union soldier. Learning he is the man who killed her only son in battle, she is about to turn him over to Southern officers when news of peace arrives. Thinking of the boy's mother, she sends him home for a family reunion. Locations at Fishkill, New York, were used for *The Fugitive*. (Two years later, Universal used an identical plot in another Civil War film,

Fortunes of War, and again in 1916 in *His Mother's Boy.*)

In mid-January 1911, Biograph released a two-part drama of the Civil War and Reconstruction, *His Trust* and *His Trust Fulfilled,* as separate segments. Griffith tried unsuccessfully to get the company to combine them into a two-reeler, but Biograph executives were apprehensive that it could not be sold in such a length! *His Trust* was released on January 16, and *His Trust Fulfilled* three days later, with many exhibitors using the second film to lure audiences back into their theaters. Production on the two pictures began on location at Fort Lee, New Jersey, on November 5, 1910, and was not completed until thirteen days later. Wilfred Lucas, a popular white actor, played the role of a devoted slave in both films. In *His Trust,* a Confederate planter (Verner Clarges) goes off to the Civil War, leaving his wife (Claire McDowell) and daughter (Adele De Garde) in the care of a trusted slave. Union troopers sack and burn the manor, and the slave hides his charges. The picture ends as he takes them to live in his cabin. *His Trust Fulfilled* picks up the story four years later. The planter has been killed in the war, the mother dies, and the slave uses his savings to educate the daughter (now played by Dorothy West). The girl falls in love and marries an English cousin, and the slave feels his trust has been fulfilled. Both pictures were commendable for a sensitive treatment of the black hero, although there was criticism in black circles for the use of a white actor in the role. The performers aged noticeably through effective makeup, and Griffith employed a camera dissolve between each scene.

Many other films about the Civil War that were not by Griffith showed a slave saving the life of his master, often at the expense of his own life. These pictures bore such titles as: *Banty Tim* (1913); *Old Mammy's Secret Code* (1913); *A Black Conspiracy* (1913); *The Common Enemy* (1910); *Domino's Devotion* (1913); *None Can Do More* (1912); *A Slave's Devotion* (1913); and *The Confederate Spy* (1910). The most elaborate was *Dan,* a feature-length production released in 1914 in which Lew Dockstader, the famous minstrel man, was a heroic slave who rescues his master after he is captured by the Union Army, but dies in the attempt. Unfortunately, many of these pictures were marred by tasteless low comedy reflecting upon black people.

Griffith's *Swords and Hearts,* released in late August of 1911, was a routine postwar drama in which a gallant Southern officer (Wilfred Lucas) returns home to find his plantation ravished by Yankee marauders. A poor white girl (Dorothy West) and a faithful slave help him to rebuild. During the same month, Griffith began work on *The Battle,* an elaborate film whose spectacular battle scenes resembled those of *The Birth of a Nation* in style and construction. The familiar story of a coward who is transformed into a hero by the scorn of his sweetheart was the framework for a series of exciting escapades. To prove his bravery, the boy rejoins his regiment and brings a convoy of ammunition wagons through enemy shellfire. A fine cast included Blanche Sweet, Charles West, Robert Harron, Lionel Barrymore, Donald Crisp, and Spottiswoode Aitken. *The Battle* was enormously successful despite Biograph's concern at its high cost, and it was reissued in 1915 to good business. Griffith's last Civil War film at Biograph was *The Informer* (1912), a drama of two Confederate brothers. One sells military secrets to the North, which results in the death of the older brother in an enemy ambush. Mary Pickford, Henry B. Walthall, Walter Miller, Harry Carey, Dorothy Gish, Joseph Graybill, and Christy Cabanne were in the exceptional cast.

Griffith left Biograph on October 1, 1913, to join Reliance-Majestic, a young production company releasing through Harry M. Aitken's Mutual Pictures complex. The parting with Biograph had not been without friction. Griffith's last picture at the studio, *Judith of Bethulia,* an elaborate biblical epic, was largely shot on location in California under conditions of great secrecy. He had been given an $18,000 budget to do the film as a two-reeler, but the final cost came to double that amount (although Griffith would later assert that he spent no more than $13,000). He returned to New York with six reels of exposed film, and with some exteriors yet to be done. *Judith of Bethulia* was later edited down to four reels, and when released the following year (1914) after a long delay was hailed as a great critical success.

Earlier in 1913, unknown to Griffith, Biograph made a deal with the Broadway theatrical firm of

In D. W. Griffith's *The Informer* (1912), Henry B. Walthall (left) was a blacksheep who sold Confederate military secrets to the North. Mary Pickford was the girl, and Walter Miller was the brother who died as a result of Walthall's treason.

Klaw and Erlanger to film some of its stage properties as feature-length specials of four to six reels. Furious at Griffith's independent attitude toward the excessive cost of *Judith of Bethulia,* and influenced by Klaw and Erlanger officials, Biograph informed Griffith that henceforth he would supervise production, but not direct. The decision was made to deliberately force Griffith out of the company, because Biograph was unwilling to finance the more expensive films (with budgets of $50,000 and perhaps $100,000) that he had in mind. After rejecting an offer of $50,000 annually from Adolph Zukor's Famous Players, Griffith negotiated the Aitken contract calling for him to personally direct more important productions, as well as to supervise a program of less costly films directed by others.

From the time shooting ended on *Judith of Bethulia* during the first week of July 1913 to his departure from Biograph on October 1, Griffith apparently worked intermittently in some vague supervisory capacity with other staff directors. Certainly, several of the Klaw and Erlanger-Biograph specials released well into 1914 (such as *Liberty Belles* and *The Wife*, both with Dorothy Gish) carried his name as supervisor. One such film, *A Fair Rebel*, not released until May but made several months earlier, had a Civil War setting. Shot at Biograph's gleaming new studio on 175th Street in the Bronx, it was a drama of a Southern girl (Linda Arvidson) who loved a Union officer (Charles West). When he is captured by Confederates and sent to Richmond's notorious Libby Prison, she engineers his escape by posing as a sentry. Dorothy Gish had a small role. The movie was highlighted by an exciting chase over the Virginia countryside. Although Griffith was billed as supervisor (most prominently in the advertising when it was reissued in 1916), it is doubtful that he had any actual connection with *A Fair Rebel*. It appears to have been produced by David Miles, a former associate who soon left Biograph to join the new Kinemacolor Corporation in Hollywood, taking Linda Arvidson with him as star.

During 1914, his first year at Reliance-Majestic, Griffith was credited with supervising at least three other Civil War pictures directed by others. These were *A Question of Courage*, with Elmer Clifton; *The Soul of Honor*, with Blanche Sweet and Henry B. Walthall; and *The Tavern of Tragedy*, with Dorothy Gish and Fred A. Turner. All were inexpensive program pictures hurriedly turned out by Griffith's Fine Arts unit to raise ready cash, and he had little if anything to do with them. Griffith was already busy with preparations for his masterpiece, *The Birth of a Nation*.

MILESTONE AND MASTERPIECE: THE BIRTH OF A NATION

One of the screen's lost films is Kinemacolor's *The Clansman* (1912), which was never completed. No fragments of this picture are known to exist. Presumably, the few scenes that were shot have been destroyed, or have long since crumbled into dust with the deterioration of its nitrate film stock. The only significance of *The Clansman* is that a portion of its story later formed the basis for the last half of D. W. Griffith's milestone of

motion-picture history, *The Birth of a Nation*.

Kinemacolor was a subsidiary of the British company of the same name that spent several years in developing a pioneer process of color motion-picture photography using a color wheel. Its films of *The Royal Visit to India* and the colorful *The Durbar at Delhi* in 1911 were a sensation, and the company moved to establish the process in the United States. After a series of frustrating differences with the powerful Motion Picture Patents Company, which did not want color films marketed in America, Kinemacolor was forced to set up its own studios—first at Allentown, Pennsylvania, and then at Whitestone Landing, New York. A California studio with three production units was established in Hollywood in 1912, using a crude building at the corner of Hollywood and Sunset Boulevards previously occupied by the Revier Film Processing Company. Kinemacolor sold this studio the following year to the Aitken interests, and it was here that Griffith filmed *The Birth of a Nation, Intolerance*, and other pictures.

During the early part of 1912, Kinemacolor contracted with a stage impresario named George H. Brennan to film *The Clansman*, a lurid novel of the Reconstruction era by Thomas W. Dixon, a Southern clergyman. Several years earlier, in 1906, Brennan had produced a dramatization of the work (also by Dixon) on Broadway with Holbrook Blinn, Sydney Ayres, and DeWitt Jennings in the leads. Although this heavy-handed play was roundly panned by reviewers after its premiere at the Liberty Theatre, it became a popular vehicle for traveling stock companies, particularly those touring in the South and West. Brennan sold Kinemacolor officials on the unique idea of using the performers of such a company—the Campbell MacCullough Players—to repeat their roles in a film version of *The Clansman*. As the troupe moved through the South, scenes would be shot in authentic locales—plantations, antebellum homes, battlefields, and historical sites—using period furnishings and costumes, and utilizing local citizens as extras.

William Haddock, who had directed for Edison, Méliès, and I.M.P. (and also for Kinemacolor at its Whitestone Landing studio) was assigned to direct. He found it difficult to do any shooting with the company jumping from town to town in a series of one-night stands. Finally, he persuaded MacCullough to lay off for two weeks in Natchez, Mississippi, where some scenes were photographed. The picture was far from complete when MacCullough insisted upon resuming the tour. Only a little more than a reel of film had been obtained when production on the ambitious project was abruptly halted. Reportedly, $25,000 was lost on the project.

Haddock offered to take over *The Clansman*, but he could not find financial backing to complete it. Finally, he went to court to secure $1,155 due him in unpaid wages. Haddock later insisted *The Clansman* was made in an early sound process.[2] (In 1907, he had directed several films for the Cameraphone Company, in which the actors mouthed words to records; the device was not successful and was demonstrated in only a few theaters.)

There are conflicting accounts for the reasons for the abandonment of *The Clansman*. One story is that the color photography by inexperienced technicians was so poor that a usable print could not be obtained. However, the cameraman, Gerald MacKenzie, was known as a competent craftsman and had photographed several pictures in the Kinemacolor process. Another report says that Haddock's direction was inept, and the acting by the stock company performers so exaggerated and amateurish as to be ludicrous. Yet another account blamed the script, which underwent several revisions, including a complete rewrite while the picture was actually before the cameras. The original idea of using Dixon's playscript verbatim was dropped after Kinemacolor executives perceived that it was too static for motion pictures. Another account of the ill-fated *The Clansman* says that all scenes were completed, which is unlikely, but that the film was never edited because of its mediocre quality. To compound the confusion, it has also been reported that the film was made without Dixon's knowledge, and alleges that he stopped its release by threatening a lawsuit for violation of copyright. (A contrasting story has it that Dixon was actually a partner with Brennan in the project.) Perhaps the most believable explan-

ation is that the backers, already stuck with $25,000 worth of unusable film, simply decided to suspend shooting and take their losses.

One of the several writers on *The Clansman* was Frank E. Woods, who was paid $200 for his efforts. Originally a pioneer film critic for *The Dramatic Mirror*, he wrote titles and many scripts for D. W. Griffith at Biograph. Woods left the company in 1912, but soon rejoined Griffith's unit after brief and frustrating associations with Universal and Kinemacolor. He followed Griffith to Reliance-Majestic, nominally as scenario editor but functioning increasingly as a production executive. He was largely responsible for the inexpensive program pictures turned out while Griffith was busy with more important features. An imposing but kindly man, Woods was for a considerable time the most influential of Griffith's associates.

D. W. Griffith did not make an auspicious beginning at Reliance-Majestic. The company was beset by financial problems and squabbling among its executives. To raise ready cash, Griffith hurriedly directed two undistinguished pictures for release in 1914, *The Battle of the Sexes* (made in only four days) and *The Escape*, as well as producing eight cheap potboilers directed by others. In February 1914, he moved his unit from New York to the new studio in Hollywood, where he immediately turned out *Home, Sweet, Home*—an episodic film based in part upon incidents in the life of composer John Howard Payne—and *The Avenging Conscience*. The latter, a psychological drama constructed from two stories by Edgar Allan Poe ("The Tell-Tale Heart" and "Annabel Lee"), had many arty touches foreshadowing the innovations of the German cinema of the twenties. With the financial tension easing, Griffith set Frank E. Woods to searching for a property that could be made into an important feature. Woods showed him the script he had written for Kinemacolor's *The Clansman* and proposed a new version of Dixon's play. With its background of the Civil War, Reconstruction, and the restoration of white supremacy through the rise of the Ku Klux Klan, the story had enormous appeal for Griffith. He was soon engrossed in the monumental film that became *The Birth of a Nation*.

The first step was to buy the rights to the play and novel from Reverend Dixon, for which the

2. Bernard Rosenberg and Harry Silverstein. *The Real Tinsel* (New York: The Macmillan Company, 1970). p. 325.

In this spectacular panoramic shot from D. W. Griffith's *The Birth of a Nation* (1915), Sherman's pillaging forces prepare to set fire to an abandoned Georgia schoolhouse.

clergyman demanded a whopping $25,000 (the figure is sometimes reported as $10,000). Eventually, Dixon settled for $2,500 cash and a share of the profits, which were to bring him a fortune. With some assistance from Woods, Griffith fleshed out a dramatic outline of the plot, but at no time was there a written script or continuity—it was all in Griffith's head. He preferred to work this way, feeling it gave a greater flexibility and freshness to his work, and associates marveled at his mental ability to keep track of all the scenes. The extent of Woods's contribution is not known, but it was sufficient for Griffith to give him screen credit. Much of Griffith's time went into a detailed research to assure historical accuracy, and at one time he employed four persons to check on the minutest details of period dress, settings, and military and social customs. He often came to the studio with

an armload of books and his pockets bulging with notes.

The cast of *The Birth of a Nation* was largely drawn from the Griffith stock company, performers whom he had discovered and developed at Biograph, and with whom he felt comfortable. There were auditions and try-outs for some parts. Blanche Sweet, his reigning star, was expected to be cast as the heroine, Elsie Stoneman, but Griffith felt a more petite and less full-bodied actress was needed. Mae Marsh was considered, but the role finally went to the fragile Lillian Gish, with Miss Marsh being wisely switched to the key role of the little sister. The thirty-six-year old Henry B. Walthall was an ideal choice for the Southern hero, Ben Cameron, combining striking good looks with an intelligent and usually restrained style of acting. Others cast by Griffith included Miriam Cooper, Elmer Clifton, Ralph Lewis, Robert Harron, Wallace Reid, Donald Crisp, George Siegmann, Josephine Crowell, Howard Gaye, Spottiswoode Aitken, and Raoul Walsh (as John Wilkes Booth). In an unusual departure from custom, Griffith put his players through six weeks of intensive rehearsals before shooting began.

The Birth of a Nation went into production on July 4, 1914 and was completed on October 31. In the interim it weathered a series of acute financial crises that promised to (and at one bad point actually did) suspend filming altogether. Griffith persuaded Harry Aitken to allocate a record budget of $40,000 for the picture, but this sum was expended on the panoramic battle scenes alone, which were completed first. Most of it went for uniforms and hundreds of horses and extras. When Reliance-Majestic's Board of Directors refused further financing, Griffith and Aitken personally took over the project. Their own funds were soon exhausted, and they raised money in small amounts here and there. Several of the cast and crew, including Lillian Gish and cameraman G. W. Bitzer, loaned their savings and went without salary. Griffith was unwilling to make any compromises to reduce the cost, and eventually $110,000 was spent on *The Birth of a Nation*, at the time a staggering investment for a single motion picture. (His four preceding films had cost between $5,000 and $10,000 each.) In its final version after last-minute cuts following the premiere, the picture ran twelve

Henry B. Walthall as "The Little Colonel" in Griffith's
monumental *The Birth of a Nation* (1915) prepares
to lead a Confederate charge on Yankee fortifications.

reels, an unheard-of length, and many exhibitors
and industry leaders predicted that it could not
be profitably shown.

Whatever reservations Griffith's competitors may
have had about it, *The Birth of a Nation* was a
sensation when it opened on February 8, 1915 at
Clune's Auditorium in Los Angeles (where it ran
for seven months). The critics were ecstatic after
its New York premiere at the Liberty Theatre a
month later, and it was shown in key cities on a
reserved-seat basis for $2 per admission. Griffith's
ambitious picture, executed with superb artistry,
was an enormous hit with audiences everywhere.
Its drama and spectacle were deeply moving, and
unlike anything yet seen on the screen. Following
a showing at the White House, President Woodrow
Wilson was reported to have said that the film was
"like writing history with lightning." (Later, after
The Birth of a Nation came under attack for its
racist bigotry, a Wilson aide denied that the President had made any comments of approbation.)

The financial success of *The Birth of a Nation*
made Griffith a millionaire, although he lost much
of his fortune on the ill-fated *Intolerance* of the

following year. Miss Gish, Bitzer (who had loaned $7,000), and other investors also reaped astronomical returns. Aitken and Griffith were both naive in motion-picture economics and failed to realize what a valuable property they had. After its road-show engagements, they foolishly sold regional distribution rights to various independent exchanges for relative pittances. One of the lucky purchasers was Louis B. Mayer, a Massachusetts exhibitor and distributor, who bought the New England franchise for $50,000 against ten percent of the net profits. This investment brought his company a return of a million dollars, enabling Mayer to branch into production and provide the stepping stone to the gigantic Loew's Incorporated and Metro-Goldwyn-Mayer combine. Aitken later alleged privately that Mayer cheated him of substantial sums by understating the box-office receipts.

Griffith originally planned to center the plot of *The Birth of a Nation* on Reconstruction and its effects upon a proud Southern family devastated by the Civil War. As his enthusiasm grew, he added a long section of battle scenes and historical incidents, including Sherman's march through Georgia, the burning of Atlanta, Lee's surrender at Appomattox, and the assassination of Abraham Lincoln. The essential story concerns two families —the Camerons of the South and the Stonemans of the North—whose friendship is ruptured by the Civil War. They are eventually reconciled after many hardships and personal tragedies. Although Griffith was careful to show the war wreaked its havoc on both North and South alike—sons of both families die on the battlefields—the sympathies of the film are clearly with its Southern protagonists, who are portrayed as decent and God-fearing people in spite of being slaveowners. Villainy is symbolized by the character of Austin Stoneman, the crippled leader of the United States House of Representatives, who keeps a black mistress and vows "to crush the White South under the heel of the Black South," as a title puts it. (Stoneman is based upon Thaddeus Stevens, the Civil War Congressional power known as "The Great Commoner.") The Griffith concept of Stoneman's final punishment is when a mulatto carpetbagger, whom he had made Lieutenant-Governor of South Carolina, asks for the hand of his daughter in marriage, and, failing to obtain it from the horrified father, at-

Ralph Lewis as the crippled Austin Stoneman in *The Birth of a Nation* (1915) introduces his protege, the mulatto Silas Lynch (George Siegmann).

tempts to rape her. In a parallel climax, the young sister of the Southern hero throws herself from a cliff rather than submit to a black renegade. These outrages are viciously avenged by the militant Ku Klux Klan, which is made to appear as a savior force.

Inevitably, *The Birth of a Nation* was bitterly attacked as a racist picture, and its showing was accompanied by numerous demonstrations and incidents, and by editorial protests in newspapers and magazines. Griffith seemed surprised at the furor his film created, and insisted that he bore no ill-will toward blacks, and that he had only shown conditions in the South as they actually existed during and after the Civil War. In all probability, he did not set out to make a bigoted picture—his friends consistently denied that he had race prejudice—but nonetheless it remains viciously racist in tone with blacks shown as objects of contempt and depravity. Those who were favorably portrayed— the family servants who came to the rescue of their former master—were caricatures from the Uncle Tom school, and were injected largely for comic relief. The controversy over *The Birth of Nation* raged for years, and the bitterness that it caused has never been erased. Even today, it is seldom shown publicly, and then mostly to film scholars.

Except for the glossy battle sequences done with great emphasis upon heroism and glory, *The Birth*

D. W. Griffith created this historical tableau of the surrender at Appomattox Courthouse for *The Birth of a Nation* (1915). Donald Crisp, right, played General Grant, while Howard Gaye, left, was General Robert E. Lee.

of a Nation provides only a sketchy glimpse of the Civil War itself. It failed to probe any of the motives or underlying causes of the conflict, although a few scenes at the outset show slaves being brought to America from Africa and sold at auction. There is no attempt to define the political or economic reasons for the struggle, nor to fathom the curious state of mind in the South in which pride and gallantry are equated with right. In the first half of the picture, the audience is stirred by the spectacle of battle, and it is not until the later section on Reconstruction that the enormities of the Civil War are brought home in personal terms. The Ku Klux Klan, which fell into disrepute soon after its organization, is made an object of admiration, which in turn contributed to the Klan's resurgence in the decade after the film's release. From the vantage point of sixty years after the first showing of *The Birth of a Nation*, its philosophies appear hollow and false today. This failure does not in any way diminish the significance of this remarkable motion picture.

The Birth of a Nation is filled with a succession of moving scenes, all marked in one way or another with Griffith's perceptive talent. The impressive battle sequences and the stirring ride of the Klans cannot be discounted, but the meat of the drama lies in the more intimate passages. These include Lillian Gish's brave good-bye to her brothers as they leave for war (only to collapse in tears in the lap of her black mammy), Mother Cameron's appeal to Abraham Lincoln for her son's life, the parting of Miss Gish and Walthall at the hospital door (with its mooning sentry), the electrically charged confrontations in Stoneman's quarters, and the heartbreaking death of the little sister. Most of all, there is the famous return of Walthall to his war-scarred home, in which he is received by a grown-up little sister in a worn dress adorned with raw cotton; the final scene of this episode, with the mother's arms reaching out from the doorway, is of classic proportion. Of the action sequences, the guerrilla raid on Piedmont has a documentary quality that gives it a pulsating life and naturalness unmarred by theatrical heroics. Only occasionally does Griffith fail, as in the archaic epilogue in which a shot of the symbolical god of war dissolves into a vision of Jesus Christ (played by Wallace Reid). It is a scene that dramatically does not age well.

The restrained acting in *The Birth of a Nation* set new standards of perfection, and few films have been so perfectly cast. Henry B. Walthall gave admirable substance to his portrait of Ben Cameron, "the Little Colonel," delineating the traditional qualities of Southern manhood that were somehow lacking in Leslie Howard's faltering interpretation of Ashley Wilkes in *Gone With the Wind*. Lillian Gish brought her sturdy fragility to Elsie Stoneman, but she is overshadowed by Mae Marsh as the little sister for whom war's privations cannot diminish the exuberance of youth. Ralph Lewis, an actor little appreciated, was powerful as the emotionally and physically crippled Stoneman. George Siegmann was on the whole just right as the fawning Silas Lynch, the mulatto carpetbagger, although his performance is blighted by overacting in the final rape scene. Joseph E. Henabery as Abraham Lincoln, Howard Gaye as Robert E. Lee, Donald Crisp as Ulysses S. Grant, Raoul Walsh as John Wilkes Booth—all are as pages from a book

The ill-fitting wig was part of the characterization that Ralph Lewis gave to Hon. Austin Stoneman in D. W. Griffith's *The Birth of a Nation* (1915).

of Civil War daguerreotypes by Brady. Perhaps the most ideally cast are Spottiswoode Aitken as the gentle Dr. Cameron and Josephine Crowell as his wife. Her performance as the bewildered mother is a masterpiece of quiet heartbreak as she weathers the long series of tragedies that strike her family. It is difficult to believe that she is the same actress who is so incredibly bad as Catherine de Medici in Griffith's *Intolerance* of the following year. It is an obvious piece of serious miscasting for which Griffith must be blamed. Later in her career, Mrs. Crowell became typed as the curmudgeon battle-axe of numerous slapstick comedies of the twenties—her role as Harold Lloyd's bossy mother-in-law in *Hot Water* (1924) is typical—and her superb work in *The Birth of a Nation* was by then all but forgotten.

In later years, fan magazines would refer to *The Birth of a Nation*, not without considerable truth, as a jinx picture for its talented cast. Many of the

In D. W. Griffith's *Intolerance* (1916), Josephine Crowell was badly miscast as the evil Catherine de Medici. Frank Bennett was the weak Charles IX.

players subsequently had disappointing and unproductive careers, while ill health and poor judgment led others into personal tragedy, obscurity, and death.

Henry B. Walthall's sensitive performance should have been the springboard of a long and distinguished professional life, but inexplicably it was rather a high-water mark of success from which he steadily declined. Only momentarily did Walthall, with his striking good looks, challenge such contemporary screen matinee idols as Francis X. Bushman and Harold Lockwood. He left Griffith soon after the release of *The Birth of a Nation*; characteristically, the great director did nothing to encourage him to remain. Walthall made the mistake of signing with the Essanay Company, a penurious and unimaginative studio lacking creative leadership, which wasted his talent on a series of cheap, mediocre melodramas in 1917 (*Little Shoes, Burning the Candle*). A stint with the ill-fated

Paralta Plays, Inc. the following year (*His Robe of Honor, Humdrum Brown*) was even more unproductive. Walthall had his own unit, but Paralta's unorthodox method of merchandising films netted only a fraction of the profits he was led to expect. By the 1920s, he was reduced to playing supporting and character roles, and work was less plentiful. He aged badly due to personal problems, and while still in his forties acquired a drawn and elderly appearance. Walthall was blessed with a good speaking voice, and talking pictures brought a greater demand for his services in bit parts. He died in 1936, a few months after participating in the emotionally charged ceremonies at which D. W. Griffith received a citation from the Academy of Motion Picture Arts and Sciences in recognition of his contributions to the screen.

Mae Marsh, the delightful but tragic little sister of *The Birth of a Nation* was cursed with much the same fate. The following year she gave a stun-

Mae Marsh added a mischievous quality to her portrayal of the ill-fated Little Sister in *The Birth of a Nation* (1915).

ning performance in the modern sequences of Griffith's *Intolerance* (1916) as the bewildered young mother beset by a series of incredible adversities. Griffith then teamed her with Robert Harron, her co-star in *Intolerance,* in several light program pictures designed to capitalize upon the popularity of the two players. When an offer came from Samuel Goldwyn, Griffith urged Miss Marsh to accept it, saying that the lucrative contract would bring her riches that he could never pay. Her Goldwyn films of 1917-19 (*Polly of the Circus, Hidden Fires*) were disappointing, although her vivacious work in *The Cinderella Man* was widely praised. The actress proved difficult to work with, and she quarreled with Goldwyn and her directors, and made unreasonable demands. Her professional reputation suffered, and for a time few roles came her way. Miss Marsh returned to Griffith in 1923 for *The White Rose*, filmed in the bayou country of Louisiana. Although she gave a fine performance, it did nothing for her faltering career. After a few pictures made abroad, she quietly left the screen to raise a family. She endured a trying marriage and saw her fortune swallowed up by poor investments and the 1929 stock market crash. A few years later, Miss Marsh filed for bankruptcy, listing debts of $5,250 and a 1931 model automobile worth $25 as her only asset.

In 1932, Mae Marsh returned to films as the mother in Fox's tired remake of the classic tearjerker, *Over the Hill*. Only thirty-seven at the time (playing the mother of twenty-seven-year-old James Dunn), she looked twenty years older and was unrecognizable as the pert Flora Cameron of *The Birth of a Nation*. She needed little makeup for the part, and fans were shocked by her haggard and dowdy appearance. *Over the Hill* was too old-fashioned and downbeat for depression audiences, and her work went unnoticed. It was her last major role. In later years she supported herself with bits in numerous films (including many directed by old friend John Ford) before her death in 1968 at the age of seventy-three.

Robert Harron started with Griffith as an eleven-year-old property boy at Biograph. He had a small part as the youngest Stoneman son in *The Birth of a Nation*. His work in *Intolerance* made him a star, and his performance as the war-weary artist-hero of Griffith's propaganda film, *Hearts of the World* (1918), was the best of his career. Harron reportedly began to brood when Griffith gave young Richard Barthelmess choice roles in *Broken Blossoms* (1919) and *Way Down East* (1920). He felt that he had lost favor with his mentor, whom he idolized, although Griffith had agreed to supervise films for Harron's own company. In New York on September 1, 1920, Harron was dressing for dinner when a revolver (which he had bought from a hungry actor) fell from his pocket and discharged. The bullet pierced Harron's lung, and he died five days later. There were peristent reports that he attempted suicide, although he denied it to a priest before his death. Harron's friends are convinced that it was an accident.

Handsome Wallace Reid had been in films since 1910, and was the star of many program pictures produced by Griffith's unit for Reliance-Majestic in 1914-15 (*The City Beautiful; Her Awakening; The Craven*). He was seen briefly in *The Birth of a Nation* as a muscular young blacksmith killed in a brutal fight in the gin mill of "White-Arm Joe." Soon afterward, Reid moved to Paramount (Famous Players-Lasky), where he won acclaim as leading man to opera star Geraldine Farrar in several spectacular films directed by Cecil B. DeMille in 1915-17 (*Carmen; Maria Rosa; Joan the Woman; The Devil Stone; The Woman God Forgot*). By the 1920s, his popularity was enormous, stemming from his familiar role as a brash young American of the Jazz Age who uses Yankee pluck to reach his goals and win the girl of his heart (usually Gloria Swanson, Bebe Daniels, Lila Lee, or Wanda Hawley). Following an injury on the set of *The Valley of the Giants* (1919), Reid was left with blinding headaches and pain from a damaged spine. At his doctor's instructions, he began to take morphine in order to continue acting, and was soon addicted. Reid's condition was further complicated by heavy drinking. In an effort to overcome the drug addiction, he entered a sanitarium, and on January 18, 1923, died of complications of influenza and renal disease. His death led to reams of sensational publicity in newspapers and magazines, and Reid's addiction did much to damage Hollywood's reputation (already tarnished by the Roscoe "Fatty" Arbuckle scandal and the unexplained murder of director William Desmond Taylor, which involved two top stars,

Mary Miles Minter and comedienne Mabel Normand).

Elmer Clifton, who portrayed Phil Stoneman in *The Birth of a Nation,* turned to directing soon afterward and in 1918-19 was responsible for a series of delightful comedies starring Dorothy Gish (*Boots; Peppy Polly; I'll Get Him Yet*) and pro-duced by the Griffith company. In 1922, he did *Down to the Sea in Ships,* a highly praised drama of New Bedford whalers that had a documentary quality. (It is more remembered as the film in which sexpot Clara Bow had her first important role.) Two years later, Clifton directed a credit-able remake of the old Civil War spy melodrama, *The Warrens of Virginia* (1924), which was his last important assignment. Jobs became scarce, and, after the advent of talking pictures, Clifton was reduced to directing Westerns, serials, and sex-ploitation pictures made on miniscule budgets. He

Elmer Clifton, who played Phil Stoneman in *The Birth of a Nation* (1915), soon switched to directing. One of his best films as a director was another Civil War opus, *The Warrens of Virginia* (1924).

never realized the promise shown earlier, and seemed to have profited little by his association with D. W. Griffith.

Others in the cast of *The Birth of a Nation* had disappointing careers. Elmo Lincoln, who was "White-Arm Joe" (as well as playing several un-credited bits), was a sensation as Edgar Rice Bur-roughs's jungle hero in the first version of *Tarzan of the Apes* (1918). Despite his beefy appearance and a ridiculous fright-wig, Lincoln had great appeal as Tarzan, but unfortunately the public did not like him in other roles. After *Romance of Tarzan* (1918) and a fifteen-episode serial, *Ad-ventures of Tarzan* (1921), and several serials at Universal in 1919–20 (*Elmo the Mighty, Elmo the Fearless, The Flaming Disc*), Lincoln got only occasional work as a bit player or stuntman, and eventually as an extra. He died in 1952, virtually penniless.

George Seigmann, a gentle man who played such brutal roles as Silas Lynch in *The Birth of a Na-tion,* the sadistic Hun officer von Strohm in *Hearts of the World,* and Simon Legree in *Uncle Tom's Cabin* (1927), had only moderate success as an actor until his early death in 1928. He aspired to be a director, but his few attempts at directing (mostly program pictures for Griffith's unit) went unnoticed. Ralph Lewis, Walter Long, Mary Alden, and Sam de Grasse were others appearing in Griffith's masterpiece who played character roles in Hollywood for years without achieving more than casual recognition. Erich von Stroheim can scarcely be said to have been in the cast of *The Birth of a Nation*—in the raid on Piedmont he is the man who falls from the roof of a house—but did serve Griffith as a third assistant director. Stroheim went on to become one of the immortals of the screen with his silent classics of directorial genius—*Foolish Wives* (1922); *Greed* (1924); *The Wedding March* (1928)—only to have his career vanish after a series of bitter controversies with studio moguls. In later years, he made a precarious living as an actor, writing scripts that seldom sold, and planning a comeback that never materialized.

There were a few significant exceptions to the jinx of *The Birth of a Nation.* Lillian Gish was to have a long and notable career on both screen and stage. She was washed up in Hollywood by the time talking pictures arrived—many felt that

Lillian Gish in a moment of classic beauty as Elsie Stoneman in *The Birth of a Nation* (1915).

Raoul Walsh, as John Wilkes Booth, leaps to the stage of Ford's Theatre in this scene from *The Birth of a Nation* (1915) after shooting Abraham Lincoln (Joseph E. Henabery). Alberta Lee was Mrs. Lincoln.

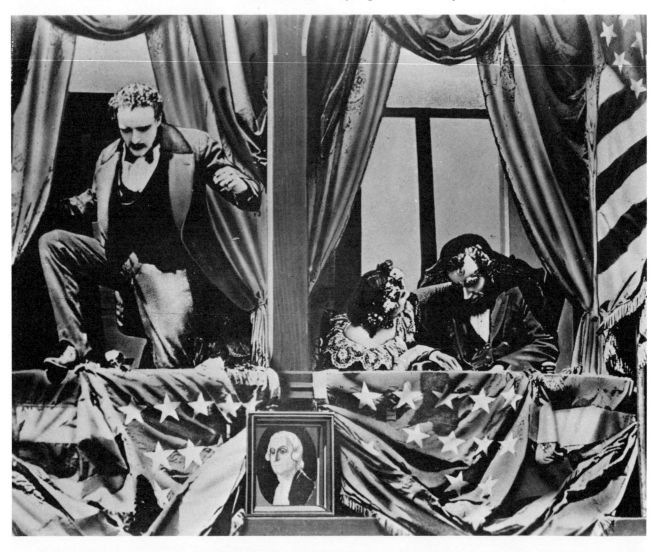

Metro-Goldwyn-Mayer had deliberately mishandled her in a series of dreary films—but for many years she was one of Broadway's brightest stars. She periodically returned to Hollywood to play character roles in such films as *Duel in the Sun* (1946) and *The Unforgiven* (1960), never failing to give an intelligent and often memorable performance.

Miriam Cooper, the older Cameron sister, was a successful albeit lesser star for ten years, mostly in pictures directed by her husband, Raoul Walsh (*The Honor System*, 1916; *Evangeline*, 1919). Her career abruptly declined, and she faded into obscurity after her divorce. Raoul Walsh, the superb John Wilkes Booth of *The Birth of a Nation*, became one of the screen's best-known directors and was responsible for a long series of commercially successful films (*What Price Glory?*, 1926; *In Old Arizona*, 1929; *The Roaring Twenties*, 1939). Always done with a sense of craftmanship, they were frequently tough, punchy dramas best suited to the talents of such stars as James Cagney and Humphrey Bogart. Donald Crisp, who was General Grant in *The Birth of a Nation*, had a lasting

Josephine Crowell was superb as Mother Cameron in D. W. Griffith's *The Birth of a Nation* (1915) as she pleads with Abraham Lincoln (Joseph E. Henabery) for the life of her son.

career as both actor and director, and was widely known for his many roles in both silent and talking pictures. (In later years Crisp would assert that he, and not Griffith, had actually directed the stunning battle scenes of *The Birth of a Nation,* an unfortunate allegation that was widely reprinted in Crisp's obituaries in 1974. At most, he served as one of Griffith's several assistants on the battle sequences.) He won an Academy Award for his role in John Ford's *How Green Was My Valley* (1941), although film buffs remember him for his portrayal of the sadistic Battling Burrows of Griffith's *Broken Blossoms* (1919). Crisp became a wealthy man through his association with the Bank of America as an advisor on motion-picture industry loans. He lived to the age of ninety-three.

Joseph E. Henabery, who was a realistic Abraham Lincoln in *The Birth of a Nation,* had some early success as director of several of Douglas Fairbanks, Sr.'s pictures, including *The Man From Painted Post* (1917) and *Say Young Fellow* (1918). Later, he worked at Paramount and for Cecil B. DeMille's unit at Pathé. After talkies came in, Henabery directed some early sound shorts in New York for Warner Brothers, but soon found his career at an end. Bessie Love, glimpsed briefly in *The Birth of a Nation,* went on to stardom in many silent hits and in the pioneer screen musical, *The Broadway Melody* (1929). After she was no longer suitable for ingenue roles, she worked as a character actress, mostly in British studios, up into her seventies.

The real significance of *The Birth of a Nation* was not in its re-creation of the drama of the Civil War and Reconstruction, but in its contribution to the art of the motion picture. Griffith's creative technique made *The Birth of a Nation* an uncommon work of art in itself, blending the elements of cinema into a masterpiece of film construction. His superb use of visual imagery, movement, stunning photography (including innovations in irising, close-ups, and the use of stills), intelligent and refined editing, and even music, established the artistic supremacy of the director. The influence of *The Birth of a Nation* was tremendous, and its impact was reflected in the best work of imaginative filmmakers around the world (particularly Eisenstein and the Russian school of the 1920s). Griffith also gave new dimensions to the spectacle

film, and with Europe poised on the brink of war, *The Birth of a Nation* forecast the frightening potentials of the motion picture as a weapon of propaganda. The film revolutionized distribution and exhibition with fresh concepts of merchandising that brought enormous financial returns to the motion-picture industry. With *The Birth of a Nation,* cinema became of age.

AFTER THE BIRTH OF A NATION

Surprisingly, the phenominal success of *The Birth of a Nation* failed to stimulate an expected flood of Civil War pictures. Only a moderate number were released in the next few years, and for the most part these were low-budget attractions that were shamelessly advertised as "another *The Birth of a Nation!*" (Griffith's earlier Civil War films for Biograph were hastily reissued and exploited with a prominent use of his name.) The Griffith spectacle was of such magnitude that Hollywood realized it could not be easily matched. The militant demonstrations and allegations of racial bias were unsettling, but more than anything the exceptionally high cost of *The Birth of a Nation* discouraged imitations. Producers were neither willing nor able to take such financial risks on another Civil War drama of questionable merit or audience appeal, despite the fabulous returns of Griffith's picture.

The more important Civil War films that appeared in the wake of *The Birth of a Nation* were Metro's *Barbara Frietchie* (1915), starring Mary Miles Minter; Thomas H. Ince's *The Coward* (1915), with Charles Ray; Universal's *Under Southern Skies* (1915), filmed on location in Savannah, Georgia, with Mary Fuller and Milton Sills in the leads; Selig's *The Crisis* (1916), perhaps the most ambitious of such pictures; Edison's *The Southerners* (1916), a drama of the Battle of Mobile Bay; Vitagraph's *A Rose of the South* (1916), with Antonio Moreno and Peggy Hyland; Lasky-Paramount's *Her Father's Son* (1916), starring Vivian Martin and directed by William D. Taylor; Lasky-Paramount's *Those Without Sin* (1917), directed by Marshall Neilan, with lovely Blanche Sweet as a Southern spy captured by Union soldiers; Triangle's *The Little Yank*

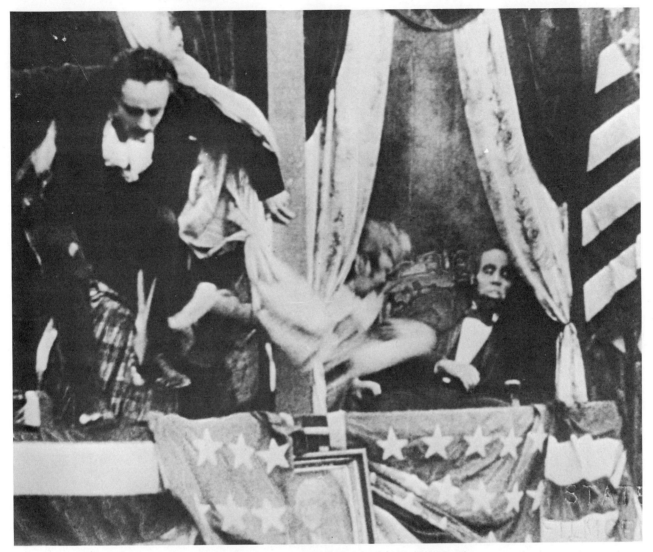

Another scene of the assassination in *The Birth of a Nation* (1915). John Wilkes Booth (Raoul Walsh) makes his escape as President Lincoln (Joseph E. Henabery) falls back mortallly wounded.

(1917), with Dorothy Gish; and Paralta's *Madam Who?* (1918), this time with Bessie Barriscale as the Confederate agent.

Selig's *The Crisis* was a sprawling twelve-reel drama obviously intended to capitalize upon the popularity of *The Birth of a Nation*. It was the longest and most expensive film that Selig, a company known for its parsimony, had undertaken to that time. Based on the 1901 best-seller (which had gone through thirty-four editions) by Winston Churchill, an American novelist of the same name as the British statesman, *The Crisis* had a rather commonplace plot. A young New England lawyer (Thomas Santschi) comes to Saint Louis, where he falls in love with a spirited Southern girl (Bessie Eyton). They differ over slavery, and at a colorful slave auction he bids against her for a beautiful quadroon, whom he sets free. When the Civil War breaks out, it tests their love against traditional loyalties; he fights for the North, but they are reconciled by Abraham Lincoln at the White House after the war. Director Colin Campbell, in some respects an early but much less competent John Ford, spent two months filming in-

Union troops assemble for the battle to come in Selig's
The Crisis (1916), directed by Colin Campbell.

Marshall Neilan (right) was a hot-tempered young
Southerner in *The Crisis* (1916). Here he glowers as
a Yankee lawyer (Thomas Santschi) pays his attentions to beautiful Bessie Eyton.

teriors at Selig's drafty Chicago studio. Other scenes were made on location at New Orleans, Saint Louis, and Charleston, South Carolina (where a re-creation of the firing on Fort Sumter was staged, although little of it was used in the finished picture). The climactic siege of Vicksburg was shot in actual locales at Vicksburg, Mississippi, where replicas of the old semiironclad and shallow-bottom gunboats were constructed. Some of the stuntwork, including a spectacular dive on horseback from a high cliff, was supposedly done by Tom Mix. On the whole, *The Crisis* was a slow and disappointing film. Although it effectively mirrored the growing tension in Saint Louis as the war approached, the battle scenes (using the Mississippi National Guard) were sparse and uninspired—"I don't believe in spectacles," Campbell once told a reporter for Photoplay mag-

Marshall Neilan (right) was still dividing his time between acting and directing when he appeared in this scene from *The Crisis* (1916) with Matt Snyder and Bessie Eyton. Later, he would direct many of Mary Pickford's greatest hits.

In *The Warrens of Virginia* (1915), Blanche Sweet, at right, and her Southern family back home roll bandages and make bullets for the Confederate troops at the front. A very young Marjorie Daw is in the center.

azine. *The Crisis* was beautifully photographed by Harry Gerstad, with additional scenes by Gerald MacKenzie. An excellent cast included George Fawcett, Marshall Neilan, Matt Snyder, Eugenie Besserer, and Sam Drane (as Lincoln). Selig's publicity made much of the fact that genuine historical documents and artifacts, including the dispatch box carried by Abraham Lincoln during his official career, were loaned by the United States government for use in the film.

Another picture that rode the crest of the success of *The Birth of a Nation* was Cecil B. DeMille's *The Warrens of Virginia*, released just one week after the premiere of the Griffith epic. It had many personal ties for DeMille, and was based on a play written by his brother, William C. de Mille (who spelled his name with a small *d*). Cecil had taken one of the leads, along with a charming youngster named Mary Pickford, when *The Warrens of Virginia* was first presented on Broadway by David Belasco in 1907. Moreover, William had fashioned his story around the experiences of their grandfather, who was captured by the federal cavalry in a raid on his North Carolina home in 1865 and kept a prisoner of war for six months. In the screen version, Blanche Sweet and House Peters were lovers parted by the Civil War—she the daughter of a Southern general, he a newspaperman who joins the Union forces. To mislead the enemy with false documents that he carries, Peters allows himself to be taken as a Yankee spy, and is sentenced to death. Lee's timely surrender at Appomattox saves him from a firing squad, and he and Miss Sweet are reunited.

The Warrens of Virginia, DeMille's eighth picture, was praised for its realism and included scenes of a ragged and starving Confederate Army in the twilight of defeat, desolate battlefields strewn with rotting corpses and abandoned equipment, devastated Southern plantations, and unrest among bewildered slaves. The superb photography of Alvin Wyckoff (dubbed "Rembrandt lighting" by DeMille) featured many innovations. The shooting of an exciting attack on an army supply train ended in tragedy when the premature explosion of a bomb cost a DeMille propertyman his right hand. In 1924, Elmer Clifton directed a new version of *The Warrens of Virginia* for Fox. Although uneven and lacking the scope of the

House Peters and Blanche Sweet were the star-crossed lovers in Cecil B. DeMille's Civil War drama, *The Warrens of Virginia* (1915). Here Miss Sweet shields a Southern agent hidden behind the draperies.

Lee's tattered army surrenders in this scene from Cecil B. DeMille's *The Warrens of Virginia* (1915), photographed at the old Providencia Ranch, later the Lasky Ranch, and now the site of the Forest Lawn Cemetery.

Elmer Clifton directed a second version of *The Warrens of Virginia* for Fox in 1924. In this scene, renegades capture Wilfred Lytell and Martha Mansfield (who was fatally burned in a studio fire soon after the film was released).

DeMille picture, it was a creditable effort with good action sequences. The cast was headed by Wilfred Lytell, Rosemary Hill, and the ill-fated Martha Mansfield (who was burned to death in a studio accident soon after the film was completed).

Paramount's *Only the Brave* (1930) had many similarities to the plot of *The Warrens of Virginia*. Gary Cooper was a Union officer who volunteers for espionage duty when he discovers his fiancée (Virginia Bruce) in the arms of another man. Carrying false plans intended to deceive General Lee, Cooper has trouble convincing the Confederates that he really is a spy! Despite the efforts of a pretty Southern girl (Mary Brian) to protect him, he is unmasked as a Northern agent and sentenced to be shot. Cooper is saved from death when the Union attacks, and after the war he and Miss Brian are married, with her former Confederate suitor (Phillips Holmes) as a forgiving best man. *Only the Brave* was an inept picture that foundered on its highly romanticized view of the war.

The granddaddy of Civil War spy dramas was William Gillette's *Secret Service*, first presented on stage in 1895, and revived with great success in 1915 (although Gillette was by then in his sixties). Robert Warwick, recently returned from France as a World War I hero, and Wanda Hawley starred in a dull screen version for Paramount in 1919, with Hugh Ford directing. It was a stagey piece of melodrama with little action. Ford, a gifted Broadway director, was frequently assigned by Paramount to transfer famous stage hits to the screen, such as *Zaza* (1915) and *Mrs. Dane's Defense* (1918). He was never able to think in cinematic terms, however, and his films had the static quality of being merely photographed plays.

In 1931, RKO Radio bought *Secret Service* as a vehicle for Richard Dix, but again it was slow-moving and an old-fashioned picture. Dix played a Northern spy who infiltrated Richmond during the siege, and managed to send a false telegram that lured the Confederate defenders away from the sector of the front where General Grant planned to attack. Although discovered, he was not given the usual penalty of death by a firing squad. In a curious ending, Dix was made to appear a hero for having brought the siege to an end, and he was allowed to enjoy the fruits of matrimony

Paramount's *Only the Brave* (1930) had a plot line similar to that of *The Warrens of Virginia*. Phillips Holmes, Gary Cooper, and Mary Brian were rather self-conscious in this publicity shot taken on the set.

Robert Warwick (right) had just returned a hero of
World War I when he played the lead in Paramount's
Secret Service (1919). Irving Cummings, later a fa-
mous director, menaces him with a gun.

with pretty Shirley Grey. (Miss Grey's Southern
accent was atrocious beyond belief.) Another
William Gillette play, *Held By the Enemy*, was
filmed by Paramount in 1920. It was a combination
of Civil War intrigue and a routine domestic triangle. Agnes Ayres was a Confederate widow who
becomes infatuated with a Union officer (Jack
Holt). When her husband (Lewis Stone), a rebel
spy, turns up alive, she remains faithful to him
and to the South. Stone is conveniently killed in
the excitement that follows, freeing the lovers to
marry after the war.

The beautiful and daring woman spy of the

early Civil War films was seldom as exotic as Mata
Hari of World War I. Gene Gauntier starred as
"Nan, the Girl 'Spy," a wholesome Dixie orphan
whose patriotism led her to espionage, in Kalem's
popular series of 1909-12. One of her best was
The Girl Spy Before Vicksburg (1910), in which
she and her lover are both Confederate agents.
When he is killed, she completes a dangerous mission to blow up a strategic bridge and to destroy
a federal ammunition train. Miss Gauntier said
later that she came to hate the role, although she
played a similar character in films for other companies after leaving Kalem, such as United's *The*

Fred Warren, right, was frequently seen as General Ulysses S. Grant in films about the Civil War. This scene is from RKO Radio's *Secret Service* (1931), with William Post, Jr. and Richard Dix.

Little Rebel (1914). In Gold Seal's *In the Fall of '64* (1914), Grace Cunard and Francis Ford were two rebel spies who steal vital war plans from under the nose of a conceited Union general. Miss Cunard acted for the North in Bison's *The Battle of Bull Run* (1913), but her espionage had a tragic consequence in the death of her sweetheart and brother. Selig's *The Baby Spy* (1914), directed by Edward J. LeSaint, had a cute premise. When Confederates occupy her farm home while her father is away fighting for the North, a precocious five-year old (Lillian Wade) plays in a room where enemy officers are plotting a surprise attack. Later, she is able to repeat every word—and even draw a map—for her mother (Bessie Eyton), who makes a dan-

gerous ride through the lines to alert the Union. The Confederates are routed by troops led by the little girl's father. The plot was not new, having been used earlier in Vitagraph's *The Little Spy* (1911) and Bison's *On the Firing Line* (1912).

Perhaps the most unbelievable of Civil War spy pictures was Marion Davies's *Operator 13*, released in 1934. No one, least of all Miss Davies and the cast, seemed to take the preposterous plot seriously. At the outset, Marion is an actress who is talked into spying for the Union by the famous detective, Allan Pinkerton. She disguises herself as an octoroon servant to Pauline Cushman, the notorious Northern agent (played by Katherine Alexander), and the two set off to infiltrate the headquarters

In Paramount's Civil War drama, *Held By the Enemy* (1920), Confederate officer Lewis Stone (left) suspects his wife, Agnes Ayres, of infidelities with a Union captain, Jack Holt.

of General J. E. B. "Jeb" Stuart, hero of Antietam. Miss Cushman is soon found out and manages to escape, while Marion remains behind to masquerade as a svelte Richmond belle and extract military secrets from a Confederate officer (Gary Cooper) with whom she falls in love. There is an exciting chase when she is found out, but Cooper allows her to escape, promising that he will return to her after the war.

Operator 13 had a stormy production history. Miss Davies was the mistress of William Randolph Hearst, and her pictures were produced by Hearst's Cosmopolitan Productions. The millionaire publisher took a great personal interest in every detail of her films, and was frequently on the set. Hearst did not get along with director Richard Boleslaw-

ski (*Rasputin and the Empress*, 1932; *Men in White*, 1934), a brilliant but temperamental man with a background in the Moscow Art Theatre. They had many heated clashes over *Operator 13*, and after one rousing row with Hearst, Boleslawski stalked off the set, but was persuaded—or ordered—to return by Louis B. Mayer. The director encouraged Marion to use her natural talents as a comedienne to play the octoroon as a sensuous, flirtatious vixen, which she did with great charm. Hearst was extremely prudish about Miss Davies's screen image and objected strongly to this concept of the role. Although he allowed the scenes to remain, he insisted that it be made clear in the later portions of the film that the heroine was a dignified and virtuous lady. Hearst arbitrarily cut other scenes he did not like, much to Boleslawski's fury, which confused the plot and gave the picture an uneven pace.

Operator 13 again presented Hollywood's usual irresponsible portrait of an unreal South built upon exaggerated male chivalry, swirling hoop-skirts, and happy darkies strumming banjos. (It had several songs, some of which were sung by the Four Mills Brothers decked out as slaves.) Except for a brief but well-done montage of battle scenes, there was no attempt to present a realistic view of the Civil War and its effects upon individuals, both black and white. *Operator 13* was done on a lavish scale, and its fine cast included Jean Parker, Ted Healy, Russell Hardie, Sidney Toler, and several silent film favorites (Wilfred Lucas, Francis McDonald, Walter Long, Wheeler Oakman, and cowboy Buddy Roosevelt). Miss Davies's famous lisp was particularly noticeable, but George J. Folsey's beautiful photography (which was nominated for an Academy Award) helped to hide the physical ravages of Marion's heavy drinking. Although the reviews were surprisingly good, *Operator 13* was a financial failure, and this (and a quarrel with Louis B. Mayer) led Hearst to move his Cosmopolitan unit from M-G-M to Warner Brothers.

Another famous agent in Civil War history, Belle Boyd, was given a fictitious screen biography in Selig's *Belle Boyd, A Confederate Spy*, released in 1913. In the same year, Selig brought out a companion film, *Pauline Cushman, the Federal Spy*, with Winifred Greenwood as the actress turned Northern agent. Charles Clary was her Southern lover.

The Heart of Maryland, based on a David Belasco play, came to the screen three times. It contained every known cliché of the Civil War drama —lovers on opposite sides, sundered family ties, battlefield heroics, and a parade of personalities that included Abraham Lincoln, Robert E. Lee, Ulysses S. Grant, and Jefferson Davis. The sensational climax in which the heroine, Maryland Calvert, prevented the capture of her lover, a hunted Union spy, by swinging on the clapper of a huge alarm bell, using her body to deaden the sound, had thrilled two generations of theatergoers. In 1895, *The Heart of Maryland* had been the first major Broadway success of Mrs. Leslie Carter, the

distinguished stage actress, and she considered it her best role. Twenty years elapsed before she starred in the first screen version of the old Belasco warhorse in 1915. Once a great beauty with flaming red hair and flashing green eyes, the fifty-three-year-old Mrs. Carter had become drawn and matronly in appearance. Unimaginative costuming gave her a postively dowdy look, and audiences were amused at the spectacle of the grandmotherly woman swaying about on the bell clapper. Mrs. Carter was ably supported by William E. Shay, who had been her leading man in *Zaza* and *DuBarry* on Broadway, and J. Farrell MacDonald, later one of Hollywood's best-known character actors.

The Heart of Maryland was elaborately done with exciting action scenes. It was produced by Tiffany Productions, an independent company headed by Herbert Brenon, a fast-rising young director, and was released through Metro. Brenon gave it a lavish premiere at the New York Hippodrome, a huge showcase of arena proportions. Mrs. Carter made a personal appearance, but the audience was more enthralled by the water ballet in the Hippodrome's huge tank, and by selections from Gilbert and Sullivan operettas preceding the film. With tongue in cheek, New York critics said Mrs. Carter acted with "her usual vigor and exaggeration." (Many went to see her out of curiosity —Mrs. Carter was constantly in the headlines through a long series of legal escapades, and as a re-

Mrs. Leslie Carter, the legendary stage star, was fifty-three when she was featured in *The Heart of Maryland*, a 1915 version of the David Belasco play. J. Farrell MacDonald is the Confederate officer.

sult of her twenty-five-year feud with David Belasco stemming from her unexpected marriage in 1905 to a man thirteen years her junior; the producer never forgave her, and she retaliated by scathingly denouncing him to the press at every opportunity.)

In 1921, Vitagraph remade *The Heart of Maryland* in a desultory fashion, this time with Catherine Calvert and Crane Wilbur as the star-crossed lovers. Hampered by the pedestrian direction of Tom Terriss, it was static and short on action, and made the mistake of following the Belasco play too closely. Miss Calvert, widow of the playwright Paul Armstrong, had a dark-eyed beauty reminiscent of Miriam Cooper in *The Birth of a Nation*. Although only thirty at the time, she brought a mature quality to the role of the proud Southern heroine. Two young actors in the cast, Ben Lyon and William Collier, Jr., later became popular leading men.

Warner Brothers' 1927 remake of *The Heart of Maryland* had the beautiful Dolores Costello as the brave Southern girl. Her swains were Warner Richmond (left) and Jason Robards, Sr.

The Heart of Maryland came to the screen again in 1927. The dewy-eyed Dolores Costello and Jason Robards, Sr. had the leads, and a fine cast included Helene Costello, Myrna Loy (in a bit as a dusky mulatto), and Warner Richmond, who had been in the earlier Vitagraph version. Although verging on bankruptcy at the time, Warner Brothers gave it a handsome mounting, lavish sets, and suspenseful action sequences. The script offered several surprises by working into the plot such Civil War personages as Abraham Lincoln (Charles E. Bull), Ulysses S. Grant (Walter Rogers), Robert E. Lee (James Welch), General Joseph Hooker (Harry Northrup), detective Allan Pinkerton (Lew Short), Mary Todd Lincoln (Madge Hunt), Jefferson Davis (Francis Ford), and General Winfield Scott (S. D. Wilcox). *The Heart of Maryland* was the first important assignment of director Lloyd Bacon, later responsible for such diversified offerings as John Barrymore's *Moby Dick* (1930), the musical *42nd Street* (1933), and *Marked Woman* (1937), a drama of clip-joint queens starring Bette Davis.

KEATON: THE GENERAL—AND OTHER CIVIL WAR COMEDIES

Buster Keaton's classic comedy, *The General* (1926), presented the Civil War in less serious terms. A long, laugh-filled chase heightened by continuous suspense, it was the high point of the frozen-faced comedian's career, from which he soon fell into personal tragedy and near oblivion. The film is a composite of the diverse elements of the Keaton technique that has made it a frequently revived screen masterpiece. Except possibly for *Sherlock, Jr.* (1924), Keaton's inventive comedy in *The General* was never equalled. His gags, often elaborately contrived, are filled with surprises and are flawlessly executed.

The General was based on an actual incident in the Civil War in which James J. Andrews, a Union spy, and a group of nineteen followers planned to steal a locomotive at Atlanta and run north to Chattanooga, crippling Confederate communications by burning bridges, destroying supply depots, and cutting telegraph lines. Andrews and his audacious band infiltrated enemy territory and made off with a train at Big Shanty, just north of Atlanta,

In this shot taken on the set of *The General* (1926), Buster Keaton demonstrates a prop used in the Civil War comedy of Northern railroad raiders.

while the crew and passengers were at breakfast. The raiders were pursued by Confederates in several other locomotives and were apprehended nineteen miles below Chattanooga. Some of the marauders were captured and hanged or imprisoned, while the first Congressional Medals of Honor were later bestowed on several who escaped.

The Andrews raid was suggested to Keaton as the plot of his next film after *Battling Butler* (1926) by his gag-man, Clyde Bruckman. The comedian was excited by its potentials and with his team of writers (Bruckman, Al Boasberg, Charles Smith) fashioned a lively script. From the outset Keaton insisted upon authenticity in costumes, sets, and period detail, particularly in the use of the narrow-gauge, wood-burning locomotives of the Civil War era. (The film drew its title from the name of an actual locomotive used to transport Union troops.) *The General* went into production in the summer of 1926 in Oregon,

where members of the Oregon State Guard were used as soldiers in the battle sequences.

In *The General*, Keaton played a hapless locomotive engineer who is refused enlistment in the Confederate Army because he is more valuable driving trains. His sweetheart, Annabelle Lee (portrayed by Marion Mack—one of those delightful, hopelessly dumb Keaton heroines—misunderstands and thinks he is a coward. She breaks off their engagement. Later, when The General is stolen by federal spies with the girl aboard, Keaton sets out in pursuit. He rescues Annabelle Lee, recovers his beloved locomotive, and lures the Union Army into a Confederate ambush. The film ends with a hilarious battle in which Keaton's ineptness as an artilleryman causes a misdirected shell to shatter a dam and flood the attacking Yankee cavalry. The engineer is acclaimed a hero, made a lieutenant in the Confederate Army, and wins the the heroine.

Keaton and Bruckman, who codirected, at times displayed an unexpected talent for striking camera compositions. The spectacular climactic battle contains several arresting long-shots of moving masses of men, horses, and equipment. (These panoramic sequences were marred slightly by clouds of gunsmoke that obscured some of the action.) Other scenes showing Union soldiers attacking in a forest as sunlight streams through the trees were later emulated in such Civil War films as *The Red Badge of Courage* (1951) and *Raintree County* (1957). Part of the delight of *The General* is the Matthew Brady quality of its photography (by J. Devereaux Jennings and Bert Haines), the rough settings of a small Georgia town of the early 1860s, and the authentic, if often ill fitting, costumes and uniforms. These values bring visual reality to the Civil War of *The General*, but it is Keaton's superb comedy that gives the film its classic proportions. (In 1939, a tired and aging Buster Keaton appeared in a Columbia two-reeler, *Mooching Through Georgia*, in which he is an unwilling spy for the North. Buster manages to escape a firing squad and capture a company of rebel soldiers. It was written by Clyde Bruckman, who a few years later borrowed a gun from Keaton and killed himself.)

The Keaton masterpiece was not the first nor the last version of the Andrews raid in motion pictures. Kalem's *The Railroad Raiders of '62*, a

The heroine in a Buster Keaton comedy was always beautiful but dumb, and lovely Marion Mack in *The General* was no exception.

A temperamental cannon with a recalcitrant fuse, perched on a flatbed railway car, leads Buster Keaton into a moment of suspenseful investigation. A scene from his classic Civil War comedy, *The General* (1926).

In *The General*, Buster Keaton rides the cowcatcher of
a runaway locomotive, imperturbably caught in a typical Keaton comedy situation.

one-reeler of 1911 directed by Sidney Olcott, was
an abbreviated account of the historic event. Four
years later, Kalem brought out a longer version
under the same title as one of the *Hazards of Helen*
series of railroad adventures starring Helen Holmes.
An old flagman tells in a flashback how he lost an
arm in the Andrews raid. It may have incorporated
some scenes from Olcott's earlier film. In 1956,
Walt Disney's *The Great Locomotive Chase* starred
Fess Parker, fresh from his success as Davy Crockett,
as the audacious Union agent. Jeffrey Hunter
played William Fuller, the conductor who pursued
his stolen train, first on a handcar and then in

another engine. Photographed in garish Technicolor with emphasis upon action, *The Great Locomotive Chase* lacked the charm and originality of
Keaton's silent comedy. To assure authenticity,
Disney retained Fuller's son-in-law, Wilbur G.
Kurtz, as technical director. An eminent Georgia
historian, Kurtz also supervised the Civil War detail of *Gone With the Wind*.

In 1948, Buster Keaton, then down on his luck
and virtually forgotten by Hollywood, was hired
as a gag writer on M-G-M's *A Southern Yankee*.
It was a broad farce of the Civil War with Red
Skelton as a bumbling hotel bellboy who inadver-

tently becomes a Northern spy. Not unexpectedly, Keaton's gags gave it the flavor of a silent comedy. One of the best laughs devised by Keaton came when Skelton is caught in the middle of a pitched battle. He dons a makeshift uniform that is Union blue on the right side, Confederate gray on the left, and escapes by making each side think he is one of their own men. When director S. Sylvan Simon became ill and had to be replaced, Keaton begged M-G-M to let him finish *A Southern Yankee,* but Louis B. Mayer would not hear of it. The picture was completed by Edward Sedgwick, director of several of Keaton's last features at M-G-M (*The Cameraman,* 1928; *Free and Easy,* 1930; *The Doughboys,* 1930). The comedian was eventually permitted to direct a few Pete Smith short subjects.

Paramount's *Hands Up!* (1926), released a few months before *The General,* was an ingenious spoof of the Civil War spy dramas. Its star was

Raymond Griffith played a debonnaire Southern spy in top hat who infiltrated the Union forces out West in Paramount's *Hands Up!* (1926). Marian Nixon was one of two girls who claimed his attentions.

the urbane Raymond Griffith, a sort of latter-day Max Linder identified by his sartorial elegance. His trademark was a well-polished silk hat, which he wore even with a Confederate uniform. *Hands Up!* was a deft combination of satire, pure slapstick, and comic anomalies. Griffith played a master spy sent west by General Robert E. Lee to obtain gold needed to purchase arms and equipment for the South. A series of absurd situations followed, from which Griffith extricated himself with cool aplomb. When Indians overtake his covered wagon, he teaches them to shoot craps and to do the Charleston, indifferent to the suffering of another hostage (the burly Mack Swain of Chaplin's 1925 classic, *The Gold Rush*) made to dance on hot coals. Griffith is twice captured by Union agents, escapes a firing squad and a hanging, and finally makes off with a gold shipment. His triumph is short-lived when General Lee surrenders and the Civil War ends. Unable to make up his mind between two pretty sisters (Marian Nixon and Virginia Lee Corbin) with whom he has fallen in love, he becomes a Mormon and marries both!

Although *Hand Up!* rated only mild reviews at the time of its release, it is more favorably received today at infrequent revivals by movie museums. (An abbreviated version is available to collectors.) The picture is no longer lost in the clutter of hundreds of slapstick comedies of the 1920s, and its satire is fresh and inventive. Part of its success is due to the clever direction of Clarence G. Badger, a little appreciated comedy craftsman who did many of the better silents of Will Rogers, Mabel Normand, and Clara Bow. (Badger's career declined sharply after talking pictures, and he lived out his life in Australia, where he had gone to make a film in 1937.) The sophisticated Raymond Griffith never seemed to catch on with audiences despite a natural bent for comedy—he worked several years as an actor, writer, and director for Mack Sennett's fun-factory. After a disastrous attempt to play dramatic leads, he had only moderate success in a series of amusing romps for Paramount (*Wet Paint,* 1926; *You'd Be Surprised,* 1926; and *A Regular Fellow,* 1925, a parody of the American visit of the Prince of Wales). In a sense, Griffith was ahead of his time with a style that came to fruition in the late 1930s with such zany comedies as Howard Hawks's *Bringing Up Baby.* Because of a voice defect, Griffith was unable to speak above a hoarse whisper, and his acting career ended when talkies came, although he had a memorable bit as the dying French soldier in the shellhole scene of *All Quiet on the Western Front* (1930). He later became a successful producer at Warner Brothers and 20th Century-Fox, turning out such hits as *Under Two Flags* (1936); *Drums Along the Mohawk* (1939); and *The Mark of Zorro* (1940). He died in 1957, aged seventy.

Afflicted with a voice defect that kept him from speaking above a whisper, Raymond Griffith (right) had a memorable but silent bit in the shellhole sequence of *All Quiet on the Western Front* (1930). The once-popular comedian played a French poilu killed by Lew Ayres (left).

A few other films used the Civil War as a background for broad comedy. M-G-M's *Advance to the Rear* (1964) was about a troop of Union misfits sent west to a lonely outpost where hopefully it could no harm to the Northern cause. Melvyn Douglas was a zany colonel who could not sit his horse, with Glenn Ford as the lieutenant who becomes involved with a beautiful rebel spy (Stella Stevens). There was much horseplay in and about a traveling whore house led by Joan Blondell, and the nutty band, more by accident than design, finally steals a gold shipment intended for the Confederacy. Cut from predictable plot patterns, *Advance to the Rear* profited from the experienced comedy direction of George Marshall.

Another M-G-M absurdity, *The Fastest Guitar Alive* (1967), showcased the talents of Roy Orbison and a group of country-music performers. In reality Southern spies, they plot to rob the San Francisco mint for the Confederacy while masquerading as dance-hall entertainers. It was strictly cornball. In *Grandma's Boy* (1922), Harold Lloyd was a country bumpkin bullied by a tramp. He gains courage when his grandmother tells him about his grandfather's heroic exploits in the Civil War. In a flashback, the grandfather (also played by Lloyd) is seen as a Union private coolly vanquishing a troop of Confederates with an umbrella while calmly reading a book! Charles Ray's *Hay Foot, Straw Foot* (1919) was about a World War I doughboy who approached every situation by asking himself, "What would General Grant have done here?" It also had comic flashbacks with Ray performing brave deeds in the Civil War. Even Mack Sennett got into the War Between the States. One of his earlier comedies, *Cohen Saves the Flag* (1913), had Ford Sterling as a Jewish lad who joins the Union Army to impress his sweetheart (Mabel Normand), only to find his commanding officer is a rival for her hand. Sterling becomes a hero in the Battle of Gettysburg and wins the girl. Sennett also did *Salome Versus Shenandoah* (1919), in which Ben Turpin, Phyllis Haver, and Charlie

Harold Lloyd's *Grandma's Boy* (1922) had a modern setting, but Harold played his own grandfather—a Civil War hero—in the hilarious flashback sequences.

Hay Foot, Straw Foot (1919) was about a World War
I dogface, Charles Ray (left), who admired General
Ulysses S. Grant. This scene is from one of the Civil
War flashbacks.

Murray burlesque Bronson Howard's old Civil
War melodrama, *Shenandoah*. The low point of
such comedies came in Columbia's slapstick two-
reeler of 1935, *Uncivil Warriors*, with the Three
Stooges as inept Union spies. This was reprised in
another Stooges comedy of 1946, *Uncivil Warbirds*.

Shirley Temple's *The Littlest Rebel* (1935) cast
the curly topped moppet as a pint-sized Virginia
rebel. When the Yankees hauled off her father
(John Boles) —a Confederate officer—to be shot as a
spy, Shirley and her faithful slave, Bill (Bojangles)
Robinson, set off to Washington to persuade Abraham Lincoln to commute the sentence. They raise
money for the trip by dancing in the streets of
Richmond, and at the White House the Great
Emancipator (portrayed by Frank McGlynn, Sr.)
shares a piece of apple pie with his young visitor.
She charms him into signing the order that saves
Boles's life. Shirley sang "Polly Wolly Doodle"
and "Believe Me If All Those Endearing Young
Charms," and no one took her hardships or the
Civil War very seriously. (*The Littlest Rebel* had
been filmed before, in 1914, with E. K. Lincoln
and child star Mimi Yvonne in the leads, only

The Civil War was all fun and games in Shirley Temple's *The Littlest Rebel* (1935). Here, she brings together Confederate John Boles and Yankee Jack Holt at an officers' mess, while Bill (Bojanges) Robinson strums a banjo.

then it was General Grant who spared the father.) Another Shirley Temple picture, *The Little Colonel* (1935), was set in the post-Civil War antebellum South. The tyke softened up her grandfather (Lionel Barrymore), an embittered Confederate colonel who disowned his daughter (Evelyn Venable) for marrying a Yankee. Barrymore played a similar role in Henry King's *Carolina* (1934), again a Southern war hero who finds it difficult to reconcile himself to the marriage of his son (Robert Young) to a Northern girl (Janet Gaynor). *Seventy and Seven* (1917) was about a tyrannical G.A.R. veteran (Julien Barton) harassed and eventually humanized by his mischievous seven-year-old grandson (Ellis Paul). Another kid picture with a Civil War setting was Hal Roach's *General Spanky* (1936), an old-fashioned burlesque of the spy drama featuring the antics of Spanky McFarland and Carl "Alfalfa" Switzer of *Our Gang* fame.

THE TWENTIES AND THIRTIES

Except for *The General*, the 1920s failed to produce any significant motion pictures about the

The wistful Jack Pickford played the lead in the first version of *The Little Shepherd of Kingdom Come* (1920), a Southern youth who betrays his heritage to become a captain in the Union Army.

In the 1928 version of *The Little Shepherd of Kingdom Come*, Richard Barthelmess enjoys a pastoral interlude with beautiful Molly O'Day before returning to the war.

Civil War. In addition to the two versions of *The Heart of Maryland* and remakes of *The Warrens of Virginia* and *Barbara Frietchie*, there were several films about Abraham Lincoln (*The Highest Law*; *The Heart of Lincoln*; and Phil Rosen's *Abraham Lincoln*), and a few Westerns with a vague relationship to the North-South struggle (*Jesse James*; *The California Mail*; *Morgan's Last Raid*). John Fox, Jr.'s sentimental novel, *The Little Shepherd of Kingdom Come*, was brought to the screen in two versions, first in 1920 with Jack Pickford, and again eight years later with Richard Barthelmess. Its rambling story provided one of the typical "soul struggles" for which those stars were famous—an orphan boy raised and educated by Kentucky secessionists cannot accept the principles of the South and becomes a captain in the Union Army. Torn by guilt, he finds peace in a small town to which his unit has been assigned, and after the war he refuses to go back to Kentucky to claim his inheritance. The Barthelmess film was dull and overlong, and its best assets were lovely Molly O'Day as the girl and the beautiful photography by Lee D. Garmes. First National originally previewed it as *Kentucky Courage*, but after the picture did disappointing business in New York it reverted to the title of the popular Fox novel. (*The Little Shepherd of Kingdom Come* was filmed for a third time in 1961, with singer Jimmie Rodgers in the lead. Independently made on a slim budget for 20th Century-Fox release, it had a slightly different ending in which the boy returned to his girl in the Kentucky mountains. Andrew V. McLaglen directed.)

Until the release of *Gone With the Wind* in 1939, the thirties were almost devoid of Civil War pictures. King Vidor's *So Red the Rose* (1935), based on Stark Young's novel, was the story of the disintegration of a proud Southern family and its plantation during and after the war. It was essentially a dishonest and deceiving film that aroused resentment in the South for its unreal portrait of Mississippians, and that antagonized black leaders with its Uncle Tom attitude toward Negroes and slavery. The protagonists are all caricatures with dripping Southern accents. Walter Connolly is "Old Massa," who goes off to war in a cocked hat amid the cheers of his slaves. The daughter (Margaret Sullavan) lives in a world of her own, petu-

lant and unwilling to accept change. Her cousin and sweetheart (Randolph Scott) is at first indifferent to the war, but rides off to join the Confederates in a fury of vengeance after an outrage by enemy marauders. Only the mother, superbly played by Janet Beecher, seems to offer some semblance of reason. *So Red the Rose* was the traditional Hollywood concept of the wealthy, slave-owning, arrogant Southern family, repeated again in *Gone With the Wind*, and far removed from the realistic Camerons of *The Birth of a Nation*.

Blacks are given an even more libelous presentation in *So Red the Rose*, perpetuating the myth of the simple-minded darky who is happy in his lowly position and devoted to his white master. The climax of the film comes when a trouble-making black (Clarence Muse) incites the slaves to revolt and plunder the plantation. With the old colonel dying in the manor house, Miss Sullavan marches manfully into the slave quarters, slaps the faces of the ringleaders, and puts down the rebellion by reminding the rioters how well they have been treated! Connolly dies peacefully, unaware of the defection of his slaves, who docilely return to the cotton fields while the Hall Johnson Choir croons a hymn. Clearly, the implication is that Negroes are an inferior people with only a thin veneer of civilization separating them from the animalistic passions of the jungle, and who must be kept in check by white oppression.

So Red the Rose rightfully offended intelligent whites and responsible black organizations, and it was widely criticized for its bigotry and falseness. King Vidor suffered from some unfortunate Paramount publicity releases that created misunderstanding as to his attitude toward blacks and the handling of black actors. Vidor has been noticeably reluctant to discuss *So Red the Rose*, and there is no mention of it in his autobiography. Despite its shortcomings, the picture is not all bad. Vidor created a stunning scene of the mother searching for her son's body on the darkened battlefield of Shiloh. A brief clash with Union raiders is excitingly done, and the love scenes between Margaret Sullavan and Randolph Scott have a tender, lyric quality. Scott is most effective in his performance that prompted Margaret Mitchell to futilely suggest him for the role of Ashley Wilkes in *Gone With the Wind*. The black actors are

Retreating Southern soldiers stream by the plantation home of Margaret Sullavan and her son, Dickie Moore, in this scene from King Vidor's *So Red the Rose* (1935).

equally good, particularly Daniel Haynes as the faithful butler (although Haynes, a distinguished stage performer, was so hurt and indignant over the portrayal of Negroes in the film that he refused all further offers to work in Hollywood). *So Red the Rose*, which was produced by silent-screen star Douglas MacLean, followed the experience of most Civil War pictures—it was a financial disaster at the box-office.

Clarence Brown's *Of Human Hearts* (1938) was a maudlin drama of a family in backwoods Ohio just before and during the Civil War. James Stewart played an ambitious son who rebelled against the authority of his father (Walter Huston), a circuit-riding minister, and goes away to study medicine. He becomes a battlefield surgeon for the Union Army and neglects to write to his self-sacrificing mother (Beulah Bondi). Thinking her son dead, she enlists the aid of President Lincoln to learn where he is buried. Lincoln (beautifully portrayed by John Carradine) lectures Stewart at the White House and sends him home on furlough. *Of Human Hearts* was too dreary and slow moving for most audiences, although the sparse battle scenes were well done.

ABRAHAM LINCOLN ON THE SCREEN

Abraham Lincoln has been the subject of several generally unsuccessful motion-picture biographies, but has also been a minor character in dozens of Civil War dramas.[3] In countless early silents, Lincoln is seen signing the order commuting the death sentence of the captured Confederate or the Union soldier who fell asleep on sentry duty. Among many films to employ this common plot device were Vitagraph's *The Reprieve* (1908), Pathé's *Abraham Lincoln's Clemency* (1910), Lubin's *A Romance of the '60s* (1911), Vitagraph's *The Seventh Son* (1912), Pilot's *When Lincoln Was President* (1913), Kay-Bee's *When Lincoln Paid* (1913), and Edison's *The Magistrate's Story* (1915). In Selig's *Lieutenant Grey of the Confederacy* (1911), Sydney Ayres was a Southern soldier sentenced to be shot as a spy. His sweetheart (Bessie Eyton) manages to wangle a reprieve from General Grant, but it is Lincoln (James Dayton) who signs the final pardon. Even D. W. Griffith used this familiar situation to good advantage in a touching scene in *The Birth of a Nation* when the anguished Southern mother (Josephine Crowell) persuades the President to spare the life of her son

Joseph E. Henabery gave a sensitive performance as Abraham Lincoln in D. W. Griffith's *The Birth of a Nation* (1915), a role that he carefully researched. Henabery later directed many of the early hits of Douglas Fairbanks, Sr.

(Henry B. Walthall). Lincoln was portrayed with great tenderness and compassion by Joseph E. Henabery. (For Southern partisans, Jefferson Davis, President of the Confederate States of America, was seen granting pardons to Union captives in Kay-Bee's 1915 drama, *The Soul of the South*.) In other pictures—such as *Court-Martial* (1928) and *Wells Fargo* (1937)—Lincoln dispatches Union agents on dangerous missions against the Confederacy, usually with a patriotic pep talk.

John Ford's *The Prisoner of Shark Island* (1936) is the story of Dr. Samuel A. Mudd, the Maryland physician who set John Wilkes Booth's broken leg after the assassination of Abraham Lincoln. It accurately portrays the public hysteria that resulted in the innocent Mudd being convicted as a coconspirator and sentenced to life imprisonment in the Dry Tortugas. He had done nothing more than fulfill his obligation as a doctor to treat an injured man, and there is no evidence that he was part of the organized plot against the President. *The Prisoner of Shark Island* gives greater dramatic emphasis to Mudd's heroism in a yellow fever epidemic at Fort Jefferson than is warranted by history, although this is seen as the reason for his ultimate pardoning. From a more realistic viewpoint, Mudd was freed when the abatement of pub-

In *Abraham Lincoln's Clemency* (1910), the President pardons a grateful Confederate captive.

3. For a comprehensive account of the subject, *see* Robert C. Roman's "Lincoln on the Screen," *Films In Review* (February 1961), pp. 87-101.

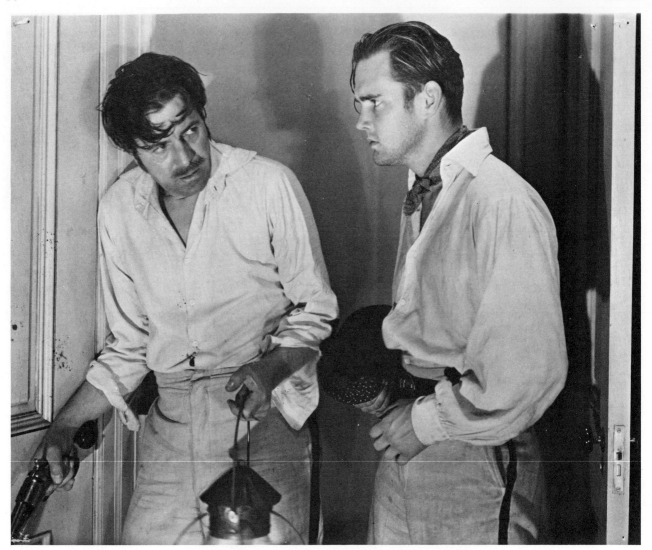

Warner Baxter (left) was the ill-fated Dr. Samuel A. Mudd in John Ford's *The Prisoner of Shark Island* (1936), the Maryland surgeon sent to the Dry Tortugas for setting the broken leg of John Wilkes Booth. Maurice Murphy is at right.

lic hysteria made it painfully apparent that a gross miscarriage of justice had taken place.

The Prisoner of Shark Island is notable for the scenes of unrest in Washington after the close of the Civil War. Included is the famous incident when Lincoln (Frank McGlynn, Sr.), responding to the clamor of a jubiliant crowd outside the White House after Lee's surrender, asks the band to play "Dixie." The assassination at Ford's Theatre is effectively staged, but there is less detail in Booth's flight and subsequent death when a soldier

shoots him in a burning barn. Warner Baxter brought dignity to the bewildered Dr. Mudd, while Francis McDonald seemed to lack both the good looks and brooding intensity usually associated with the role of John Wilkes Booth.

Another film in which the Lincoln assassination is recreated in vivid detail is Philip Dunne's *Prince of Players* (1955), a biography of actor Edwin Booth, brother of the killer. John Derek gave an interesting if somewhat flashy performance as a more immature John Wilkes Booth. *Prince*

John Derek (center) played John Wilkes Booth in *Prince of Players* (1955). Richard Burton was the Shakespearean tragedian, Edwin Booth, whose own career was seriously damaged by the backlash of the Lincoln assassination.

of Players contains several historical inaccuracies—Wilkes did not escape from the front door of Ford's Theatre, but used the stage entrance at the rear; he did not shout "Sic semper tyrannis!" from Lincoln's box (if indeed he shouted anything at all), but from the floor of the stage; Booth did not commit suicide in the burning barn, but was shot by a soldier.[4] *Prince of Players* does show the

personal anguish that his brother's act caused to Edwin Booth, and its effect upon the great tragedian's career (although the incident of Edwin Booth being pelted on the stage with rotten fruits and vegetables is untrue). In Bison's *The Toll of War* (1913), Lincoln frees a Southern girl (Ethel Grandin) sentenced to be executed for spying against the North. After her release, she witnesses the assassination at Ford's Theatre. The President is carried to her room nearby and dies in her bed as she kneels in prayer—a fanciful bit of cinematic fiction. An earlier attempt by a gang of

4. These and other errors, including the picture's fictionalized account of Booth's presence at Harper's Ferry, are described by Robert Downing in *Films in Review* (February 1955), pp. 79–81.

John Derek (left), as John Wilkes Booth, is stopped
by Union soldiers in 20th Century Fox's *Prince of
Players* (1955). Stanley Hall played Abraham Lincoln
in a few brief scenes.

Southern sympathizers to kill Lincoln on the train
taking him to his first inauguration was described
in M-G-M's *The Tall Target* (1951), directed by
Anthony Mann. Dick Powell was a private detective who foiled the plot, and Leslie Kimmell
played Lincoln.

Ralph Ince was the first major screen actor to
be associated with the role of Abraham Lincoln,
although he seems a most unlikely choice to those
who remember him as the sadistic sea captain
Wolf Larsen in *The Sea Wolf* (1926) or as the
gangland boss Pete Montana in *Little Caesar*
(1930). A brother of producer Thomas H. Ince,
he appeared on the stage with Richard Mansfield

before joining Vitagraph in 1908, where he directed or acted in over 500 films during the next
ten years. Ince first portrayed Lincoln in *One Flag
At Last* in 1911, a mediocre one-reeler in which a
Union officer, in love with a Southern girl, induces
the President to release her captured brother. Ince
said later that he got the job because he was the
tallest man in the Vitagraph Company. His impersonation was accomplished through makeup
and a dark wig that hid his curly red hair.

Ince subsequently appeared as Abraham Lincoln
in several Vitagraph films of 1911-14, many of
which he also directed. He had only a small role
as the President in *The Battle Hymn of the Re-*

public (1911) a much-praised picture that purported to be an account of how Julia Ward Howe came to write the famous Civil War marching song. In an early scene, Mrs. Howe (Julia Swayne Gordon) and Lincoln visit a Washington recruiting center that is empty of volunteers. That night, she dreams the words to the hymn, which are superimposed over such diverse sequences as the Nativity, the Crusades, and Lincoln striking huge chains symbolic of slavery. The song sweeps the North, inspiring thousands of men to enlist in the Union Army. *The Battle Hymn of the Republic*, directed by Lawrence Trimble, was a sensation in better theaters when accompanied by a large orchestra playing the stirring music, but it lost some of its

impact in tiny nickelodeons fortunate to have only a tinny piano. The film was slightly shortened and brought out again in 1917 as propaganda to create a feeling of patriotism during World War I.

Some of the other Vitagraph pictures with Ralph Ince as Lincoln bore such titles as *The Seventh Son* (1912); *The Songbird of the North* (1913); and *Lincoln's Gettysburg Address* (1912). They had a dreary sameness in which the President frequently pardoned a convicted spy or rebel sweetheart. The most popular of these films was *Lincoln the Lover* (1914), a sensitive retelling of the Ann Rutledge tragedy. Returning to the White House after his inauguration as President with the cheers of the crowd still ringing in his ears, Lincoln sits before

Bessie Eyton and Sydney Ayres were the reconciled lovers in *Lieutenant Grey of the Confederacy* (1911), who paid a visit to Abraham Lincoln in the White House (James Dayton).

the fire in his study. His mind wanders back over the years, and in flashbacks Lincoln is seen in the first days of his flirtation with Ann (played by Anita Stewart). He helps her with lessons in grammar—most accounts have it as Ann teaching Lincoln—and her warm personality and beauty do much to soften his somber spirit. Their idyll is interrupted when she becomes infatuated with another man, John Neil, and promises to marry him. Ann's fiancé goes East to see about an inheritance, but never returns. By the following spring she has recovered from the depression caused by her broken love affair, and returns to Lincoln. Ann becomes ill and dies before they can be married. The picture ends as an old Negro servant tiptoes into the study, and, thinking the President asleep, quietly steals out of the room.

Ince had three particularly fine scenes in *Lincoln the Lover* that he did with great dignity and sensitivity, the first as a heart-broken swain manfully congratulating his rival for winning Ann's hand. There is a poignant moment when, as postmaster of New Salem, he gives Ann the letter containing the news that Neil will not return, silently sharing her anguish. Finally, there is a glimpse of a bitter and disconsolate Lincoln standing forlornly at her grave in a swirling snowstorm. On February 12, 1914, at the Vitagraph Theatre at Broadway and 44th Street, Ince was a smashing success in a Lincoln's Birthday stage prologue to *Lincoln the Lover*. The setting showed an artist working on a portrait of Lincoln; he falls asleep, and in a dream Ince as Lincoln is seen standing in silhouette against a distant view of the White House. The lights came up as Ince turned and faced the audience to deliver a ringing rendition of the Gettysburg Address. Waves of applause brought him back for several curtain calls.

In 1920, Ince again portrayed Lincoln in *The Land of Opportunity*, a two-reeler about the President's early years in Illinois, which he also directed. It was produced by Lewis J. Selznick on commission from the Americanization Committee, and was first used to indoctrinate aliens seeking United States citizenship. The film did so well in subsequent theatrical showings that Ince was permitted to direct and star as Lincoln in a feature, Selznick's *The Highest Law* (1921). The plot was conventional—the old cliché of Lincoln pardoning

a condemned soldier who deserted the Union Army to visit his dying mother. It was told in flashback by an old G.A.R. veteran to two World War I doughboys. *The Highest Law* was Ince's last appearance as Lincoln, and thereafter he was seen mostly in villainous roles far removed from his characterization of the Great Emancipator. In later years Ince became beefy and bull-necked, and was frequently cast as a brutal sea captain (*Breed of the Sea*, 1926; *The Singapore Mutiny*, 1928) or a tough gangster (*Chicago After Midnight*, 1928; *The Big Fight* 1930). Ralph Ince continued to direct minor program pictures both in Hollywood and England, and was klled in an automobile accident in London in 1937, aged fifty.

Benjamin Chapin was a deeply religious man whose lifelong study of Lincoln became an obsession with him. He first won attention as a Lincoln impersonator on the Lyceum Circuit and in vaudeville, and in 1906 took the title role in an unsuccessful Broadway play that he wrote, *Abraham Lincoln in the White House*. From 1913 through 1917, Chapin starred in a series of films, mostly short subjects, designed to trace the dramatic highlights in the life of the martyred president. The project was incomplete at Chapin's death in 1918, and had progressed only through Lincoln's inauguration and the outbreak of the Civil War.

The production history of these films is obscure. They were shot in the East, with Chapin producing and directing from his own scripts. Originally, there were ten films in the series — *Lincoln's Thanksgiving Story* (which may never have been released); *My Father; My Mother; Myself; The Slave Auction; Down the River; Tender Memories; Under the Stars; The President's Answer;* and *The Call to Arms*. Although praised for their inspirational value, these pictures did not readily find a major distributor for theatrical release, and were shown primarily in churches and schools. At various times these short films were pieced together into feature-length attractions, sometimes using scenes that Chapin had previously deleted. *Old Abe* (1915) was a five-reeler about the Ann Rutledge romance, largely a composite of several of the shorts. In the spring of 1917, Chapin showed four of the original films as *The Lincoln Cycle* in a lengthy run at the Globe Theatre on Broadway. Their success led to a distribution contract with

Paramount-Artclass, and in 1918 the material was reedited into two full-length features, *Children of Democracy* and *Son of Democracy*, which did poor business. In the 1920s, the Chapin pictures were sold to a documentary producer, and portions were later used in historical films for classroom study. Chapin enjoyed denying that he resembled Lincoln, but in later years he took to dressing like the President, appearing in public with the beard, stovepipe hat, and shawl.

In 1924, two brothers, Al and Ray Rockett, brought out *Abraham Lincoln*, a scholarly twelve-reel biography that followed the martyred president from his birth in a Kentucky log cabin through the assassination at Ford's Theatre. Despite major flaws, it was one of the best films about Lincoln ever produced, although it was singularly unsuccessful in terms of general public acceptance and financial returns.

The Rocketts, described by friends as "intensely patriotic, idealistic young men," had for years harbored the idea of making a definitive motion picture of Lincoln's life. They had been in the film industry since 1914, working mostly as publicists and production assistants, and even before, Al Rockett had played the piano in a nickelodeon for five years. After failing to interest a major studio in the costly project, they scraped together enough money to produce *Abraham Lincoln* independently. Frances Marion, a highly paid scenarist for Mary Pickford and Norma Talmadge, was persuaded to write the script and to invest $50,000 of her own money. A distribution contract was negotiated with Associated First National, and the film premiered to rave reviews under the title, *The Dramatic Life of Abraham Lincoln* (which was shortened when exhibitors complained that it would not fit on small-town marquees).

The Rocketts said later that they spent two years in a nightmare of financial crises and intricate production detail. Five months went into meticulous research for *Abraham Lincoln*, much of it conducted in archives of the Library of Congress and the Smithsonian Institution in Washington. Yellowed newspaper and magazine files were sifted for every scrap of contemporary information about Lincoln and his era. Great care was taken to reproduce authentic costumes and coiffures, and the sets were modeled on dozens of paintings,

drawings, and daguerreotypes. Many old-timers who had actually known Lincoln, men and women in their eighties and nineties, were interviewed for anecdotes.

The research produced some questionable facts that were at variance with the familiar Lincoln legend. For instance, the Rocketts asserted that Lincoln did not write his immortal Gettysburg Address on the back of an old envelope, nor was it jotted down on his shirt cuff during the train ride to Gettysburg. One of the Lincoln cronies located was a 101-year-old gentleman named Cornelius Cole, who had been a United States Senator from California during the Civil War. Senator Cole said that he had ridden with Lincoln to Gettysburg after trying futilely to get an appointment with the President during the preceding five days. They talked of political matters throughout the trip, Cole declared, and at no time did Lincoln stop to make notes for his speech. The Senator further alleged that the President delivered the famous Gettysburg Address extemporaneously. The audience, although worn out by a two-hour oration by Edward Everett, was bitterly disappointed at both the brevity and content of Lincoln's remarks.

Cole recalled that a newspaper reporter had tried to take down the Gettysburg Address verbatim on the back of a worn yellow envelope. Later, he approached the President and asked him to fill in several missing sentences and key phrases. The reporter's copy, annotated by Lincoln, was later mistakenly identified as the President's own original notes—or so Senator Cole said. His recollections do not correspond to eyewitness accounts, and his name is not among those listed by John Hay as accompanying Lincoln on the train to Gettysburg. Whatever the truth of Cole's reminiscences at the age of 101, his version of the historic day found its way into the Rocketts' film.

Frances Marion's plodding script for *Abraham Lincoln* was divided into four sections—the Kentucky and Indiana period, which recorded Lincoln's birth and early boyhood; the New Salem period, which centered about the heartbreaking romance with Ann Rutledge and her death; the Springfield period, in which the country lawyer became the standard bearer of the Republican Party; and the Washington period, from the inaugural through the war years and the tragic assassination. The major fault of *Abraham Lincoln* and the cause of its ultimate failure was the insistence upon including all of the key occurrences in Lincoln's life in exhaustive detail. As a result, the picture was episodic and had the quality of a school textbook in which the traditional concept of Lincoln was presented in an interminable series of historical highlights.

Abraham Lincoln was strewn with familiar incident. Lincoln is shown trudging twenty miles through a January winter to return a book he has borrowed. As postmaster of New Salem, he both reads and writes letters for the town's mostly illiterate population. He outsmarts a country charlatan who offers to trade horses sight unseen by swapping a carpenter's sawhorse for a swaybacked nag. There is the historic fight with the town bully, Jack Armstrong, and a display of strength as Lincoln lifts a heavy barrel of whiskey and drinks from the bunghole (only to spit the liquor on the floor). Lincoln arrives on a mule, his long legs brushing the ground, late for the famous debate with Senator Stephen A. Douglas after stopping to rescue a pig caught under a gate. His children interrupt the ceremony at which he learns of his nomination as a presidential candidate to summon him to the dinner table. And, of course, there is the obligatory scene in which the President succumbs to the plea of an anguished mother and pardons a Union soldier (A. Edward Sutherland) condemned to death for falling asleep while on sentry duty.

The role of Abraham Lincoln was played by an unknown, George A. Billings, who had never acted before. A fifty-two-year-old foreman for the Los Angeles Municipal Department, he bore a startling resemblance to the President. (When Senator Cole first saw him in makeup during the filming of the ballroom scene, he threw his arms around the actor and wept.) Billings was originally selected for the part over twenty-two other candidates, but was fired after a disappointing screen test revealed his shortcomings as an actor. Ray Rockett was unable to forget his uncanny resemblance to Lincoln, and at the producer's insistence Billings was recalled and given a crash course in acting. He did much better in a second test and was awarded the coveted role. In spite of his inexperience, Billings

William Moran, as John Wilkes Booth, takes aim on George A. Billings, as the martyred President, in the assassination scene of *Abraham Lincoln* (1924). Billings was so typecast by the role that he could not get other work in Hollywood.

gave a workmanlike performance and was highly praised by most critics. His portrayal of Lincoln proved his downfall, however, and for years virtually the only work he could get was to repeat the role in such films as *Barbara Frietchie; The Man Without a Country;* and *Hands Up!* Frustrated by his failure, Billings disappeared from Hollywood and was later found destitute in a Chicago flophouse. Ray Rockett brought him back for a Christlike character in *The Greater Glory* (1926), a drama of a wealthy Viennese family ruined by war. Late in 1928, Billings wrote and starred in an early Fox Movietone talking picture about Lincoln, a short subject that ran only a few minutes. He continued to impersonate Lincoln in vaudeville, before school groups, and on the lecture circuit, appearing in full makeup, but he had only a few bit roles in movies prior to his death at age sixty-three in 1934.

The Rockett-Marion film was not as carefully cast as D. W. Griffith's *Abraham Lincoln* would be six years later, and it was handicapped by uneven performances. There was uniform praise for Nell Craig in the role of Mary Todd Lincoln. A onetime leading lady for Essanay, she was excellent as the President's wife, fussing about his wrinkled clothes and aghast at the dirty condition in which she found the White House. (Yet, there was no attempt to show Mrs. Lincoln as a jealous, emotionally disturbed woman who would be institutionalized after her husband's death.) Irene Hunt was good as Lincoln's mother, Nancy Hanks, and William Humphrey, a former Vitagraph director, did well in a rather unsavory characterization of Stephen A. Douglas. On the minus side, director Phil Rosen permitted many of the performers in the New Salem sequences to outrageously overact in their roles as frontier hayseeds, possibly in a misguided attempt to inject comic relief.

The most difficult of the four sections, the Ann Rutledge story, was surprisingly the best handled. Much of its success was due to a sensitive performance by Ruth Clifford, a beautiful blonde actress who had starred in many pictures at Universal. She brought a natural quality to the role of Ann Rutledge, and portrayed her as an intelligent, self-reliant woman, rather than the all-too-frequent concept as a rather helpless and coy ingenue. The part did little for Miss Clifford's declining career, which did not survive talking pictures. Lincoln and Ann Rutledge were seen in a gentle relationship, again emphasized by incident, such as his

George A. Billings had the title role in *Abraham Lincoln* (1924). In this scene, he meets with his cabinet just prior to the assassination at Ford's Theatre.

demonstration of the new phenomenon of sulphur matches. Inevitably, the death scene became somewhat mawkish, but it was constructed with taste and delicacy.

Abraham Lincoln opened at the Gayety Theatre in New York on January 21, 1924, with a large orchestra playing a special score composed by Joseph Carl Breil, author of incidental music for *The Birth of a Nation*. Critics acclaimed it a significant motion picture and praised Billings and Miss Clifford, as well as the beautiful photography (by H. Lyman Broening and Robert E. Kurrle). Ecstatic at such reviews, Al and Ray Rockett were totally unprepared for what followed. *Abraham Lincoln* proved a failure at the box-office and lost a substantial portion of its investment. Except for those partnered in Associated First National, few major chains would book the picture. Exhibitors complained that it lacked name stars and that the terms asked by the Rocketts were too high. The film was twice the length of an ordinary feature, reducing the number of performances that could be profitably scheduled in a day. Second-run contracts with smaller theaters were few.

Audiences found *Abraham Lincoln* much too long and out of step with the peppy movie fare demanded by the Jazz Age. (Surprisingly, readers of *Photoplay* magazine later voted it the best motion picture of 1924.) More than anything, the familiarity of its subject matter robbed it of dramatic surprise. Part of the problem lay in a lack of action—most of the scenes were static and occasionally saccharine—and only seldom did it move with physical excitement and suspense. The Civil War sequences were short (probably deliberately so due to cost factors), and were mostly devoted to the defense of Washington after the first battle of Bull Run. Lincoln's assassination at Ford's Theatre came across with such impact that critics thought it too savage and gruesome, and urged that it be cut somewhat. A discriminate paring of Frances Marion's script, something she urged without success at the time, seems in retrospect an easy solution to the picture's multiple problems.

The Rocketts' *Abraham Lincoln* also suffered from the pedestrian direction of Phil Rosen, when more innovative techniques were clearly indicated. A onetime cameraman (best known for his photography of George Loane Tucker's *The Miracle Man* in 1919), Rosen first won attention as director of several of Wallace Reid's charming Paramount comedy dramas of the early 1920s (*The World's Champion*; *Across the Continent*). He later did *The Young Rajah* (1922) for Paramount, a ridiculous but highly profitable film in which Rudolph Valentino was an Indian prince who became a popular athlete at Harvard University! After nearly a year's work on *Abraham Lincoln*, Rosen directed several domestic dramas at Warner Brothers (*This Woman*, 1924; *Bridge of Sighs*, 1925) with Alice Joyce and others. He moved to Metro-Goldwyn-Mayer for a brief stay, where his principal assignment was to largely remake *Escape*, a Mae Murray vehicle begun by the erratic but brilliant Josef von Sternberg, which was ultimately released as *The Exquisite Sinner* (1926). Rosen directed the ill-fated Barbara La Marr in *Heart of a Siren* and *The White Monkey* in 1925, which were to be his last top assignments at a major studio. For the next twenty-two years (1927-49), virtually all of his work was at Hollywood's poverty row studios—Sterling, Tiffany, Chesterfield, Liberty, Monogram, Republic, and others. Rosen's ability to turn out any kind of film—dramas, mysteries, Westerns, comedies—on a miniscule budget with shooting schedules of less than a week made him the dean of independent directors.

Eventually, scenes from *Abraham Lincoln* were used in educational pictures made for use in schools, for which the Rocketts received only nominal compensation. Al Rockett became a successful producer at First National and Fox (*The Patent Leather Kid*, 1927; *The Barker*, 1928; *High Society Blues*, 1930), while Ray Rockett left the industry after producing several undistinguished films for First National in the 1920s.

Despite the financial failure of the Rockett-Marion-Rosen version, yet another biography of Lincoln came to the screen in D. W. Griffith's first talking picture, *Abraham Lincoln* (1930). The great director's career had been in decline since the release of *Orphans of the Storm* in early 1922. A Revolutionary War drama, *America* (1924), proved ponderous and old-fashioned, and a touching study of young lovers in post-World War I Germany, *Isn't Life Wonderful?* (1924), was out of step with the carefree times. Griffith tried a mixed bag of comedy, fantasy, and light drama in several films as a contract director at Paramount (*Sally of the Sawdust; That Royale Girl;* and *The Sorrows of Satan*), but without success.

In 1927, Joseph M. Schenck offered Griffith a contract whereby his films would be financed by Schenck's Art Cinema Corporation and released through United Artists. Schenck was then President of United Artists, and a major factor in the Griffith deal was that Schenck would vote a large block of stock that the director held in the company. The cagey Schenck reserved the right of script approval over Griffith's films and certain other key veto powers, which effectively robbed Griffith of any real autonomy. Under this arrangement, Griffith made three disastrous silent pictures, *Drums of Love* (1928); a second version of *The Battle of the Sexes* (1928); and *Lady of the Pavements* (1929), which had synchronized sound effects and songs by Lupe Velez. Their failure brought him to a critical low point in his career. Griffith's relationship with Schenck had so deteriorated at this time that he was unable to get an interview with the executive for several months. When Schenck finally consented to see him, Griffith managed to sell the idea of a new screen biography of Lincoln; no one was more surprised than the director himself, who went to the conference fully confident that Schenck would fire him.

Griffith's selection of this subject for his comeback film may have seemed surprising for a man with such intense loyalties to the South. As evident from his sympathetic treatment of Lincoln in *The Birth of a Nation*, Griffith had great admiration for him and felt that had Lincoln lived the South would not have been subjected to such humiliation and tyranny during Reconstruction. Griffith asserted later that he had been planning a film about Lincoln for twelve years, although there is little indication that he made any move toward it until the crisis with Schenck developed. (At the time, Griffith had been reading extensively about Sam Houston, and often spoke of doing an epic picture on Texas independence, climaxing with the historic Battle of the Alamo.)

In preparation for his presentation to Schenck, Griffith found the works of Carl Sandburg on Lincoln to be of immense value, and he proposed that the poet and historian be engaged to write the script. Although a generous budget for *Abraham Lincoln* was approved—about $400,000—Schenck was unwilling to pay the substantial fee that Sandburg demanded. Griffith then signed the distinguished American poet, Stephen Vincent Benét, to prepare a scenario. Benét had spent two years in Paris on a Guggenheim Fellowship writing his epic poem, *John Brown's Body*, and had read hundreds of books on Lincoln, Lee, Grant, Jefferson Davis, John Brown, and a host of other figures of the Civil War. He fell in with Griffith's suggestion that *Abraham Lincoln* be predominantly a Civil War film, with the story to revolve around a young Union soldier whom Lincoln pardons after a battlefield court-martial for cowardice under fire.

Benét's script was torn apart in a humiliating conference with Schenck and his assistant, John W. Considine, Jr., who brutally condemned it as worthless. Benét was sacked and left Hollywood a few days later, filled with a bitterness for the film industry that he never overcame. A new scenario fashioned by Griffith and Gerrit Lloyd fell back upon the familiar milestones of Lincoln's life, although some of Benét's dialogue was retained. Lloyd, a former publicity man who had written the scripts for *Drums of Love* and *The Battle of the Sexes*, said later that he spent nearly a year in research for the film.

Griffith was unwell during much of the shooting of *Abraham Lincoln*, and his physical and mental condition suffered from the heavy drinking to which he had become addicted. He frequently quarreled with Considine, whom Schenck assigned to supervise production, and was overruled by Considine on many issues. When filming was completed, Griffith abruptly left Hollywood for Mineral Wells, Texas—reportedly to dry out—and *Abraham Lincoln* was edited and scored without his participation. He did not see the completed picture until shortly before its New York premiere, at which time Considine refused to make several changes that Griffith suggested. The film opened at the Central Theatre on October 25, 1930 to generally favorable reviews.

Although Griffith seemed comfortable with sound, *Abraham Lincoln* was essentially a self-conscious film done with an old-fashioned technique that showed no originality in style or construction. Griffith had abandoned the unreal pathos that detracted from his silent classics, but he was obsessed by the sanctity of Lincoln as the savior of the Union. As a result the picture frequently lacked warmth, a defect accented by the episodic, isolated sequences that tried to cover too much of Lincoln's life. Once again, as in Phil Rosen's *Abraham Lincoln* of six years earlier, the plot simply offered no dramatic surprises.

As in most Lincoln films, the Civil War and the Presidency were subordinated to the more personal drama of the New Salem days and the Ann Rutledge tragedy. Griffith included scenes of Union and Confederate soldiers marching off to war, the firing on Fort Sumter, and the Yankee rout at the first Bull Run. The action was the suspenseful ride of General Sheridan (Frank

Sam D. Drane was one of several actors who made a career of playing Abraham Lincoln in movies and on the stage. His best-known appearance as the President was *The Crisis* (1916), Selig's answer to *The Birth of a Nation.*

Campeau) to rally his troops in the Shenandoah Valley, effectively done in a style reminiscent of the ride of the Klans at the climax of *The Birth of a Nation,* Lincoln is shown visiting a battlefield, where he interrupts a court-martial to pardon a young offender and send him back to his unit, and in salty conferences with General Grant (Fred Warren). *Abraham Lincoln* had the popular myth, retained from Benét's aborted script, of Lincoln remarking on Good Friday before the assassination that he had dreamed of a ship with white sails, which he interpreted as an omen of death. For some reason Griffith inserted a scene in which Lincoln speaks from the box at Ford's Theatre, repeating portions of his inaugural address. No such historical incident occurred. *Abraham Lincoln* had a dramatic ending in which the confusion after the assassination blends into sobbing, a voice calls, "Now he belongs to the Ages," and the film ends with a conventional shot of the Lincoln Memorial in Washington.

Walter Huston, a distinguished stage actor who had made a three talking pictures in 1929 (*Gentlemen of the Press; The Lady Lies; The Virginian*), gave a technically superb but somewhat mannered performance as Lincoln. He was particularly natural in his dialogue, avoiding the common tendency of Lincoln impersonators to declaim their lines. When asked by Griffith if Huston could play Abraham Lincoln, George M. Cohan replied, "Hell, man, he could play Grover Cleveland!" Huston spent several months preparing for his role, digesting a mass of Lincoln material, and experimenting with makeup and hair styles that would change the shape of his head above the eyes. His performance, although felt by some critics to lack warmth, is the best thing in the picture. (Huston had previously appeared as Lincoln in *We Americans,* a Paramount two-reeler of 1929 written and directed by John Meehan, which recounted the President's appointment of Ulysses S. Grant as head of the Union Army in the face of cabinet opposition.)

Griffith attempted to show that Lincoln's life was influenced by the death of Ann Rutledge. In contrast to the 1924 version, the New Salem segment was the weakest part of Griffith's *Abraham Lincoln.* Una Merkel, a young actress who first attracted attention because of her resemblance to

Walter Huston gave an impressive but somewhat man-
nered performance as Lincoln in D. W. Griffith's
Abraham Lincoln (1930). Fred Warren (right) was
General Ulysses S. Grant.

Lillian Gish (and who had been an extra in
Griffith's *The White Rose* in 1923), was chosen
to play Ann Rutledge, although she was originally
tested for the role of Mary Todd Lincoln. Unlike
the resolute characterization by Ruth Clifford, she
portrayed Ann as a coy, doll-like ingenue usually
dressed in a spotless dimity gown or billowing
crinolines. When Abe impulsively kissed her, she
fell in surprise from a pile of rails, expectedly
showing her new lace pantaloons. Ann's death
came during a frightful storm, with Lincoln barely
arriving in time to kiss her goodbye. It was, once
again, the traditional Griffith concept of frail

womanhood to be sheltered and cherished, as best
exemplified by the characters played by Lillian
Gish. The shortcomings in Miss Merkel's interpretation stemmed from Griffith's explicit direction.
Admittedly, it is difficult to reconcile her subsequent performances as a wisecracking, honey-
accented Southern blonde in dozens of sophisticated comedies with the pristine Miss Rutledge.

There were more than 150 speaking parts in
Abraham Lincoln, which were cast by Griffith with
great care. Particularly effective were Ian Keith as
the fanatical John Wilkes Booth and Kay Hammond as a gentle Mary Todd Lincoln. In the cast

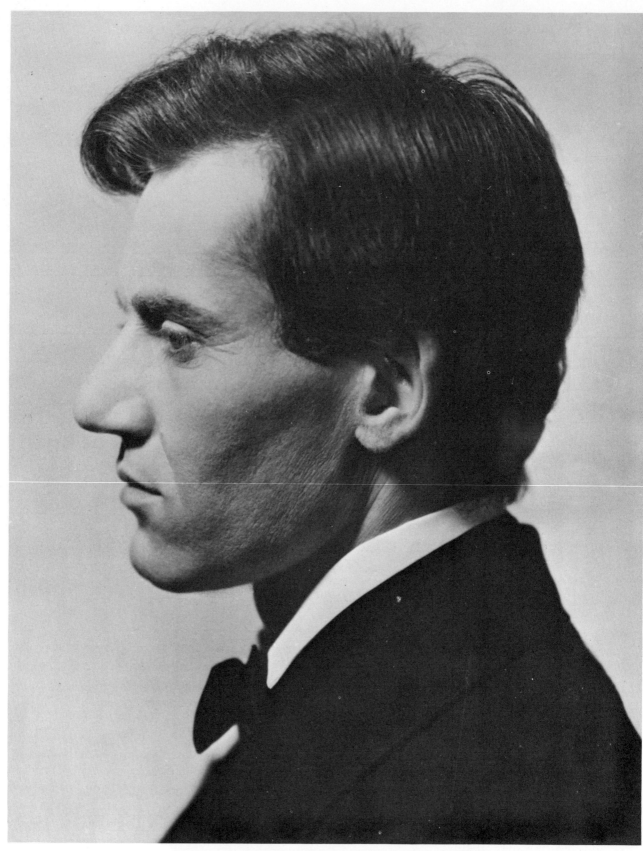

Henry Fonda was superb as *Young Mr. Lincoln* (1939) but director John Ford had to talk him into undertaking the role.

were two of the leads from *The Birth of a Nation,* Henry B. Walthall and Ralph Lewis.

Abraham Lincoln was highly praised by most but not all critics, although some felt its episodic construction made it more of a scholarly biographical sketch of Lincoln than a warm, human portrait of the Great Emancipator. Charitable reviewers thought Griffith's old-fashioned technique appropriate to the subject, and Benét's dialogue was consistently applauded, although in truth only a little of his material was used. (Griffith later asserted that he made a serious error in not insisting upon the Benét script, and said his original concept with Lincoln as an important but subsidiary character would have resulted in a more intimate and perceptive study of the physical and emotional ravages of the Civil War.) Although hailed as Griffith's best film in a decade, *Abraham Lincoln* did nothing for his faltering career. A contract with Schenck for a fifth picture was canceled by mutual consent. After one more talkie, *The Struggle* (1931), a morose drama of alcoholism produced in New York on a tiny budget, Griffith was through.

Two later Lincoln films of merit, John Ford's *Young Mr. Lincoln* (1939) and John Cromwell's *Abe Lincoln in Illinois* (1940), were limited to Lincoln's early life and did not touch on the Civil War. The Ford film was graced by a natural performance by Henry Fonda in the title role, perhaps the best Lincoln impersonation yet seen on the screen. It is interesting that one of Fonda's earliest acting jobs was appearing in vaudeville in a Lincoln skit with George A. Billings. *Abe Lincoln in Illinois* retained most of the beautiful lines of Robert E. Sherwood's play. Physically well suited to the part, Raymond Massey recreated his Broadway role as a more mature Lincoln saddened by the loss of Ann Rutledge. His performance was much admired, and he subsequently appeared as Lincoln in M-GM's *How the West Was Won,* (1961), and in television and on radio.

In addition to those already named, Abraham Lincoln has been portrayed in motion pictures by many other actors. One of the best known in the role was Frank McGlynn, Sr., a former lawyer who first acted the part in Edison's *The Life of Abraham Lincoln* in 1915. Some of his other performances as the martyred President were in *The*

Raymond Massey was Lincoln in John Cromwell's *Abe Lincoln in Illinois* (1940), which was largely limited to the early years of the President before he went to Washington for the second time.

Littlest Rebel (1935), *The Prisoner of Shark Island* (1936), *Wells Fargo* (1937), and Cecil B. DeMille's *The Plainsman* (1936), and in several of Warner Brothers' patriotic short subjects of the 1930s and 1940s.

The Reverend Lincoln H. Caswell was a New York clergyman with a great resemblance to Lincoln, as well as being a gifted amateur actor. He became a leading authority on the President, and for many years lectured on the subject in all parts of the United States. For these appearances he would dress in authentic Lincoln costume, including the stovepipe hat and shawl, and his presentation included many dramatic extracts from Lincoln's speeches and writings. In 1927, Caswell appeared as the President in *Lincoln's Gettysburg Address,* a Warner Brothers short subject that was one of the earliest Vitaphone talking pictures. He enjoyed being called, "The Living Lincoln." Cas-

Francis Ford, later a popular serial star, appeared as
Abraham Lincoln in Ince's *On Secret Service* (1912).
Judging from the disarray of Ford's hair with its revealing streaks of gray, this was probably a candid
shot taken between scenes.

Frank McGlynn, Sr. played Lincoln in films more times than any other actor. Here he is in makeup for a scene in Shirley Temple's *The Littlest Rebel* (1935).

Francis Ford again played Lincoln in Ince's *When Lincoln Paid* (1912), which used the same set and properties of the earlier *On Secret Service*. In this scene, Lincoln and his cabinet hear the familiar appeal of a distraught Southern mother for the life of her captured son.

well was quite a film buff. In the 1920s, when he was pastor of the Crawford Memorial Methodist Church at 218th Street and White Plains Avenue in New York, he began showing films at the church on Saturday evening—free of charge—and would preach on the moral of the picture the following day. The B. and B. Theatre of Williamsbridge furnished suitable features without cost, as well as posters for advertising purposes. These showings drew huge crowds, but were discontinued after area exhibitors complained that they hurt business. Caswell occasionally persuaded popular movie stars to make personal appearances at his church, and some of those who came were Lillian Gish and Mary Carr (of *Over the Hill* fame).

Sam D. Drane, who appeared as Lincoln in Selig's *The Crisis* (at a salary of $200 weekly), was a native Virginian who had moderate success

"His heartstrings torn by the stories of defeat and death," read the title for this scene in *Abraham Lincoln's Clemency* (1910).

A native Virginian, Sam D. Drane in costume for his role as Abraham Lincoln in Selig's *The Crisis* (1916).

as a character actor on the stage and in films with Biograph, Universal, Lubin, Nestor, and other studios. While his face lacked the craggy features of a Huston or a Massey, he did creditably well in the part. Drane claimed that he turned down the role of Lincoln in Griffith's *The Birth of Nation* because it was only a bit. After his appearance in *The Crisis*, he announced the formation of the Made In America Film Company to produce a series of one-reelers about Lincoln, starring himself. However, none of these films appears to have materialized.

Other Lincoln impersonators in motion pictures and television have included Francis Ford (*The Heart of Lincoln*, 1915), Willard Mack (*The Battle of Gettysburg*, 1913), Charles E. Bull (*The Iron Horse*, 1924), Frank Austin (*Court-Martial*, 1928), Victor Killian, Bruce Bennett, Chic Sale, Charles Middleton, Royal Dano, Meyer F. Stroell, William Clifford (who also appeared as John Wilkes Booth), George Stelle, Stanley Hall, Leslie Kimmell, James Dayton, and Hal Holbrook.

LEE, GRANT, AND OTHERS

Many other historical personages of the Civil War have been seen in various films. Robert E. Lee was a character in such early pictures as Thomas H. Ince's *With Lee in Virginia* (1913),

Lubin's *Between Two Fires* (1914), Reliance's *A Man's Duty* (1912), and Kalem's *The Love Romance of the Girl Spy* (1910). In Champion's *Service Under Johnston and Lee* (1911), it was the Confederate general who pardons a condemned sentry for deserting his post to search for a lost child. *The Heart of General Robert E. Lee* (1928), directed by R. William Neill, was an ambitious two-reeler that also showed him pardoning a Union spy, as well as the surrender at Appomattox. It was one of a series of short subjects produced by the Technicolor Corporation to show off its improved two-color process. More often, a tired but proud Lee is only glimpsed in Civil War films, frequently in the heartbreaking surrender, and without any real attempt at characterization. Such a vignette was inserted in *The Birth of a Nation*, with Howard Gaye (who later played Christ in Griffith's *Intolerance*) as Lee.

James Welch, a character actor with a striking

Howard Gaye was Robert E. Lee in *The Birth of a Nation* (1915). The following year he played Christ in Griffith's *Intolerance*.

resemblance to Lee, portrayed the Southern general in many silents (most notably in Phil Rosen's *Abraham Lincoln* and in *The Heart of Maryland*). J. Barney Sherry, who was Lee in the 1924 remake of *The Warrens of Virginia*, was too portly and melodramatic for the role. Perhaps the best Lee was Hobart Bosworth, a matinee idol of the early screen, in D. W. Griffith's *Abraham Lincoln*. With his beautiful white hair and erect bearing, he brought great dignity to the part. Others who have appeared as Lee are John H. Elliott (*Only the Brave; Operator 13*), Moroni Olsen (*Santa Fe Trail*), and Robert Osterloh (*Seven Angry Men*), William Johnstone did the role in *Sunset at Appomattox*, a 1959 television film, and Dean Jagger was Lee in *Gentleman's Decision* (1961), an episode of the "Our American Heritage" TV series.

Since the mid-sixties, producer-director Roger Corman has periodically announced plans for a definitive screen biography of Robert E. Lee budgeted into the millions, but it has never materialized. Richard Burton is reportedly confirmed for the leading role, and Corman also hopes to get George C. Scott as General Grant, Burt Lancaster as General Sherman, and Michael Connors (television's private eye of the "Mannix" series) as Abraham Lincoln! Corman, best known for his low-cost horror dramas (*The House of Usher*) and tasteless motorcycle exercises in violence (*The Wild Angels*), has also talked of filming the life of General Grant. It is interesting that his choice for the Union leader is also Richard Burton! In late 1974, producer James Ellsworth announced formation of Richmond-Confederate Productions (reportedly financed by Virginia businessmen) to make a ten-million dollar film about Robert E. Lee. Scenes are to be made on actual Civil War battlefields, the Custis-Lee mansion in Arlington, and in the Confederate White House. Another actor with plans to play Lee is Cameron Mitchell. In 1973, Mitchell and a South Carolina industrialist formed a company to produce the Lee story "with a cast of thousands—the most massive ever assembled," according to the publicity. A year later, Mitchell filed for bankruptcy, declaring that he owed $2,400,000 in debts. His assets totaled $306, including $200 in clothing and $80 in household goods.

Because of his unconventional approach to life and war, General Ulysses S. Grant has been a colorful character in many Civil War dramas. Like Lee, the Union hero has never been given a full-length portrait in motion pictures, and he is usually seen as the traditional unkempt, cigar-smoking, whiskey-drinking rakehell intent upon a Northern victory at any price. Grant was treated in more respectful terms in early silents such as Vitagraph's *The Bugle Call* (1909), Selig's *Lieutenant Grey of the Confederacy* (1911), and Champion's *Grant and Lincoln* (1911). The absurd plot of the latter had a young woman pull a pistol on Grant and extract a written pardon for her brother, a Northern soldier accused of treason. Donald Crisp was a more realistic Grant in *The Birth of a Nation*, and in the 1920s a minor character actor named Walter Rogers impersonated him in several films (Phil Rosen's *Abraham Lincoln; Flaming Frontier; The Heart of Maryland;* and *The Little Shepherd of Kingdom Come*). Joseph Crehan was frequently seen as Grant in such talking pictures as *They Died With Their Boots On* (1942) and *Silver River* (1948). He had a memorable bit in *The Adventures of Mark Twain* (1944) as Grant in his last years, a sick and discredited ex-President saved from poverty by the generosity and assistance

of the American writer. A television special of 1960, *Shadow of a Soldier*, also showed Mark Twain (Melvyn Douglas) describing Grant's downfall. James Whitmore played the General with admirable restraint. Other actors who have taken the role of Grant include Wilbur J. Fox, Fred Warren, Guy Oliver, Henry Morgan, Stan Jones, and Morris Ankrum. For Selig's *Lieutenant Grey of the Confederacy*, cameraman Alvin Wyckoff was drafted to play Grant. (Wyckoff later photographed most of Cecil B. DeMille's silent pictures.)

John Ford directed the brief Civil War segment of M-G-M's sprawling episodic film, *How the West Was Won* (1962), which has General Ulysses S. Grant and General William Tecumseh Sherman as principal characters. On the evening of the first day of the Battle of Shiloh, Grant (Henry Morgan) and Sherman (John Wayne) meet to assess their military shortcomings. A Texas Confederate deserter (Russ Tamblyn) is thwarted in an attempt to kill Grant by a young Union soldier (George Peppard), and the segment ends with a few random shots of the battle. Dramatically meaningless, it does little other than to bridge parts of the plot, and except for one telling scene—an exhausted army surgeon operating in an abattoir of human blood—it conveys nothing of the horror of war. It is, like his earlier *The Horse Soldiers* (1959), the John Ford conception of the Civil War, hampered by an unreal set obviously constructed on a studio soundstage, distracting art direction and garish color photography, and melodramatic dialogue. The two Union generals are stiff and mannered, and Morgan somehow fails as Grant in *How the West Was Won*, possibly because it is difficult to separate him from his image as a television policeman in the "Dragnet" series. Wayne, looking remarkably like the Matthew Brady photograph of General Sherman, succeeds only in being John Wayne.

Sherman's devastating march through Georgia to the sea has been unaccountably neglected in Civil War films. There are brief panoramic scenes of it in *The Birth of a Nation*, and it is referred to, but not seen, in *Gone With the Wind* (1938) and Clint Eastwood's *The Beguiled* (1971). Edison's *Hearts and Flags* (1911) showed the more grim aspects of the march. The hero, one of Sher-

Joseph Crehan (right) played a sick and discredited Ulysses S. Grant in *The Adventures of Mark Twain* (1944), who is saved from poverty by the distinguished writer (Fredric March).

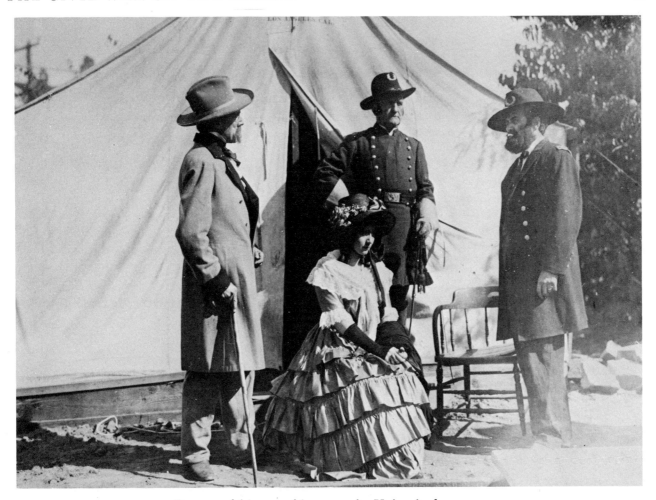

Because of his resemblance to the Union leader, cameraman Alvin Wyckoff played General Ulysses S. Grant in *Lieutenant Grey of the Confederacy* (1911). Others in the scene are Fred W. Huntley, Bessie Eyton, and Frank Richardson.

man's officers, is overcome with remorse at the destruction caused by his men, and he prevents them from plundering and burning the plantation of his Southern sweetheart. Bison's *When Sherman Marched to the Sea* (1915) also depicted the ravages of the campaign and the futility of the Confederate rearguard action. The postwar Sherman briefly associated with quelling the Indian uprisings was a character in Tim McCoy's *Spoilers of the West* (1927), played by Charles Thurston. (It is interesting that President Richard M. Nixon, while campaigning for reelection in California in 1972, suggested to industry leaders that a film about Sherman's life be made.)

Other Union and Confederate military heroes were occasionally portrayed in Civil War movies. General Philip Sheridan was idolized in such early silents as Vitagraph's *Sheridan's Ride* (1908), Selig's *In the Shenandoah Valley* (1908), Champion's *With Sheridan at Murfreesboro* (1911), and Kalem's *Shenandoah* (1913). David Bruce played him as a young man in *Santa Fe Trail* (1940), and the older Sherman of the Indian wars was impersonated by John Litel in *They Died With Their Boots On* (1941), and by J. Carrol Naish in John Ford's *Rio Grande* (1950). General P. G. T. Beauregard of Bull Run fame was the central figure of Kalem's *The Darling of the C.S.A.* (1912), which starred Anna Q. Nilsson. General George C. Meade, one of the Union heroes at Gettysburg, was the subject of Champion's *General Meade's Fighting Days* (1911), and he was also portrayed by Alfred Allen in the 1924 *Abraham Lincoln*.

Among other Civil War personages seen in motion pictures have been "Fighting Joe" Hooker, in *The Heart of Maryland* (1927); Thomas J. "Stonewall" Jackson, in Kalem's *To the Aid of Stonewall Jackson* (1911) and *The Bugler of Battery B* (1912), and in Champion's *With Stonewall Jackson* (1911); and James Longstreet, in Champion's *With Longstreet at Seven Pines*, another in the company's popular series of Civil War adventures released in 1911-12. J. E. B. "Jeb" Stuart, played by Errol Flynn, was the hero of Warner Brothers' *Santa Fe Trail* (1940), which also included scenes with Longstreet, George Pickett, John B. Hood, Jefferson Davis, and George Armstrong Custer as young cadets at West Point. Stuart was also a central character in Kalem's *The Battle of Pottsburg Ridge* (1912). General Custer, whose fame rests more on the tragedy at the Little Big Horn, had a genuine record of bravery and valor in the Civil War. In Raoul Walsh's film about him, *They Died With Their Boots On*, Custer is given an honest interpretation (also by Errol Flynn) as the irresponsible, foolhardy captain who led three cavalry charges that decimated his Michigan Brigade at Gettysburg. Kalem's *The Fire-Fighting Zouaves* (1913) was a unique account of the famous New York company of firefighters that became a crack Union regiment in the Civil War. It was built around the exploits of Colonel Elmer Ellsworth, the nineteen-year-old leader of the colorfully uniformed Zouaves, who became one of the North's first heroes when he was killed during the occupation of Arlington, Virginia.

Two notorious leaders of Confederate irregulars, John Morgan and William Clarke Quantrill, have been indiscriminately pictured by Hollywood as both hero and villain. Their audacious, often bloody raids in Kansas, Missouri, and Kentucky were frequent plot devices for disguised Westerns, and seldom was there any attempt to seriously portray this aspect of the North-South struggle. Morgan, a bearded Kentuckian whose gang of plunderers did not wear uniforms, was a character

in many silent films. In Kalem's *The Chest of Fortune* (1914), Morgan attacks a Union officer and his family at their home; faithful servants escape with a four-year-old son, the only survivors of the massacre. Reviewers criticized the film for its excessive brutality and killing. Universal's *Morgan's Raiders* (1918) was a Cinderella story of a poor relation (Violet Mersereau) who lived with a wealthy Kentucky family. When the Civil War breaks out, she masquerades as a boy and joins Morgan's men, and keeps them from burning the plantation. Eventually, she marries a handsome Union officer (Edward Burns) who comes to her rescue when her disguise is discovered. Others in the cast were Frank Holland, Barbara Gilroy, and a very young Ben Lyon. Wilfred Lucas's direction of *Morgan's Raiders* earned him a term contract at Universal. The best film about the renegade chief was M-G-M's *Morgan's Last Raid* (1929).

In *Morgan's Last Raid* (1929), a drama about the Confederate marauder, Tim McCoy (right) tussles with villain Wheeler Oakman.

expertly directed by Nick Grinde, with swarthy Allan Garcia in the title role. Tim McCoy played a Tennessean who refused to fight for the South when his state seceded, and was thought a traitor by his girl (Dorothy Sebastian). He redeemed himself later by joining Morgan's guerrillas and rescuing her after she was captured by a Union spy (Wheeler Oakman). Morgan and his men were also villains in Jack Pickford's 1920 production *The Little Shepherd of Kingdom Come*.

A lesser known Confederate partisan, Colonel John Singleton Mosby, although over seventy at the time, appeared as himself in an independent film, *All's Fair in Love and War*, released in 1910.

It purported to be a true account of how his daughter, although married to a Union officer, had served as a spy for the Confederacy. Broncho's *The Pride of the South* (1913) retold the same story in more sentimental terms and showed how Mosby (Joseph King) forgave his daughter for her transgression in marrying a Yankee, but not until he found her living in poverty after the war. Kalem's *The Old Soldier's Story* (1909) was about Mosby and his marauders outsmarting General Grant.

William Clarke Quantrill was the infamous leader of a band of 400 Confederate renegades who pillaged and burned much of Lawrence, Kansas, on August 21, 1863, destroying a Union arsenal

Joseph King played Colonel John Singleton Mosby in Broncho's *The Pride of the South* (1913).

In Raoul Walsh's *The Dark Command* (1940), Walter Pidgeon was William Clarke Quantrill the mild-mannered schoolmaster who led the vicious Kansas raids of the Civil War. His portrayal bore little resemblance to the real-life guerrilla chief. Claire Trevor was the girl he loved and lost to John Wayne.

and butchering 182 men, women, and children. The best film about Quantrill was Republic's *The Dark Command* (1940), although it presented a highly fictionalized account of the events that led up to the massacre. Walter Pidgeon was fine as "Will Cantrell," the embittered schoolteacher who organized the gang. The cultured actor had little resemblance to the real Quantrill, a small-time horsethief who hid from the law by living with Indians under the name of "Charley Hart." John Wayne was the federal marshal who killed him in a manufactured ending. (Quantrill actually died in a knife fight in Kentucky in 1865, two years after the tragedy at Lawrence.) As directed by Raoul Walsh, *The Dark Command* was impressively done, particularly the exciting raid featuring Republic's stable of famous stuntmen under the supervision of Yakima Canutt. Earlier portions of the picture bogged down in a conventional triangle involving Wayne, Pidgeon, and Claire Trevor.

Allied Artists' *Quantrill's Raiders* (1958) was also built around the Lawrence raid, but was done with less scope and imagination by director Edward Bernds. Steve Cochran was the Southern officer sent to contact Quantrill (Leo Gordon) and arrange the attack on the arsenal. He finds the rebel leader to be a scoundrel using the Confederacy as an excuse for killing and stealing, and alerts the

town and helps it to fight off Quantrill. Although imprisoned as a traitor, he returns after the war to marry a pretty Lawrence belle (Diane Brewster) with whom he had fallen in love. In Paramount's *Red Mountain* (1951), Alan Ladd was an undercover agent for the South who made Quantrill a scapegoat for Confederate crimes. Ladd knifes him to death in a bloody fight. John Ireland was a colorful Quantrill of dark and angry moods. Vitagraph's *Quantrell's Son* (1914) —the name was misspelled in the title—was one of the few films to show the guerrilla chief as a compassionate man. When his son, a Union soldier, is captured in a raid, Quantrill allows him to escape. Fred Thomson's *Jesse James* (1927), a highly fictionalized biography of the Missouri outlaw, depicted Quantrill's partisans as noble Confederate heroes fighting for the honor of Southern womanhood. In contrast, another picture about Jesse James, *Kansas Raiders* (1950), painted Quantrill as a black villain. The role was indifferently played by Brian Donlevy, who repeated it three years later in *The Woman They Almost Lynched*, an insignificant period piece. Allied Artists' *Kansas Pacific* (1953) was about a government agent (Sterling Hayden) sent west to stop Quantrill's attacks on a railroad under construction. Many Westerns with a post-Civil War background showed the remnants of Quantrill's gang as outlaws terrorizing the frontier. Among such films were *Arizona Raiders* (1965), with Audie Murphy as an ex-Confederate officer who tracked down Quantrill (Fred Graham), and *Rough Night in Jericho* (1967), with Dean Martin.

Although it did not identify him by name, Gold Seal's *A War Time Reformation* (1914) had some similarities to Quantrill's early life as a Western outlaw. The hero, a fugitive from frontier justice, is denied the opportunity to serve in the Confederate Army. He becomes the leader of a band of guerrillas that harass the advancing Union troops. In a wholly fictionalized ending, the renegade expiates his crimes by sacrificing his life so that his Southern sweetheart and her father can escape capture.

GONE WITH THE WIND

David O. Selznick's production of *Gone With*

Fred Thomson was a member of Quantrill's Rangers
in the silent version of *Jesse James* (1927), which took
great liberties with Civil War history.

In Paramount's *Jesse James* (1927), Fred Thomson
avenged the maiming of his mother by Union sympathizers after he returned home from the Civil War.

Allan Dwan turned the story of Quantrill, the butcher
of Lawrence, into a parody in *The Woman They
Almost Lynched* (1953). Brian Donlevy (right), styl-
ishly dressed for the Confederate raider, does not seem
much alarmed at the threat from James Brown, Jim
Davis, and Audrey Totter.

the Wind (1939), based on Margaret Mitchell's
sprawling novel of the Civil War and Reconstruction, is the most popular and possibly the most
famous of all motion pictures. It is also a superb
achievement in filmmaking, put together with
consumate skill by an orchestra of talents under
Selznick's baton. In more recent years, a younger
generation of critics, weaned on sordid and tasteless dramas of sexual perversion and drug addiction, have found it fashionable tó viciously deni-
grate Selznick's masterpiece. Admittedly, *Gone

With the Wind* is a pretentious film marred by
moments of great shallowness. It illustrates, in
retrospect, much of what was both good and bad
about the star system and (although it was basically an independent production) the big studio
concept of filmmaking. Nevertheless, by any standards it remains a high-water mark in screen entertainment, a milestone from which the motion
picture began a long, slow decline.

The public odyssey of *Gone With the Wind* is
now quite familiar, although its true production

Rhett Butler helps Scarlett O'Hara and Melanie Wilkes begin their escape from the burning Atlanta. Vivien Leigh, Olivia de Havilland, and Clark Gable in *Gone With the Wind*.

In this tense scene from *Gone With the Wind*, Rhett Butler (Clark Gable) and Ashley Wilkes (Leslie Howard) pretend to be returning from a night on the town. Ward Bond is the Union Officer, and Olivia de Havilland is at left.

history may never be fully told. The publication of David O. Selznick's famous memos have added some light, as have the reminiscences of George Cukor, the original director. Death has prevented the significant contributions that might have been made by Clark Gable, Vivien Leigh, Leslie Howard, director Victor Fleming, and others associated with the picture. The essential highpoints of the *Gone With the Wind* story include the following chapters.

First there was Selznick's reluctance to purchase the screen rights to the Margaret Mitchell bestseller while it was in galley form—he was only too well aware of the dismal box-office history of Civil War films—and their eventual acquisition for a paltry $50,000.

Second was the public insistence that Clark Gable play Captain Rhett Butler, for which he was so ideally suited, despite Gable's own disinterest in the role. To obtain the services of the actor from Metro-Goldwyn-Mayer, Selznick was forced to sign away the distribution rights and half the profits, and subject himself to the interference of his father-in-law, Louis B. Mayer.

Then there was the well-publicized search for an actress to play Scarlett O'Hara, which dragged on for months with fanfares of publicity. Some of those mentioned—and for the most part totally unsuited to the role—were Norma Shearer, Katharine Hepburn, Irene Dunne, Miriam Hopkins, Joan Crawford, and, inexplicably, Tallulah Bankhead. Others suggested were Claudette Colbert, Ann Sheridan, Carole Lombard, and Margaret Sullavan. Screen tests were given to Jean Arthur, Lana Turner, Loretta Young, and several unknowns including Susan Hayward and Margaret Tallichet. Selznick might have settled for Bette Davis, a prime candidate in public favor, but Warner Brothers would not lend her. He was reported to have decided upon Paulette Goddard when his brother, agent Myron Selznick, brought a vivacious English girl to the set where the scenes of the burning of Atlanta in *Gone With the Wind* were being shot. In Vivien Leigh he found an incomparable Scarlett O'Hara.

An incessant problem with the script evolved throughout the production, with Selznick personally rewriting numerous drafts prepared by such prominent writers as Sidney Howard (who re-

ceived the final screen credit and the Oscar), Ben Hecht, Oliver H. P. Garrett, John van Druten, Jo Swerling, and the erratic F. Scott Fitzgerald, then trying to earn a living in Hollywood amidst a welter of personal troubles.

A complete surprise was the replacement of George Cukor as director after only two-and-a-half weeks of shooting, for reasons that are still unclear. Some possible explanations for the shift were disagreements between Cukor and Selznick (although they remained lifelong friends), the producer's concern that Cukor's reputation as a "woman's director" made him unsuitable for a film of such epic proportions (an untenable theory), and that Clark Gable may not have wanted Cukor and was uncomfortable working with him. Victor Fleming, an M-G-M staff director of some distinction (*Captains Courageous*, 1937; *Red Dust*, 1932; *Test Pilot*, 1938), was engaged to replace Cukor. Later, when Fleming collapsed—whether from overwork or pique at Selznick's interference—a third director, Sam Wood, was brought in. Many action sequences and other inserts were directed by others, including Otto Brower, B. Reaves Eason, and the film's production designer, William Cameron Menzies.

The final chapter involves the glamorous premiere of *Gone With the Wind* in Atlanta, its enormous and enduring box-office success, and the winning of ten Academy Awards. Over the next thirty-five years it was reissued seven times, always to heavy returns—the 1969 revival alone produced $23 million. In 1972, John Schultheiss recomputed the $74 million domestic gross of *Gone With the Wind* to compensate for inflation in theater prices and arrived at an adjusted total of $114,200,000.[5] On one occasion, a completely new negative of *Gone With the Wind* was made through computerized techniques that converted it to a wide-screen projection ratio, added stereophonic sound, and restored its fading Technicolor hues.

Unlike *The Birth of a Nation*, which re-created many historical highlights of the Civil War and Reconstruction, *Gone With the Wind* is essentially a film about people, rather than events and places. There are no deeds of heroism, no epic battles or

5. *Films In Review* (August–September 1972), pp. 438–39.

Vivien Leigh was all innocence and crinolines as the
young Scarlett O'Hara of *Gone With the Wind* (1939).

stirring cavalry charges, no last-minute reprieves from the firing squad granted by a compassionate Abraham Lincoln, no attempt to ennoble the fallen South by the Ku Klux Klan and no happy ending. The nearest approach to traditional screen action comes in the escape of Scarlett and Melanie from the chaos of burning Atlanta to the war-ravaged Tara. Even an attack on the squatter's camp in retaliation for the attempted rape of Scarlett is only referred to and not shown. The only intimacy with the physical side of the Civil War in *Gone With the Wind* is found in the memorable scenes of dying men in the overcrowded

hospital, the magnificent pull-back shot of the wounded in the railway yards, and the headlong flight of panic-stricken civilians and soldiers as Sherman's men converge upon Atlanta. These sequences, along with a compelling scene where the casualty lists are received, convey the enormity of war in grim and bitter reality.

Few of the protagonists in *Gone With the Wind* are admirable or sympathetic people. The heroine (if indeed she can be so described), Scarlett O'Hara, is transformed by the circumstances of war from a pampered darling of Georgian aristocracy to an aggressive and greedy woman with a meaningless

The defeat of the South looms as wounded and exhausted Confederate soldiers sprawl in the railway yards of Atlanta in David O. Selznick's *Gone With the Wind*.

A bored and ungrieving widow whose husband has been lost early in the Civil War, Scarlett O'Hara shocks Atlanta society by accepting the bid of the dashing Rhett Butler for a dance at a charity ball. Vivien Leigh and Clark Gable in *Gone With the Wind*.

life. She is at once both a strong and a weak person: strong in her determination to overcome defeat and win back what the war has cost her; weak in her persistent emotional immaturity that prevents her from ever finding happiness. Stunningly played by the beautiful Vivien Leigh, Scarlett O'Hara is a totally fascinating character about whom all of *Gone, With the Wind* revolves. Rhett Butler, the rich blockade-runner who marries and eventually deserts her, is another nonhero, a Civil War incarnation of the distinctive personality of Clark Gable. His background and motivations are never explained, but Gable portrays the picaresque Captain Butler with such style and charm as to conceal this defect. It is interesting to note that Gable felt that he was unsuited to the part, and for a time resisted efforts to cast him in it.

The gentle Melanie (Olivia de Havilland) is a calculated contrast to the fiery Scarlett, an overdrawn example of pristine goodness and sweetness in Southern womanhood that is ultimately unconvincing. By far the most unreal character is Ashley Wilkes, a caricature of the gallant Southern gentleman impoverished in both spirit and pocketbook

by the war. The fault is largely the unwise selection of Leslie Howard for the role, a major error
that is increasingly apparent with the passage of
time. He is at best a dull bore and completely unlikely as the object of Scarlett's unrequited passion;
one can only wish that Ashley might emulate Rhett
by seizing Scarlett (or even Melanie) and carrying
her up the stairs, two steps at a time, to an ornate
bedroom!

In contrast, D. W. Griffith had clothed the Cameron family of *The Birth of a Nation* in a gentility
that wears well, and they are more believable (if
less interesting) than the emotional misfits of *Gone*
With the Wind. Griffith's portrait is less intimate,
and from time to time impressive historical panoramas move across the screen. When the focus
comes back to the Camerons, it is to consistently
depict them with great nobility, despite their being
slaveowners and a party to the terrorism of the Ku
Klux Klan. Walthall's Ben Cameron is a creature
of inherent dignity and quiet masculinity, a more
realistic image of the man Scarlett imagines Ashley
Wilkes to be.

It is unthinkable that the Griffith heroines of
The Birth of a Nation could behave as Scarlett
did. They are cut more from the cloth of Melanie

The grand staircase at Twelve Oaks sets the scene for
Scarlett's rebuff by Ashley Wilkes. Vivien Leigh and
Leslie Howard in *Gone With the Wind.*

Vivien Leigh and Leslie Howard as Scarlett O'Hara and Ashley Wilkes in the Reconstruction sequences of *Gone With the Wind*.

—Mae Marsh with the radiant charm of youth and innocence as the little sister who flings herself from a cliff to escape a rapist, Miriam Cooper sedate in dark-eyed beauty in the near meaningless role of the older sister, and finally, Lillian Gish as the fragile Elsie Stoneman, epitomizing Griffith's own concept of purity in womanhood. The implications of the scene in which Miss Gish, flushed with excitement from Walthall's declaration of love, kisses and caresses a bedpost with phallic characteristics may be safely discounted. Griffith's protagonists are a greater part of the Civil War and Reconstruction, while those of *Gone With the Wind* merely react to it.

The Reconstruction portions of *Gone With the Wind* are anticlimactic and disappointing after the impact of the Civil War sequences. The film soon degenerates into a commonplace and maudlin account of the matrimonial problems of Rhett and Scarlett, and becomes tiresome. Only a few of the more immediate disorders of Reconstruction are hastily sketched—starvation on a desolated plantation, confused slaves insecure in newfound freedom, and the arrogant tool of the carpetbagger (Victor Jory), who threatens to buy Tara for taxes. In contrast, the Reconstruction of *The Birth of a Nation* is finely etched, building on what has gone before to a massive final climax. Griffith delineates both the history and personal trials of this angry period, from the startling shots of a black legislature in session to freed slaves abusing their former master. The Camerons strive to overcome the injustices of Reconstruction and begin a new life, first by honest attempts at conciliation with the carpetbagger government, and finally by spilling the blood of their oppressors; Scarlett O'Hara uses Reconstruction only as an opportunity to grow rich in the lumber business. It is Griffith who paints the broader if less intimate picture, who accents the issues more than individuals. The ideological controversies of *The Birth of a Nation* will never be resolved; admirers of *Gone With the Wind* can only debate the shallow question of whether Scarlett ever won Rhett Butler back. (Of course, she didn't—Rhett's departure into the night was as final as Nora's door-slam in *A Doll's House!*)

Notwithstanding its craftsmanlike construction and remarkable track record at the box-office,

Gone With the Wind will ultimately, with the passage of time, become something of a curiosity in movie museums, perhaps even an object of high camp. That fate will be met when it no longer holds nostalgia for those who go to the movies. Already it shows signs of wear—the cumbersome and tasteless titles that sweep from right to left across the screen, the garish color of an outmoded process no longer used, the unreality of the blacks, Max Steiner's dated music, and the unbelievability and triteness of Scarlett's closing speech. Hopefully, its final demise is light-years away.

Much of the charm and nostalgia of *Gone With the Wind* stems from its superb cast. Besides the fabulous personalities of Clark Gable, Vivien Leigh, Olivia de Havilland, the miscast Leslie Howard, Thomas Mitchell, and the never-to-be-forgotten (and Academy Award winning) Hattie McDaniel, there is a continuous parade of gifted performers, stars of the silents, young hopefuls on their way to fame, and the legion of talented bit players. One waits expectantly for the next familiar face to appear, and is never disappointed.

At the outset there is handsome George Reeves as one of the Tarleton twins, yet to become television's Superman and eventually to die a suicide's death. The many others included: Ann Rutherford, Andy Hardy's petite, wide-eyed sweetheart, and a teenage leading lady to John Wayne and Gene Autry; Evelyn Keyes, the warm, wonderful wife of *The Jolson Story*, and real-life wife to John Huston and Artie Shaw; Howard Hickman, leading man to Bessie Barriscale in many silents; Rand Brooks, Scarlett's ill-fated, young first husband, remembered by many filmgoers as one of Bill Boyd's sidekicks in the Hopalong Cassidy Westerns; Carroll Nye, a Warner Brothers' hero of the 1920s as the bewildered Frank Kennedy, Scarlett's second husband; Isabel Jewell, a fey personality but accomplished actress whose talents were never fully appreciated by Hollywood; Ona Munson, star of early talkies (and also a suicide), perfectly cast as Belle Watling, the whore with a heart of gold; handsome Tom Tyler, one of the great cowboy stars, in a bit as a Confederate officer herding a work-gang of slaves to dig trenches on the Atlanta front; Ward Bond, a rugged favorite of director John Ford, who found his greatest success in television's "Wagon Train"; Paul

In the wedding scene in *Gone With the Wind*, Scarlett O'Hara's poignant face cannot conceal her love for Ashley Wilkes. From left to right: Leslie Howard, Olivia de Havilland, Thomas Mitchell, Barbara O'Neill, Vivien Leigh, and Rand Brooks (as Scarlett's first husband).

Belle Watling (Ona Munson), at right, was the whore with a heart of gold in *Gone With the Wind*. Melanie (Olivia de Havilland) thanks her for hiding her husband when authorities hunt him after a raid on a squatter's camp—but Scarlett (Vivien Leigh, at left) is unreconciled.

Hurst, a director of early silents, just right as the Union deserter whom Scarlett kills and buries at Tara; Yakima Canutt, king of Hollywood stunt-

men, in a memorable bit as the brutal squatter who tries to rape Scarlett; Jane Darwell, the unforgettable Ma Joad of *The Grapes of Wrath*; Eddie (Rochester) Anderson, of the Jack Benny radio and television programs; handsome young juveniles William Bakewell and Eric Linden; fluttery Laura Hope Crews, a great name in the American theatre, as Aunt Pittypat; Cliff (Ukelele Ike) Edwards, Harry Davenport, George Meeker, Robert Elliott, Jackie Moran, Mary Anderson, Olin Howlin, and the fine black players, Ernest Whitman, Oscar Polk, and Butterfly McQueen. The list seems endless—it is a film buff's dream cast.

Although he received an Academy Award for his direction (but refused to attend the ceremonies), Victor Fleming has been accorded little recognition for *Gone With the Wind*. While he directed perhaps only half of this impressive motion picture under conditions of great personal stress, it is invariably referred to as the creation of its brilliant producer, David O. Selznick. At the time, a flood of studio publicity consistently minimized Fleming's work and stressed Selznick's enormous input and control over every aspect of production. Fleming has been accused of fashioning his direction to conform to Selznick's daily instructions, and also of simply following the detailed production design (which included each camera set-up) prepared by William Cameron Menzies. In view of Fleming's previous experience dating back to the early silents, and his record of hit pictures, it is unjust to overlook what is undoubtedly a significant contribution to *Gone With the Wind*.

There has been confusion as to what scenes were directed by George Cukor before his removal, although it is now established that he did only four major sequences. For years, it has been fashionable among the George Cukor cult to speculate on what a better film *Gone With the Wind* might have been under his direction. More recently, unjustified significance has been attached to the frequent visits of Vivien Leigh and Olivia de Havilland to Cukor's home during the course of production, where both actresses bitterly complained about Fleming and sought Cukor's counsel on the interpretation of their roles. Without doubt, George Cukor, a masterful talent, would have created an equally fine or better picture, with or without Selznick's interference. Working under the most difficult of circumstances, Victor Fleming did an admirable job on the construction of *Gone With the Wind*. He has had a bad shake, and deserves far more recognition than he is likely to ever receive. In lesser hands unable to bring a leveling influence to Selznick's dictums, *Gone With the Wind* could have been an incredible disaster.

THE FORTIES, FIFTIES, AND SIXTIES

The stunning artistic and financial success of *Gone With the Wind* surprisingly failed to stimulate an anticipated flood of Civil War films, repeating the experience of *The Birth of a Nation* in this respect twenty-four years earlier. World War II was on the horizon, and Hollywood soon turned to a remarkable combination of propaganda and escapist entertainment that had no place for dramas of a divided America.

Virtually the only film about the Civil War in the 1940s was Walter Wanger's uneven and melodramatic production of *Tap Roots* (1948), based on James Street's popular novel. An unbelievable plot centered about a Mississippi family that op-

Wearing a velvet gown made of window draperies, Scarlett O'Hara (Vivien Leigh) comes to borrow money from Captain Rhett Butler (Clark Gable), but finds him in jail. A scene from *Gone With the Wind* (1939).

Tap Roots (1948) was about a Southern family that resisted secession. Susan Hayward, Van Heflin, Ward Bond, and Richard Long figure in this scene.

posed secession and resisted the Confederacy when the war came. Susan Hayward was a spirited Southern belle with a touch of Scarlett O'Hara (a role for which she was once considered) who spends the night with a rebel officer (Whitfield Connor) to delay an enemy attack. Her true love (Van Heflin) forgives her, and they start life anew on a mountain top after her plantation is burned. Indifferently directed by George Marshall, *Tap Roots* is burdened with clichés of the Old South, and its principal asset is the beautiful color photography by Lionel Lindon and Winton C. Hoch. It had several good action scenes, and

Boris Karloff was delightful as Tishomingo, a Choctaw Indian medicine man.

Of interest to Civil War buffs was Warner Brothers' misnamed *Santa Fe Trail* (1940), starring Errol Flynn as a young Jeb Stuart. It was about the radical abolitionist John Brown and his final martyrdom at Harper's Ferry in an abortive attempt to free slaves, an event that indirectly stimulated the North-South conflict. Raymond Massey was superb as the wild-eyed fanatic, and in 1955 he repeated the role in Allied Artists' *Seven Angry Men*, a less elaborate picture but with a more human portrait of Brown.

Raymond Massey as the fanatic John Brown goes to
the gallows in *Santa Fe Trail* (1940). Addison Richards
at left.

Raymond Massey (center), a famous Lincoln impersonator, portrayed John Brown, the fanatical Kansas
abolitionist, in Allied Artists' *Seven Angry Men*
(1955). (Jeffrey Hunter and Debra Paget are the
couple at right). Earlier, Massey had played the role
in Warner Brothers' *Santa Fe Trail* (1940).

A minor revival of Civil War films in the 1950s
was sparked by John Huston's *The Red Badge of
Courage* (1951). Based on Stephen Crane's classic
story of a young Yankee soldier who panics during his first exposure to combat but courageously
redeems himself in a subsequent battle, it is a
hauntingly beautiful motion picture. Directed
with consummate artistry, perfectly cast and acted,
and expertly photographed (by Harold Rosson)
to resemble Matthew Brady daguerreotypes, *The
Red Badge of Courage* constructs an intensely personal experience of the Civil War into unforgettable drama. It sensitively explores, as did *The
Big Parade* (1925) and *All Quiet On the Western
Front* (1930) for a later war, the self-doubts of
men going into battle for the first time, the un-
certainty of what has brought them to this ordeal,
and the nagging worry of how they will behave
under fire. The picture is a succession of deftly
executed vignettes of human understanding that
build into a whole of remarkable power.

The plot of *The Red Badge of Courage*, completely faithful to Crane's original, is deceptively
simple. A farm youth (Audie Murphy) is followed
through inadequate training in a disorganized
Union camp to his company's first encounter with
the Confederates. When the line is overrun by the
enemy, he flees to the rear in panic and is struck
by a fellow soldier of whom he seeks information.
Concealing his cowardice, the youth manages to
rejoin his unit and performs heroically in driving
back the rebels on the following day, although
many of his comrades die. The film ends on a
note of irony as the soldiers, matured by their
blood bath, learn the battle was of no practical
importance. The decisive struggle had been fought
by greater masses of troops several miles away.

The Red Badge of Courage had an interesting
history that was chronicled in fascinating detail
by Lillian Ross in her book, *Picture*. Louis B.
Mayer, then on his way out as M-G-M's production chief, was bitterly opposed to making the
film, feeling it too downbeat and devoid of romance. Eventually authorized by Dore Schary,
Mayer's successor, *The Red Badge of Courage* was
brought in for $1,642,000, approximately $200,000
over budget. M-G-M panicked at the response to
a series of sneak previews where audiences jeered
and many persons walked out. In John Huston's

Glenn Ford (left) and William Holden (right) learn
the Civil War is over in this scene from Columbia's
The Man From Colorado (1948).

absence—he had by then gone to the Belgian Congo to begin shooting on *The African Queen* —the picture was drastically cut in a frantic attempt to give it popular appeal. Many key scenes and characters were eliminated, and a narration (taken directly from Crane's story and spoken by James Whitmore) was added. In its final form, it bore little resemblance to Huston's original, and he disclaimed any responsibility for the mutilated version. While the critics were almost unanimous in praise of *The Red Badge of Courage*, audiences disliked the film, and it failed miserably at the box-office. M-G-M was unable to secure major showcase bookings and finally resorted to selling it at reduced rentals for the lower half of a double bill.

Despite the fragmentation of its style and lapses in continuity produced by flawed and haphazard editing, *The Red Badge of Courage* has astonishing vitality. Most impressive are the battle scenes, the acting of John Dierkes as the Tall Soldier, and the wealth of incident that cumulatively reflects the horrors of war. Audie Murphy flowers under Huston's direction, and his performance is far removed from his wooden cowboy heroes. He brings a subtle realism to the role of the confused youth, no doubt psychologically influenced by his own moving experiences in World War II. Even cartoonist Bill Mauldin, an untrained actor, is just right as the Loud Soldier. If the philosophical tenets of Crane's masterpiece are at times obscured by the brilliance of Huston's direction, *The Red*

On the edge of battle, anxious Union soldiers find a moment's humor in this scene from John Huston's *The Red Badge of Courage* (1951). World War II hero Audie Murphy was the sober-faced hero (center), and Bill Mauldin, famed wartime cartoonist (second from left), was the Loud Soldier.

Badge of Courage is a perceptive and magnificent telling of a great story.

Only in recent years has *The Red Badge of Courage* come to be recognized as a classic motion picture, due in part to the emergence of the rabid cult of Huston worshippers. (It is much admired by a younger generation whose own conflict over the Vietnamese War might be expected to produce ambivalent feelings toward the film—identification with the confused hero on one side, and rejection of its positive emotions of honor, valor, and patriotism on the other.) Too much attention

has been given to useless speculation on the merits of Huston's lost version, rather than to an objective appreciation of what remains. In 1972, Huston said that M-G-M was considering reissuing *The Red Badge of Courage* in its original form. Such a restoration, if effected with Huston's assistance, could be a great contribution to film history. Conceivably, it could also be a major disappointment.

The Red Badge of Courage has undoubtedly suffered irreparable damage from Lillian Ross's book, *Picture*. It is not an inaccurate account— even Huston admits that—but her concentration on the foibles and personal idiosyncracies of its makers (particularly Huston, producer Gottfried Reinhardt, and writer Albert Band) has created a lasting prejudice against the film. However brilliant and entertaining her reporting, it serves to deepen the tragedy of this fine motion picture.

William Wyler's *Friendly Persuasion* (1956) is a charming account of a Quaker family of southern Indiana whose religious beliefs forbid their participation in the Civil War. The son (Anthony Perkins) is torn between his faith and a sense of duty to the Union, and, like the youth in *The Red Badge of Courage*, fears that he will be found wanting under fire. When Morgan's raiders approach, the boy joins the Home Guard and is wounded in the skirmish that follows. His father (Gary Cooper), experiencing the same struggle of conscience and self-doubt, goes to seek him. He captures a rebel bushwhacker, but cannot bring himself to kill the man and lets him go. Wyler's scenes of the Civil War are taut and surprisingly violent, played for shock value to counterpoint the gentler qualities of the film. Much of *Friendly Persuasion* is devoted to the quaintness and naiveté of the simple Quaker life, which provides frequent opportunities for comedy and quiet displays of family love. Gary Cooper and Dorothy McGuire are fine as the compassionate parents seeking to preserve the ordered morality of their beliefs in war times.

M-G-M's grandiose picturization of Ross Lockridge, Jr.'s tedious novel, *Raintree County* (1958), was a seemingly endless exercise in audience endurance. Montgomery Clift was a dreamy Indiana adolescent of the 1860s, a born loser who spent most of his time splashing around a swamp looking for a mystical raintree supposedly planted by the legendary Johnny Appleseed. Burdened by a plethora of other unbelievable characters, the picture follows Clift through a succession of woes, including two marriages (one to a woman lapsing into insanity) and the Civil War. The Battle of Chickamauga is recreated, and Atlanta is again burned by Sherman, all in gaudy Technicolor and 65mm widescreen, which only heighten the unreality of these sequences. Like the novel, *Raintree County* tried to encompass too much, and the impact of the Civil War on the bewildered hero is lost in the film's episodic style. Shooting was interrupted by the near-fatal automobile accident of Montgomery Clift—only one in a series of disasters that skyrocketed production costs to over $5,000,000—and much of his acting was that of a sick man. M-G-M attempted to exploit *Raintree County* as a Civil War epic, which it was not, with a series of elaborate premieres in the South rivaling those of *Gone With the Wind*. The tiresome picture drew mixed notices and lost money. Edward Dmytryk directed.

One of the multiple plot lines of *Raintree County* concerned Elizabeth Taylor as a Southern belle who went mad because she thought she had Negro blood. (For her bravura performance Miss Taylor received an Academy Award nomination.) Earlier, in 1957, another Civil War opus, Raoul Walsh's *Band of Angels*, was about the daughter (Yvonne de Carlo) of a Southern aristocrat who is sold into slavery when it is believed that her mother was a black Creole. An aging and obviously tired Clark Gable played a Rhett Butler-type with a shady past who bought her on the slave block. He installs her on his plantation, and predictably they fall in love. The Civil War breaks out, and the couple is trapped by the siege of New Orleans. A rebellious slave (Sidney Poitier) helps them to escape. An absurd, cliché-ridden motion picture that was offensive to both blacks and whites, *Band of Angels* had no semblance of realism. Several early films about the Civil War used the theme of the heroine who finds she has Negro blood and gives up a white lover. These included Kay-Bee's *The Crimson Stain* (1913) and Rex's *A Gentle Volunteer* (1916). In the latter, Dorothy Phillips was a Virginia girl who falls in love with a Northern officer (Ben Wilson). Learning that her real mother was a slave on the family plantation, she goes to tell her sweetheart that they can never marry. She takes a Confederate bullet intended for him in an ambush and dies in his arms.

John Ford's colorful *The Horse Soldiers* (1959) was based on the famous Grierson raid, an audacious sortie by Union cavalry 300 miles inside Mississippi to cut Confederate lines at Vicksburg. It was a characteristic Ford study of the types of men who make war, but the film's best parts were its magnificent combat sequences, particularly in the exciting sack of Newton Station. John Wayne as the tough leader of the troops bore little resemblance to the real Colonel Benjamin H. Grierson, a small-town music teacher who hated horses (he had been kicked in the face by one when a child). William Holden played a cynical Union Army surgeon who competes with Wayne for the attentions of a beautiful blonde hostage (Constance Towers).

The most memorable scenes of *The Horse Soldiers* were those of an aged headmaster marching his corps of military-school cadets, mere boys of ten to fourteen, to repel the invaders. Although played for comedy to a certain extent, these sequences have an undercurrent of profound emotion. Such an incident actually took place in 1863, but Ford was too soft hearted to follow history and show the massacre of the children that occurred. Instead, Wayne calls a retreat of his men when the old Colonel leads a charge in a buggy—shades of Roaring Jake Griffith! *The Horse Soldiers* was not vintage Ford, due in part to a banal script, but it was rich in entertainment value. Among Ford's stable of marvelous bit players was a white-haired and almost unrecognizable Hoot Gibson, the veteran cowboy star whom Ford directed in Harry Carey Westerns at Universal in 1917.

Drums In the Deep South (1951) was a conventional tale of two West Point buddies, James Craig

Drums in the Deep South (1951) was a drama of two West Point buddies who fought on opposite sides. James Craig and Barbara Payton had the leads.

The historic sack of Newton Station in Mississippi was the action highlight of John Ford's *The Horse Soldiers* (1959). William Holden, kneeling in the street, played a cynical but compassionate Union Army surgeon.

and Guy Madison, whose loyalties separate them when the Civil War comes. The Confederate officer is killed by his Union friend in a battle over a Southern stronghold. Director William Cameron Menzies seemed uninspired by his work as production designer on *Gone With the Wind*. In *The Proud Rebel* (1958), a saccharine tearjerker, David Ladd was a Southern boy who becomes a mute after witnessing his mother murdered by Sherman's men. His speech is restored by the affection of a frontier woman (Olivia de Havilland). *Shenandoah* (1965) told of a dour patriarch (James Stewart) in a border state who resisted attempts of the Confederacy to draft his six sons into the Army. He also fights off Northerners trying to impound his animals. When one son is mistaken for a rebel and taken prisoner by the Union, Stewart and his sons set out to rescue him. Their search fails, one son is killed by a nervous youth in a Confederate uniform, and they return

One of the best pictures of the Civil War in the border states was Universal's *Shenandoah* (1965). James Stewart (second from right) was the dour patriarch who resisted attempts to draft his six sons into the Confederacy.

home to find looters have murdered another son and his wife left to protect the farm. *Shenandoah* effectively portrayed the agony of a confused man who wanted only to be left in peace, but who cannot evade the terrible consequences of a war not of his making. Andrew V. McLaglen directed.

Hollywood's last effort at a large-scale Civil War drama was Edward Dmytryk's *Alvarez Kelly* (1966), which cast William Holden as a paunchy rancher who delivers 2,500 head of cattle to the Union in Virginia in 1864. Richard Widmark, a one-eyed Confederate guerrilla, coerces him into stealing the herd back for the South. *Alvarez Kelly* was another of those tiresome accounts of two men on opposite sides who come to respect each other.

There were several diversions to the plot, including Holden's penchant for Widmark's sexy girlfriend (Janice Rule), some cloak-and-dagger espionage in wartime Richmond, and a psychopathic rebel henchman (Richard Rust) intent upon killing the hero. Neither Holden nor Widmark had any warmth or believability, and both seemed bored by the whole thing.

THE CIVIL WAR WESTERNS

Dozens of Westerns whose plot threads held tenuous links with the Civil War flooded the screen during the 1950s and 1960s. Most were

Miriam Hopkins and Randolph Scott were both Confederate spies in Warner Brothers' *Virginia City* (1940), a drama of North-South espionage in the West.

cheaply made B-films with no pretense at reflecting history. The prototype of such pictures was Warner Brothers' rousing *Virginia City* (1940), but few were done with such style and verve. Errol Flynn, then at the height of his career, was a dashing Union officer who escapes from Richmond's Libby Prison. He is sent west to divert a Confederate gold shipment into Northern hands. Flynn spars with Randolph Scott, a suave Southern officer entrusted with getting the gold wagons through the lines, and falls in love with Miriam Hopkins, a Confederate agent masquerading as a dance-hall girl. Scott and Flynn have a grudging admiration for each other, and they finally team up to beat off a rascally half-breed outlaw (Humphrey Bogart) who wants the gold for himself. Scott is killed, and Flynn, in a most unlikely ending, buries the gold for use later in helping to

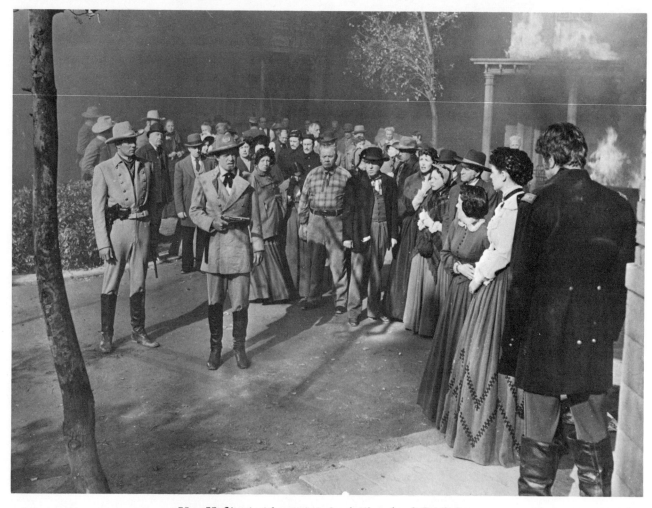

Van Heflin (with gun) led a jailbreak of Confederate prisoners to terrorize a Vermont town in *The Raid* (1954).

rebuild the defeated South. The Union-Confederate squabble over a gold shipment was the basis of numerous Westerns, including Ken Maynard's *The California Mail* (1929), *The Outriders* (1950), *Westbound* (1959), *Thirteen Fighting Men* (1960), *Incident at Phantom Hill* (1966), and the Italian-made *The Hills Run Red* (1967).

A favorite setting of the Civil War Western is the frontier prison in which Confederate captives help to fight off hostile Indians or outlaws. This theme was used with variations in such films as Robert Wise's *Two Flags West* (1950), *Hellgate* (1953), *Escape From Fort Bravo* (1953), and *The Long Ride Home* (1968). In Sam Peckinpah's *Major Dundee* (1965), Charlton Heston was a

Union officer who drafted twenty Confederate prisoners to augment a punitive expedition against the Apaches and marauding Mexican bandits. Less believable was *Arizona Bushwhackers* (1968), in which Howard Keel, in a respite from musicals, was a tough Confederate officer released from a Union prison to clean up a lawless guntown. Yvonne de Carlo made a pretty rebel spy. In *The Raid* (1954), well directed by the Argentinian Hugo Fregonese, Van Heflin led a group of Southern soldiers in an escape from a military prison near the Canadian line. They sack a Vermont town as a ploy to draw Yankee troops away from the front. *The Man From Dakota* (1940) was a routine Civil War melodrama in which two Union

Director Hugo Fregonese made a fast-moving attack by Confederates upon a New England town the action highlight of *The Raid* (1954).

soldiers, Wallace Beery and John Howard, escape from a Virginia prison with the aid of a Russian-born girl (Dolores Del Rio). They make their way through Confederate lines to Grant's head-quarters.

Regrettably, MacKinlay Kantor's *Andersonville,* a monumental novel of the infamous Civil War prison in Georgia, has never reached the screen. It was planned for several years by producer-direc-tor Stanley Kramer, and later was on Columbia's schedule with Fred Zinnemann as director. The project was abandoned when estimates of the pro-duction cost exceeded $12,000,000. Few properties offer such exciting potentials for a realistic view of this aspect of the Civil War. (In 1909, Kalem had brought out a fifteen-minute drama, *Escape*

From Andersonville, in which six Union captives flee the prison by stealing a locomotive.)

In one way or another, the Civil War figured in varying degrees in other Westerns. In *Belle Starr* (1941), Randolph Scott and Gene Tierney played the notorious outlaws, Sam and Belle Starr, who plunder to finance the rebellion. A sordid life of crime was justified in the name of loyalty to the South. *In Rocky Mountain* (1950), Errol Flynn was a Confederate officer sent west to secure New Mexico for the South, but his troop was nearly annihilated by Indians; *War Drums* (1950) and *Column South* (1953) were among many films with similar plots. In *The Last Outpost* (1951), Ronald Reagan and Bruce Bennett were two brothers on opposite sides in the Civil War out

In 20th Century-Fox's *Belle Starr* (1941), Randolph
Scott was a Confederate officer who turned to banditry.

Betty Compson played Belle Starr, the notorious woman outlaw in Columbia's *Court-Martial* (1928). Jack Holt was the Union officer whom General Grant sent to break up her gang of Confederate raiders.

West, but they join forces to fight off the redskins. John Dehner played the commandant of a frontier post in *Revolt at Fort Laramie* (1957); after secession, he is torn between loyalty to his native Virginia and his duty as a federal officer when Southern soldiers plan an uprising. Jacques Tourneur's *Great Day In the Morning* (1956) showed how the outbreak of the Civil War divided the townspeople of a Colorado mining community.

Undercover agents for the North and South set the pace for action in many Westerns. In *Border River* (1954), Joel McCrea was a rebel officer sent to Mexico to buy guns for the Confederacy. *The Redhead and the Cowboy* (1950) was about a plains drifter (Glenn Ford) who inadvertently got involved with a sexy spy (Rhonda Fleming) sent west by General Lee. Other Westerns followed the problems and fortunes of Civil War veterans in the West after the surrender at Appomattox, with many becoming soldiers of fortune, outlaws, or just simple men seeking peace. Some of the better films of this type were *South of St. Louis* (1949), *Horizons West* (1952), *Copper Canyon* (1959), *Young Guns of Texas* (1962), and *The Undefeated* (1969), in which veterans of the Blue and Gray team up to fight the remnants of Maximilian's forces in Mexico.

RECONSTRUCTION; THE VETERAN; THE CIVIL WAR AT SEA

Many aspects of the Civil War remain to be properly explored in motion pictures. Except for *The Birth of a Nation* and *Gone With the Wind*, the Reconstruction era has been largely neglected. Particularly absent has been any comprehensive and understanding account of the adjustment of former slaves to freedom. For most blacks, the Civil War produced little immediate change in living conditions, education, and opportunity— either in the South or the North. The carpetbagger governments are seldom defined in films, nor the bitterness portrayed that existed in the border states and lasted more than half a century. The unrest that arose in the Northern cities during the Civil War, and the draft riots that followed, have never been depicted on the screen. Neither has there been an intelligent cinematic appraisal of the root causes of the war, nor any intimate study of the leaders of the Confederacy.

Mutual's *My Fighting Gentlemen* (1917), directed by Edward Sloman, attempted to show the problems that a Southerner who fought for the North (William Russell) encountered when he returned home after the war. Francelia Billington was the girl who could not at first forgive him for his disloyalty. In M-G-M's *Stars In My Crown* (1950), directed by Jacques Tourneur, Joel Mc-Crea was a preacher assigned to a new church in a Southern town immediately after the Civil War. He fights the Ku Klux Klan and works with freed slaves in trying to improve their lot, and incurs the enmity of the local bigots. Kay-Bee's *An Orphan of War* (1913) pictured the psychological difficulties of a bitter, young Union veteran in trying to live in the South after the Civil War. In Paramount's *The Vanquished* (1953), John Payne was a Confederate veteran who fought against the carpetbagger government and its corrupt boss (Lyle Bettger). Kalem's *The Northern Schoolmaster* (1909) showed the Ku Klux Klan persecuting a Yankee schoolteacher in a Southern town. In *Drango* (1957), Jeff Chandler was a Union Army officer assigned to the occupation of a Southern town shortly after the surrender. He encounters great difficulty in a sincere attempt to rebuild the community.

The disgraceful treatment given to both Union and Confederate veterans seems an unlikely topic for motion pictures, but dozens of early films had such a theme. Broncho's *The Veteran* (1913) was about an aged Civil War hero who becomes impoverished. His wife dies of starvation, and his old buddies finally rally to care for him. Selig's *A Soldier of the C.S.A.* (1914) concerned a Southern veteran who makes a precarious living by playing the violin on street corners. Dispossessed by his landlady, he pauses before a statue of Robert E. Lee and for a moment relives the war years. Starving, the old soldier enters a fine antebellum home to steal food. A reunion of his old Confederate company is in progress. He picks up a loaf of bread and wraps it in a Southern flag, but is caught by the butler. When his former comrades learn of his plight, they wine and dine him, and flashbacks show his heroism on the battlefield. The saccharine film ends on a happy note as his old commander finds a job and a new home for the forgotten veteran.

In Universal's *The Medal of Honor* (1912), a destitute G.A.R. veteran is seen pawning a medal he won for bravery. Hodkinson's *The Old Fool* (1924) told of an eccentric Civil War veteran (James Barrows) who is rejected by his son. He eventually finds a home out West with a more compassionate grandson (Lloyd Hughes). In *His Last Parade*, a Lubin brevity of 1911, a Union veteran leaves a sickbed to march in a Memorial Day parade, and then dies of exhaustion. On a lighter note, Thanhouser's *The Reunion* (1916), directed by William Parke, was an account of two lovers, a Confederate nurse and a wounded Northern soldier. He promises to return to her after the war, but it is not until forty years later that they meet at a G.A.R. reunion and renew their romance. Chic Sale gave a touching performance as a Confederate veteran who knew Lincoln in an early Fox two-reel Movietone talkie, *Marching On* (1929).

A few of the many other films about the neglect of Civil War veterans were Vitagraph's *The Only Veteran In Town* (1913), Selig's *A Soldier of the U.S.A.* (1914), Rex's *Ashes of Remembrance* (1916), Universal's *Corporal Billy's Comeback* (1916), Vitagraph's *The Empty Sleeve* (1909), Broncho's *The Grand-Dad* (1913), Lubin's *A Veteran of the G.A.R.* (1910), and Edison's *The Sunset Gun* (1912). There is no evidence that any of these pictures did anything to improve the Civil War veteran's lot.

The Civil War at sea has received scant attention in motion pictures. One of the few such films was Edison's three-reel drama, *The Southerners* (1914), which climaxed with the Battle of Mobile Bay. The highlight was the historic moment when old Admiral David G. Farragut (Duncan McRae), directing the fight from the rigging of the flagship *Hartford*, shouted, "Damn the torpedoes! Full speed ahead!"

The plot of *The Southerners* offered no surprises. The hero (Allen Crolius), scion of a wealthy Alabama family, is an officer in the United States Navy. When secession comes, his decision to remain faithful to the Union disgraces him in the eyes of his father (Bigelow Cooper), a general in the Confederate Army. His sweetheart (Mabel Trunnelle), a fanatic about the Southern cause, scorns him and turns to another suitor. The son redeems himself in the Battle of Mobile Bay by a heroic attempt under heavy fire to rescue sailors from the *Tecumseh*, which swiftly sank after hitting harbor mines. After the war he is reunited with his family and his girl, whose Southern fiancé (Herbert Prior) has been conveniently killed at Chickamauga.

Although an elaborate and costly film, *The Southerners* was marred by the artificial quality of its battle scenes. The action was mostly photographed in the studio against painted backgrounds of ship decks and fortress walls, and there were few glimpses of the sea needed to give these sequences perspective and reality. Moreover, the climactic exploit of the hero in saving the survivors of the *Tecumseh* while exposed to a hail of cannon fire was not actually shown, but was covered by expository titles! Despite these faults, *The Southerners* was a popular and engrossing picture, well directed by Richard Ridgely. Although inexplicably neglected by Edison's publicity corps and consequently little known, Ridgely was an able director who handled many of the company's more important films including two other 1914 hits, *The Message of the Sun Dial* and *The Colonel of the Red Hussars*.

On the early morning of March 27, 1914, while

The Southerners was still in production, a fire severely damaged the Edison studio at Bedford Park, New York. A main structure housing five stages was gutted. Several members of the Edison Company who lived nearby—Ben Wilson, Mary Fuller, Miriam Nesbitt, Duncan McRae, Marc MacDermott, and others—carried films and records to safety before firemen arrived. However, the negatives for several completed scenes for *The Southerners* were destroyed, as well as a complex set representing the forward bow of the *Hartford* in collision with the Confederate ram *Tennessee*. Ridgely was on location in Florida, and another director, John H. Collins, hastily reshot the scenes lost in the fire. Although Edison was able to resume shooting seventy-two hours after the disaster, several key scenes for *The Southerners* were abandoned in order to meet a scheduled release date for the film in early May.

Another picture about the Civil War at sea was *Hearts In Bondage* (1936), cheaply made by Republic under the direction of Lew Ayres (his only film as a director). It used the old theme of two friends (James Dunn and David Manners) on opposing sides in the historic struggle of the two ironclads, the *Monitor* and the *Merrimac*. The famous battle in Hampton Roads was largely created by special effects, convincingly done by Howard and Theodore Lydecker. There were

Hearts In Bondage (1936), directed by Lew Ayres, was one of the few films to be made about the historic sea battle of the *Monitor* and the *Merrimac*. James Dunn (left) was a Union naval officer.

scenes of John Ericsson trying to sell his idea of an ironclad to Admiral Farragut (Henry B. Walthall) and President Lincoln (Frank McGlynn, Sr.).

Kalem's *The Confederate Ironclad* (1912) was about a Union attempt to steal the plans for the *Merrimac*. Selig's *A Daughter of the Southland* (1917) had an improbable premise—a Virginia girl disguises herself and takes her wounded brother's place on the *Merrimac*. Later, she marries the Union naval officer (Harold Vosburgh) who commanded the *Monitor*. A television film, *The Ship That Shook the World* (1955), directed by Robert Stevenson, showed the controversy that raged over the construction of the *Monitor*.

SLAVERY AND UNCLE TOM'S CABIN

Hollywood has never taken a serious look at human slavery in America nor intelligently probed it as a cause of the Civil War. The subject received some attention in the two films about John Brown, *Santa Fe Trail* and *Seven Angry Men*. Most pictures caricatured slaves as simple, contented darkies faithful to their white masters, and ready to make any sacrifice for them. Such an absurdity was Pathé's *For Massa's Sake* (1913), which told of a devoted slave who tried to get himself sold so that his feckless young owner (Crane Wilbur) could pay gambling debts! Life in the slave quarters was seldom portrayed, although an occasional early film, such as Edison's *In the Days of Slavery* (1914), touched broadly upon its problems. All too often, slaves were seen as protected, beloved servants whose lot in life was seemingly not bad; at times, they were shown as living rather high by sharing the sumptious fare prepared in the plantation kitchen. The white folks from the big house—Barbara O'Neill as Mrs. O'Hara in *Gone With the Wind* is an example—were frequently down at the cabins ministering to a sick child, delivering a baby, or toting up how much clothing and supplies would be needed for the winter. John M. Stahl's *The Foxes of Harrow* (1947) had a more realistic glimpse of slave life on a New Orleans plantation of 1820, although blacks objected to the emphasis upon sex and baser emotions that marred the film.

The plight of the slave in the hands of a vicious

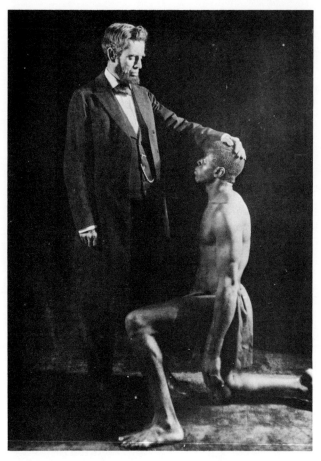

Abraham Lincoln (Sam D. Drane) was seen in this symbolic scene from Selig's *The Crisis* (1916).

the hands of Simon Legree, and the ascent of Little Eva into Heaven never failed to move the unsophisticated audiences of the ninetenth century.

Uncle Tom's Cabin came to the screen for the first time in 1903 under the guidance of the pioneer film director and cameraman, Edwin S. Porter, whose *The Great Train Robbery* made motion picture history the same year. This archaic version of the Stowe classic for the Edison Company, only 508 feet in length, was nevertheless one of the most advanced films yet produced. Porter utilized double exposures, optical tricks, miniatures, stopmotion photography, and combinations of live action and painted backgrounds. Filmed in fourteen scenes each introduced by titles, Porter's *Uncle Tom's Cabin* featured a violent thunderstorm, a race between riverboat steamers, and slides showing Abraham Lincoln, Ulysses S. Grant, Robert E. Lee, and scenes of fighting between the North and the South. The picture was shot from a single camera position (as an audience might see it as a play in a theater), and utilized both white and black actors in the cast.

In 1910, three different companies—Vitagraph, Pathé, and Thanhouser—each brought out *Uncle Tom's Cabin*. The Pathé version was in three reels, with each reel issued separately on successive weeks. Vitagraph's *Uncle Tom's Cabin* was elaborately mounted and personally directed by

owner was seldom explored other than in the several versions of the inevitable *Uncle Tom's Cabin*. Harriet Beecher Stowe's inflammatory novel of 1852 was a catalyst in the development of the Abolitionist movement and indirectly helped to provoke the Civil War. Within a few weeks after its publication, *Uncle Tom's Cabin* was adapted to the stage, and a pirated version (so hastily written that it left out Topsy and Eva) opened in New York in August. George L. Aitken's classic edition of the play, authorized by Mrs. Stowe, premiered in Troy, New York, on September 27, 1852, with Cordelia Howard as Topsy. It was a sensational hit, and for the next seventy years *Uncle Tom's Cabin* was standard fare for dozens of stock companies traveling throughout the United States. The antics of the impish Topsy, the escape of Eliza while pursued over the ice by bloodhounds, the brutal death of Uncle Tom at

World's *Uncle Tom's Cabin* of 1914 had all the elements of the popular novel, including an impish Topsy.

production chief J. Stuart Blackton, with an all-star cast that included Maurice Costello, Earle Williams, Clara Kimball Young, Norma Talmadge, Julia Arthur, and Charles Kent. I.M.P.'s 1913 version was also in three reels, and the following year saw the release of World's feature version directed by William Robert Daly. Included in the cast were Irving Cummings, child star Marie Eline (as Little Eva), and the distinguished black actor Sam Lucas, as Uncle Tom. In 1918, Marguerite Clark, one of Mary Pickford's principal rivals, played dual roles as Topsy and Eva in Famous Players-Lasky's *Uncle Tom's Cabin.* Frank Losee, a white actor, was Uncle Tom. J. Searle Dawley's direction lacked originality, but Miss Clark was beautifully photographed by H. Lyman Broening.

In 1927, Universal made *Uncle Tom's Cabin* its principal attraction of the year, laying out $1,500,-000 for an elaborate version that was roundly panned by the critics as hopelessly old-fashioned. The picture was excessively maudlin, caricatured both blacks and Southern whites, and contained much low comedy. Although director Harry Pollard (who played the role of Uncle Tom in blackface in the 1913 version) professed to have followed Mississippi River iceflows through a bitter winter to make the climactic chase, most of the scenes were shot in the studio—and showed it.

Eliza was much too surefooted as she leaped across the moving ice while clutching her baby. Two white performers, Margarita Fischer and Arthur Edmund Carewe, played the slave lovers and were unconvincing as blacks. As Simon Legree, the cruel slavemaster, George Siegmann (the Silas Lynch of *The Birth of a Nation*) overacted badly, and he was made into such a monstrous brute as to make the role totally unbelievable. The story was somewhat altered and moved forward to the period of the Civil War, with brief scenes of Lincoln and Sherman's march through Georgia. A major fault was Pollard's unrestrained direction, and many sequences were cut up with a distracting plethora of short shots from every conceivable angle.

With the advent of talking pictures, Universal refurbished *Uncle Tom's Cabin* in 1928 with sound effects and a musical score. This time the baying of the hounds was heard as Eliza made her perilous escape. There were the inevitable Negro spirituals and an annoying repetition of "Dixie" on the sound track. Since much of the market had been milked by the silent, many theaters rejected the new sound edition in favor of the all- or part-talking pictures that were being made available by other studios.

DOCUMENTARIES

Many documentaries, used primarily for teaching purposes, have added to the store of responsible Civil War history. One of the best is M-G-M's *The Battle of Gettysburg* (1936), a thirty-minute tour of the historic Pennsylvania battlefield. Produced with unusual care, it profits from a fine script by Dore Schary and the creative cinematography of George J. Folsey. The U.S. Park Service of the Department of Interior brought out a series of short subjects in the 1950s that visited the national military parks at Vicksburg, Shiloh, Stone Mountain, Chickamauga, Fredericksburg, and other battlefields. Warner Brothers' *The Blue and the Gray* (1935) also visited many historical monuments and sites commemorating the Civil War. As part of its long series of patriotic short subjects on American history, Warner Brothers dramatized several events of the North-South struggle with popular casts and competent directors. The best

Mona Ray and Virginia Grey were Topsy and Eva in Universal's 1927 production of *Uncle Tom's Cabin.* Miss Grey later became a popular leading lady at M-G-M and other studios.

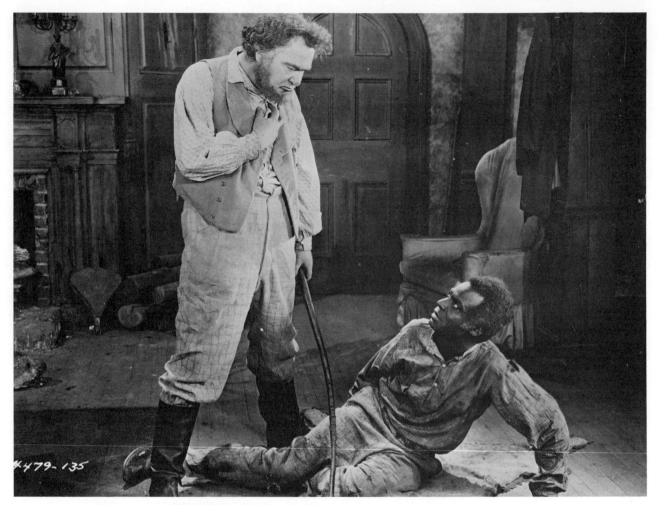

George Siegmann, the Silas Lynch of *The Birth of a Nation*, played another archvillain, the sadistic Simon Legree, who took the whip to his slaves in Universal's *Uncle Tom's Cabin* (1927).

of these were Nick Grinde's *Under Southern Stars* (1937), William McGann's *Lincoln In the White House* (1939), Jean Negulesco's *The Flag of Humanity* (1940), and Crane Wilbur's *I Am An American* (1944). All were widely shown during World War II for propaganda purposes. The annual encampments of the Grand Army of the Republic, as well as the reunions of the United Confederate Veterans, were extensively filmed by Edison, I.M.P., and other companies during the early part of the twentieth century. As the number of survivors dramatically declined, these touching events were only briefly reported in contemporary newsreels.

The great injustice in Hollywood's concept of the Civil War is to the people of the South, both white and black, who have been so caricatured and cliché ridden that any responsible, realistic presentation of them seems beyond hope. D. W. Griffith's *The Birth of a Nation* comes closest to abandoning the morass of false notions about Southerners of the Civil War era, and attempts to show them in intelligent and understanding, if not always admirable, terms. It is unlikely that the facade of the antebellum South, so carefully manufactured in more than a century of irresponsible literature, drama, and motion pictures will ever be eradicated.

2

Nazimova

AT the height of her screen popularity just after World War I, Alla Nazimova was called "the star of a thousand moods." Her striking, exotic appearance, accented by a shock of blue black hair and burning eyes, gave credence to her roles as a bizarre vamp or passionate native girl. Yet her curiously sexless *Salome* was a disastrous failure, while her greatest successes were the intensely emotional and intelligent, if neurotic, women who recalled the Ibsen heroines for which she first established an international reputation as a gifted stage actress.

Nazimova's silent-film career spanned a brief ten years, centering about a series of costly films she did for the old Metro Company in 1918-21. While she once made the mistake of portraying a Mary Pickford gamine, mostly she played a suffering woman who fell into sin and temptation, and paid for her transgressions with her life or was regenerated by the love of a decent man. It was a basic formula employed with enormous success by her contemporary, Norma Talmadge, but refined by Nazimova with more imagination and sophistication.

Later, Nazimova would squander her fortune on two highly individual films, the widely divergent Ibsen's *A Doll's House* and Oscar Wilde's *Salome*, which American audiences neither understood nor enjoyed. Her career in motion pictures was soon over, and she returned to the more appreciative audiences of Broadway and London's West End. In the forties, badly in need of money, Nazimova came back to Hollywood and was seen in a few insignificant character roles, no longer identifiable as the tempestuous toast of the silents.

Despite the sparseness of her films, Nazimova had a profound influence upon Hollywood. She created the vogue for a provocative new screen heroine—the sensitive, mature woman of the world, at once both intelligent and passionate, and tinged with a flair for adventure. It was a type that would come to fruition later with such exciting personalities as Pola Negri, Mae Murray, Gloria Swanson, Greta Garbo, and Marlene Dietrich.

Nazimova was also the first of the regal movie queens who dominated the 1920's. She lived with a man not her husband in a fabulous home that, like herself, became part of the Hollywood legend. Reams of studio publicity about her, much of it fiction and little of it fact, helped to build up the image of a glamorous, completely fascinating, and somewhat mysterious Hollywood star.

EARLY BEGINNINGS IN RUSSIA

Alla Nazimova—her real name was Adelaide Leventon—was born on June 4, 1879, in Yalta, Russia, a small town in Crimea on the Black Sea. Her parents, Yacov and Sofia Leventon, were

Jewish, both from wellborn but only moderately well-to-do families. The father was not a physician, as often reported later, but a chemist or pharmacist whose small shop included Tsar Alexander III among its customers. Alla's parents separated when she was three, and at six she went with her father, brother, and sister to Montreaux, a Swiss village on Lake Geneva. There she learned French, and when the family returned to Russia a few years later, she was left in a private school at Zurich, where she also became fluent in German.

At twelve, Alla rejoined her father in Yalta. He wanted her to be a musician, and sent her to the Philharmonic Music Academy of Odessa. She became an accomplished violinist, playing in school orchestras conducted on occasion by Tchaikovsky and Rimsky-Korsakov.

Nazimova's introduction to the theatre came quite by chance. When her boarding school at Odessa burned, she was sent to live with a family active in amateur theatricals. She was permitted to attend rehearsals, and eventually to hold the promptbook. Alla said later that she asked one of the players to carry something of hers on stage at each performance, a bit of ribbon or costume jewelry, so that she could feel a part of the play. Totally fascinated by this new world of make-believe, the fifteen-year-old girl resolved to become an actress.

Her father was too ill to be asked for permission, and her older brother, Voloyda, a newspaperman, was aghast at the idea of an actress in the family. He refused her pleas, but relented when the highstrung Alla threatened to run away from home. After some coaching by a former actress living in Yalta (who was dismayed by her multiple accents), she applied for admission to the Moscow Dramatic School, a branch of the Philharmonic Academy.

Alla auditioned by reading poetry, but the director, the brilliant Vladimir Ivanovich Nemirovitch-Dantchenko, declared he could not understand a word she said. However, he accepted her as a pupil, along with sixty others, because of her beautiful voice. Nazimova was unattractive as a child, being quite fat—unkind schoolmates called her "The Barrel"—and during the next year she was physically made over through rigid dieting and training in ballet.

During the winter of 1897-98, her second year as a drama student, her Christmas gift was a pass to a performance of Hauptmann's *The Sunken Bell*, staged by a group of amateur actors under the direction of the gifted Constantin Sergeivich Stanislavsky. Nazimova was enormously impressed and excited by his revolutionary techniques in acting, and was elated a few weeks later when Stanislavsky and Nemirovitch-Dantchenko merged their schools to form what became the world-famous Moscow Art Theatre.

As a student, Alla appeared in crowd scenes or tiny parts in such plays as *Magda* (her first public appearance), Tolstoy's *Tsar Fyodor Ivanovitch*, Shakespeare's *The Merchant of Venice* (in which she was a flower girl), Goldoni's *La Locandier* and *The Happiness of Gretchen*, Chekhov's *The Sea Gull,* and prophetically, Ibsen's *Hedda Gabler.*

During her fourth year, she spoke her first line in a performance of Tolstoy's *The Death of Ivan the Terrible,* and also appeared in bit roles in Hauptmann's *Drayman Henschel* and *Lonely Lives,* and Chekhov's *Uncle Vanya.* For her graduation exercises, conducted on stage at the Small Imperial Theatre of Moscow, she did scenes from Ibsen's *Little Eyloff,* and from *Gold,* a play by her teacher, Nemirovitch-Dantchenko. Nazimova was awarded a gold medal, the first to be given since the gifted Lyeshkovskaya received it a few years earlier. She never got the medal itself because she had no money to pay for it.

Nemirovitch-Dantchenko advised her to gain experience by playing in stock companies in the provinces, and for a few weeks she worked in Bobruisk, a small town near Minsk. The tiny, ill-equipped theater depressed her, and she returned to Moscow and pleaded with Nemirovitch-Dantchenko for a job. She was too inexperienced for the Moscow Art Theatre's resident company, but he let her watch him (and occasionally Stanislavsky) direct from a seat in the back row of the auditorium for nearly a year. Nazimova said later it was one of the greatest experiences in her professional life. Her father had died, leaving little in the way of an estate, and her months of inactivity were a drain on the family finances.

Alla blossomed into a beautiful young woman, and in 1900, while vacationing in Saint Petersburg, a young Army officer and friend of the Tsar became madly infatuated with her. To escape his attentions, she signed with a provincial theater in Kostroma, a small town near the White Sea in northern Russia. The winter months were bitterly cold. She played the lead in two new plays each week, performing some twice in the same evening for the enthusiastic peasant audiences that crowded into the tiny theater. After a season in Kostroma, she was sent to Vilna, where she appeared in a wider variety of roles, including a stint as a soubrette in musical comedy. Mostly she did plays by Molière, Suderman, Shakespeare, Hauptmann, the classic Russian dramatists, and the rising young Norwegian, Henrik Ibsen. A third year was spent with a traveling stock company in the provinces, with the troupe remaining a month to seven weeks at each town. By then she was using the stage name of Alla Nasimoff.

PAUL ORLENEFF

In 1904, Nazimova was offered a contract with the Nemetti Theatre, a repertory group in Saint Petersburg. To her intense disappointment, it was housed in a nondescript building in a shabby part of the city and catered to the working classes. It was here that she attracted the attention of the distinguished Russian actor and director, Pavel Orlienieff—known outside Russia as Paul Orleneff. He was much taken by her poise and expressive voice, and began coaching her privately for more challenging roles. Soon she was performing with him at better theaters in Saint Petersburg and Moscow.

Paul Orleneff, then thirty-six years of age, was something of an eccentric, although recognized as an actor of great ability, if not of genius. He was famous for his performance of Raskolnikov in Dostoevski's *Crime and Punishment*, and as Mitka Karamazov in *The Brothers Karamazov*, at Youzhny's Variety Theatre in Moscow. He was a dedicated actor, intent upon extracting every nuance of human emotion from the part he was playing. Although somewhat short—he built up his height with high-heeled boots—Orleneff was handsome and quite attractive to women.

Orleneff was restless and impatient, and tended to flit from one project to another, never fully realizing the potentials of his great talent. After a stunning success in a popular play, he would become bored and abandon his role to organize a traveling stock company, or start an acting school, or perhaps squander his money in an experimental theater that the tradition-bound Russians neither understood nor patronized. He was continually brimming with new ideas, but few were ever realized.

The coming Russian Revolution of 1905 brought chaotic economic and social conditions, and many theaters were closed. Orleneff was openly critical of the Tsar's government. Although not a Jew himself, he was much disturbed at a strong wave of anti-Semitism that swept the country, openly condoned and possibly encouraged by the government. An inflammatory play called *The Contrabanders*, which was extremely anti-Jewish in character, was playing to huge crowds. To protest the persecution of the Jews, Orleneff organized a company of Jewish players, with Nazimova as leading lady, to do Eugene Tchirikov's pogram drama, *The Chosen People*. However, Saint Petersburg officials would not let the play open, and warned the cocky Orleneff he was close to being thrown into prison. His close friend, dramatist Maxim Gorky, was already in a cell for his criticism of the government.

Orleneff and his troupe were finally permitted to leave Russia for Berlin, where *The Chosen People* was performed, in Russian, at a small theater for several weeks. The company then went to London, where Orleneff hoped the play would encourage the British government to protest to the Tsar about the treatment being accorded Jews in Russia. Orleneff and his players were virtually penniless when the London producer and critic, J. T. Grein, finally came to their aid by arranging financing and a week's booking at the Avenue Theatre.

Nazimova's first recognition outside Russia dated from the London opening of *The Chosen People* on January 21, 1905. The Jewish community of Whitechapel turned out in huge numbers, and the premiere was sold out in advance with hundreds turned away. The controversial play attracted many government leaders and other celebrities to its first night, including Madame Olga de Novikov, leader of Mayfair fashion and the unofficial emissary of the Tsar, who noisily walked out during the first act. *The Chosen People* was an impressive critical success, with one reviewer writing that the troupe had "voices like harps in the air."

It was a night of glory for Alla Nazimova. Grein remembers that at a backstage reception after the performance, she sat on a tiny stool, weeping with emotion and exhaustion. She kissed Grein's hands, and thanked him for all that he had done to help the company open in London, modestly brushing aside his compliments on her sensitive performance as Leah. Despite the impact of the play and the publicity it garnered, its run was limited by the Russian dialogue, and *The Chosen People* closed two weeks later. The profits were £226, which were soon eaten up in living expenses for the actors. Orleneff was anxious to take the play to the United States, but there was no money for steamship fares. The necessary funds were finally raised when Dame Ellen Terry, Laurence Irving, and others arranged a benefit matinee.

Even more difficult times awaited the Russian performers in New York. Unable to afford the subway, Orleneff and Nazimova walked miles to call upon unresponsive Broadway producers, struggling to convey through an inadequate English interpreter their enthusiasm for *The Chosen People*. Eventually, enough money was scraped together, and the play opened on March 10, 1905, at the Herald Square Theatre for a limited run. Despite the praises of a few hardy reviewers who ventured downtown, it quickly closed.

Orleneff and his troupe were again penniless when their plight came to the attention of Emma Goldman, the Russian-born anarchist, whose demonstrations and literary broadsides advocating the overthrow of the government had landed her in jail on more than one occasion. She impulsively invited the destitute actors to her home on Hunter Island, New York, where some of them lived in tents on the beach throughout the summer of 1905. The evenings were often spent sitting around a huge bonfire of driftwood, with Orleneff strumming a balalaika, and everyone joining in on the choruses of Russian ballads and drinking songs. Mrs. Goldman was much impressed by Orleneff, and he was quick to see in her a way out of his precarious condition. Through her Tchirikov So-

ciety, a so-called cultural organization of local Russians, she began raising financing for a season of Russian repertory.

Although the exact dates are now somewhat uncertain, Alla returned to Yalta in mid-1905 after a quarrel with Orleneff. Her family cabled her the passage money. It was a bad time to return to Russia, where the abortive revolution was about to break. Years later, Nazimova would weep while recalling cossacks whipping a group of frightened Jews and political prisoners bound for Siberia. The country was in a state of fear and economic paralysis, and she was elated when a letter containing enough money to get her back to the United States arrived from Orleneff. He wrote glowingly of plans for a new theater and a triumphant season; Alla was to return at once, bringing with her certain performers from the Moscow and Saint Petersburg stages.

After a rough crossing during which she was violently seasick, Nazimova landed in New York to find Orleneff's grandiose plans already in difficulty. The Tchirikov Society was aghast at substantial bills that Orleneff had run up for scenery and costumes—which were quickly repossessed—and in importing actors from Russia, and the venture was soon in dire financial straits. Instead of the elaborate Broadway theater he had promised Nazimova, Orleneff was forced to settle for an ancient stable on East 3rd Street just off the Bowery. It had been used more recently as a lecture hall, and was easily converted into a shabby theater, although Mrs. Goldman complained that she spent much of her time in arbitrating Orleneff's disputes with the workmen. Nazimova remembered it as housing a dancehall on the second floor, and said sounds of music and dancing were often heard through the ceiling. Others recall a noisy bowling alley was located next door. Instead of seats, the make-shift theater had benches, and the curtain was made from tattered blankets scrounged from a nearby thrift shop.

Orleneff's Russian Lyceum opened on November 3, 1905, with *Vanyushin's Children*, a somber, four-act play about worthless children who bring ruin to a respected family. Nazimova, for some unaccountable reason, was not in this first play. Mrs. Goldman had persuaded a number of influential critics to attend, and they were lavish in praise of Orleneff's realistic performance. Others noted the acoustics were bad, the stage too small, and the scenery ugly and uninspired.

The company lived a precarious existence as it presented a different Russian or Yiddish play each evening. Admission was ten cents, and those who could not afford a dime were admitted free. A package of cigarettes was often as welcome as money. To be nearer the theater, which occupied all her waking hours, Nazimova moved from Brooklyn, where she had been living with relatives, to a cold and depressing room in the Bowery. In addition to playing the lead (or perhaps a bit), she was property master and wardrobe mistress, painted scenery, and with the other actors swept out the theater each afternoon. She even composed incidental music for the plays, which was performed by unpaid musicians from the Russian-Jewish community. After several months, the theater was finally closed as a public hazard by the New York Fire Department.

Although she was sorely tried by Orleneff and his explosive temperament, which was often directed at unappreciative critics, Mrs. Goldman tried valiantly to keep the project alive. At times she discretely hid her identity as an incorrigible revolutionist by posing as "E. G. Smith," and representing herself as Orleneff's press agent. For a time it was fashionable for the New York theater crowd to visit the 3rd Street auditorium, and among those who came were Ethel and John Barrymore, but the novelty soon wore off. On January 31, 1906, Orleneff's troupe moved to the Criterion Theatre, where a few perforances of Tolstoy's *Tsar Fedor Ivanovitch, Son of Ivan the Terrible* were presented. It was a role Orleneff had done in Russia more than 1,000 times. Later, Mrs. Goldman arranged bookings in Boston and Chicago, where the company was often entertained by some of her coworkers in the revolutionary movement.

In late February 1906, Orleneff began to talk of returning to Russia unless his sponsors could guarantee funds for several seasons. A committee of New York cultural leaders was formed to assist Orleneff out of his difficulties, and a fund of $10,000 was to be raised. The principal benefactors were Mrs. Frances Hellman, Ernest Crosby, Owen Johnson, Paul Herzog, Arthur Hornblow, and playwright Charles Klein. One of the first sub-

scribers was the millionaire-industrialist Andrew Carnegie. Eventually, $16,000 was subscribed for a limited season of Russian repertory at the Berkeley Theatre, with the veteran impresario Daniel Frohman keeping an eye on Orleneff.

Hardly had the project been announced when Mrs. Goldman and the Tchirikov Society threatened suit, pointing out that Orleneff was under exclusive contract to them, a fact he had not revealed to his new backers. The savior committee withdrew in disgust. Orleneff moved quickly to restore himself in Mrs. Goldman's good graces by proposing to direct Nazimova in a benefit performance of Strindberg's *Countess Julia* to raise money for a new left-wing magazine (*The Open Road*) that she was attempting to launch. He assured his benefactor it was little enough to do in repayment for her many kindnesses.

Orleneff's troubles came to a head when he was arrested on March 24, 1906, on charges of grand larceny. The complainant was one Joseph Goldstein, who said he gave Orleneff $1,500 for a part-interest in *Tsar Feodor Ivanovitch, Son of Ivan the Terrible*. Goldstein was made company treasurer at a salary of $30 a week, which he received for only two weeks. He got $15 the third week, and only five dollars the fourth. Goldstein demanded his money back, but Orleneff had already spent it to satisfy his creditors. When the actor returned from an engagement in Boston, he was jailed for two days amid front-page newspaper headlines. The charges were eventually withdrawn after someone, possibly one of Mrs. Goldman's supporters, made restitution to Goldstein. Although the benefit performance of *Countess Julia* was only two weeks away, Orleneff was so upset that he cancelled the production. Soon afterward, he and Nazimova and the remnants of the Russian Lyceum Players did appear in Ibsen's *Ghosts*, but only a paltry $250 was realized for the new magazine.

THE SWEET SMELL OF SUCCESS

With the collapse of his prospects, Orleneff sailed for Russia, possibly with the encouragement of immigration officials who looked with suspicion upon his friendship with Emma Goldman. As for Nazimova, she resolved to remain in the United

States and pursue her career. She said later that in spite of her early hardships in New York, she had fallen in love with America and never felt the slightest urge to return to her homeland. In 1927, she would become a naturalized citizen.

Nazimova had made friends with a number of influential Broadway personalities who came to the Bowery theater to see Orleneff and his exotic leading lady. Among those much impressed by her talents were actresses Grace George and Margaret Anglin, who touted her to such producers as William A. Brady and Henry Miller. She also found a warm friend in Janet Gilder, whose father, Richard Watson Gilder, was coeditor of the highbrow *Century* magazine.

Providentially freed of a professional and emotional involvement with the erratic Orleneff, Nazimova turned to the problem of her inability to speak English. Janet Gilder arranged for her to be interviewed by the Broadway impresario Lee Shubert. Actor-playwright Owen Johnson, who spoke French, went along as interpreter. The canny Shubert offered her a five-year contract, during which her salary would go from $50 to $350 weekly. Her contract was signed on May 10, 1906, and she moved the same day from her dingy room in the Bowery to the warm and clean Judson Hotel.

Shubert hired Caroline Harris, a Shakespearean actress somewhat down on her luck at the time, to teach English to Nazimova. She was a hard but patient taskmaster, and for the next five months up to ten hours a day were spent with Alla. Mrs. Harris's eleven-year-old son often played with his toys at their feet—a decade later, as Richard Barthelmess, he would first win fame as Nazimova's son in her initial motion picture, *War Brides*.

By fall Nazimova was ready for Broadway. Encouraged by Janet and Richard Gilder, and with Lee Shubert's permission, Henry Miller agreed to sponsor her in a limited series of matinee performances of Ibsen's *Hedda Gabler* at the Princess Theater in Herald Square. A fine supporting cast included John Blair, Dodson Mitchell, and Laura Hope Crews. With an incredible command of the English language, Nazimova opened on November 13, 1906, to rave reviews. Acton Davies of the New York *Evening Sun* compared her to Duse, and the New York *Times* called her portrayal "a brilliant achievement" and praised her expressive voice—

"she speaks English better than nine-tenths of others in the theatre." In answer to demands for a curtain-call speech, Alla emotionally pleaded, "Let me feel—not speak!"

Nazimova's stunning Broadway debut made her a star overnight with American audiences. Originally, only seven matinee performances of *Hedda Gabler* were planned, but these were extended to every Monday, Tuesday, Wednesday, and Friday afternoon. She began evening performances as Nora Helmer in Ibsen's *A Doll's House* at the Princess Theatre on January 14, 1907, to even greater critical acclaim. It was to become her most famous role. In March, she migrated to the Bijou Theatre and alternated the Ibsen classics.

The glamorous Russian actress was fabulous copy as scores of newspaper and magazine writers clamored for interviews. They marveled at her jet black hair and large eyes, and her extraordinary poise—one reporter said Alla was "the very typification of all the Russian countesses," but noted she also had "a more feminine side." For her part, Nazimova went into raptures about the United States and declared she would never return to Russia. She immodestly asserted that she had never had any artistic difficulties in the United States—only financial ones! She pontificated about drama, and said she hated characters like Zaza, the butterflies, the adventuresses, the abandoned women—the very types she would later play on the screen with success—and preferred a role like Hilda Wangelin in *The Master Builder*, in which the character *thinks*!

Nazimova spoke of Paul Orleneff "with motherly tenderness and indulgence," and described him to the New York *Times* as "a man of dreams . . . with the most beautiful visions which are not at all practical. He thinks a thing can be done, and in his mind it is already accomplished." Adding that he was "such a baby," Alla said she was all the more fond of him for his unworldliness. She claimed to have discouraged Orleneff from returning to the United States to present Ibsen's *Brand*, which he had done in Moscow and Oslo that summer with marked success. Nevertheless, Orleneff sent an agent (who could not speak English) to New York in a futile attempt to rent the Academy of Music and to borrow money.

The New York *Times*, in an interview published on December 19, 1906, identified her for the first time as the wife of Paul Orleneff, which she did not publicly deny. It is possible that such a marriage may have taken place after they first met in Saint Petersburg. Most of her friends doubt it, and say that through long years of acquaintance Nazimova never referred to Orleneff as her husband. There is little question but that she was his mistress during their association in Russia, and probably through most of the early months in America. Another story is that Nazimova was married in Russia, not to Orleneff, but to a minor actor named Golovine, identified only as a jealous, heavy-drinking bear of a man. There is nothing to confirm or deny this report. In none of the obituaries published at her death is there any mention of a marriage to Paul Orleneff. After Alla's decision to remain in the United States, he returned to Russia in a state of deep depression, although eventually he came to speak rather bitterly of her to close friends.

The extent of Paul Orleneff's professional influence upon Nazimova is not to be minimized. Of paramount significance is that he taught her the extraordinary technique of using body movement to enhance the mood and emotion of her role. Actually small in stature (5'3"), she was able to give an impression of rising to a commanding height for climactic emphasis, or by contrast, to crouch in a tiny ball of despair and defeat. There are innumerable references to Nazimova's "towering figure," which seems to linger in the memory of all who saw her on the stage. Coupled with her beautiful and expressive face, it gave a characteristic style to her acting. In later years, she tended to overdo the body movements, and was criticized for her "contortions" and "posturings." Exaggerated by the close-up, they were even less adaptable to motion pictures, and annoyed many audiences.

Some stage historians felt Nazimova never surpassed her early performances in the United States, when she still reflected Orleneff's gifted tutelage. Oliver M. Sayler would write in his book, *The Russian Theatre*, that "it is apparent to everyone in America now, as it was clear to many at the time . . . that the farther the actress got from her preceptor and the roles he taught her, the more artificial she became." Certainly, Nazimova's exciting interpretations of the Ibsen heroines were

directly traceable to Orleneff's analytical concepts.

For a change of pace, she opened on Broadway on April 12, 1907, in *Comtesse Coquette*, a wispy comedy that ran for seventy-five performances. Alla wore beautiful gowns designed by Mlle. Frederica de Wolfe. Her leading man was Sir Guy Standing, later replaced by Walter Hampden, with whom she would subsequently co-star many times. In the fall of 1907, she revived *A Doll's House* at the Bijou with a stellar cast that included Hampden, Warner Oland, and Glady Hulette. It alternated in repertory with another Ibsen classic, *The Master Builder*, with Hampden again in the male lead. Nazimova closed the year by premiering on December 30 in another comedy, *The Comet*, the first play of her friend and booster, Owen Johnson. It was only moderately successful. Although she was under contract to the Shuberts, all of these plays were produced by Henry Miller.

Throughout 1908 and part of the following year, Nazimova toured the United States for the Shuberts, performing her Ibsen heroines as well as such popular hits as *Zaza, Magda,* and *The Passion Flower*. She was widely acclaimed everywhere, and charmed the local press with her frank views on love, marriage, politics, and the stage. For the first time she insisted, as she would throughout most of her life, on being billed and addressed as *Madame* Nazimova. With her success came money, and she bought a lovely home (christened "Who-Torak") in Port Chester, New York, which had been built during the Revolutionary War. It was here that her older sister, Nina, recently divorced, arrived in 1909 from Russia with her two children, Lucy and Vladimir. The boy, an imaginative and shy lad, grew up to become Val Lewton, a writer and producer of low-budget horror films (*The Cat People; Bedlam*) much admired by screen buffs. For a time Nina served as her sister's secretary.

To capitalize on Nazimova's growing fame, the Shuberts built a beautiful new theater on 39th Street, and named it the Nazimova Theatre in her honor. She opened it on April 18, 1910, with the first American performance of Ibsen's *Little Eyolf*. Brandon Tynan and Ida Conquest headed a fine supporting cast. She starred in *The Fairy Tale, The Other Mary,* and *The Marionettes* (with Frank Gilmore) in 1910-11. In 1912, Nazimova had a smash hit in *Bella Donna*, a play based on Robert Hichens's novel of an adventuress who tried to poison her husband so she could marry an Egyptian native scalawag. As the ruthless Mrs. Chepstow, she found a role that in every way measured up to her exotic public image. Alla spent most of 1913 touring the play throughout the United States.

ENTER CHARLES BRYANT

Nazimova's leading man in *Bella Donna* was a handsome thirty-three-year-old Englishman named Charles Bryant. A passionate romance sprang up, and although it soon cooled, they continued a curious relationship for the next twelve years, living openly as man and wife although no marriage ceremony was ever performed. At various times, when pinned down by interviewers, Nazimova told conflicting stories—that she and Bryant were married backstage during rehearsals of *Bella Donna*, or in Europe, or in a New England town by a justice of the peace. The date varied from 1911 to 1913.

The son of a prominent British solicitor, Charles Bryant acted in amateur theatricals while working in London's financial district. He disliked commercial life, and in 1900 made his professional

Alla Nazimova and Charles Bryant lived together as man and wife for fourteen years, but no marriage ceremony was ever performed.

debut with Mrs. Bandman-Palmer's stock company. He then worked in a touring production of *Lady Tetley's Divorce*, starring Mrs. Patrick Campbell, and in 1901 made his first London appearance in Sir Arthur Wing Pinero's *Iris* at the Garrick Theatre. During the next ten years, Bryant had leading roles in numerous plays in England, Europe, and America, appearing in support of such stars as Cyril Maude, Arthur Bourchier, and Sir Johnston Forbes-Robertson. A versatile actor, he played a variety of parts ranging from Shakespeare's *Macbeth* to drawing-room comedies (*All-Of-A-Sudden Peggy; Is Matrimony A Failure?*) to domestic drama (*A Fool There Was*). Bryant had appeared in the supporting cast of the original London production of *Bella Donna*, and was brought to the United States to repeat his role. At Nazimova's insistence, he was soon recast in the male lead.

In 1913, Nazimova and Bryant went to Europe to finalize plans for a world-wide tour under the management of Charles Frohman. To extend over a period of twenty months, it was to begin in September in Detroit, Michigan, thence to California, Australia, Japan, China, India, South Africa, and concluding in eight European countries. She planned a repertoire of seven plays, including Ibsen, Barrie's *Half-Hour*, and, of course, *Bella Donna*. Only a portion of this grandiose tour materialized, and although Nazimova was acclaimed everywhere, it was a financial fiasco due in part to heavy transportation costs in the Orient. More losses were incurred when the outbreak of World War I forced cancellation of the profitable European dates. Nazimova returned to New York, where she and Bryant opened in *That Sort*, a negligible comedy drama, at the Harris Theatre on November 6, 1914. It ran only twenty-five performances.

The failure of her world tour left Nazimova strapped for money, and she reluctantly signed a lucrative contract to appear in vaudeville, which was considered a comedown for the actress. *War Brides*, a one-act dramatic sketch based on a magazine story by Marion Craig Wentworth, was selected as a vehicle, and Alla opened on January 25, 1915, at the Palace Theatre in New York, the mecca of American vaudeville. Bryant, Mary Alden (soon to win fame as the mulatto mistress in D. W. Griffith's *The Birth of a Nation*), and Gertrude

Berkeley were in the cast. Although the playlet was overlong and somber in its antiwar message, she was enthusiastically received.

Displaying the same disciplined performance as she had her roles in the legitimate theater, Nazimova. toured *War Brides* from coast to coast with great success for more than a year. She disliked the drudgery of vaudeville—the multiple daily performances, drafty and inadequate theaters, and long train rides—but said later it exposed her talents to thousands who otherwise would never have seen her. Unlike many of her contemporaries, Alla was not actually resentful of appearing in vaudeville, and counted it a new experience in her professional career. She frankly admitted that she was in it for money, and laughed when some of her fellow performers called her, "No Mazuma," a ploy on her name meaning that she was broke.

Nazimova in her first film, *War Brides* (1916).

WAR BRIDES; BRENON AND SELZNICK

In 1916,. Nazimova was approached by Herbert Brenon, a rising film director, to expand *War Brides* into a feature motion picture. He had attracted attention with two Annette Kellerman mermaid spectacles, *Neptune's Daughter* (1915) and *A Daughter of the Gods* (1916), and several films with Theda Bara at Fox. Alla was introduced to Brenon by a mutual friend, and she was impressed by his Irish personality and background as an actor with the Shakespearean company of Walker Whiteside. Nazimova had received movie offers before—most recently Essanay had wanted her for the screen version of her play, *That Sort*, but she disliked the idea of working at the company's Chicago studio, and was miffed at the niggardly terms that were proposed. (Eventually, the role in *That Sort* went to Warda Howard, a young California actress whom Essanay tried unsuccessfully to make into a vamp.) After seeing some of Brenon's work at a private screening, Alla promised to think about his suggestion, but told him everything depended upon how good a deal he could offer.

Brenon had signed a contract to independently produce and direct several films for distribution through Lewis J. Selznick Enterprises, which was to provide the financing. A former diamond salesman, the flamboyant Selznick had risen to be a major power in the film industry in the short space of four years. If legend is to be believed, he became General Manager of Carl Laemmle's Universal Pictures by simply appropriating a desk in the New York office, printing up a supply of stationery listing his new title, and giving orders in an authoritative manner. Later, fired by Laemmle from a job for which he had never been hired, Selznick gained control of World Pictures Corporation, enticing such Broadway favorites as Lillian Russell, Holbrook Blinn, and Lew Weber into its fold. In 1915, he set up Selznick Pictures, with his twenty-one-year-old son Myron as production chief. The new company's principal asset was the buxom Clara Kimball Young (in whom the elder Selznick had more than a strictly professional interest). Her titilating domestic dramas were highly popular and profitable, partly because of daring advertisements displaying Miss Young's ample charms.

Theodora Warfield, Nazimova, and Gertrude Berkeley
in a dramatic scene from *War Brides* (1916), the antiwar preachment that Alla first did as a vaudeville skit.

Selznick was quick to recognize the box-office potentials of the Nazimova name, and he readily agreed to underwrite a handsome offer to the actress. Brenon was literally shunted aside as Selznick personally undertook negotiations. Nazimova signed a contract calling for her to be paid $30,000 for thirty days' work, with a bonus of $1,000 for each day production went over schedule. Moreover, the money was to be paid daily, and the publicity-wise Selznick was often photographed handing his exotic star a $1,000 bill or a stack of gold coins.

War Brides was shot in a small studio in Hud-son Heights, New Jersey, just across the river from Manhattan. Brenon was a volatile personality, often impatient and arrogant, and Selznick feared he would clash with Nazimova. They got along surprisingly well, however, and Alla found her initiation into motion pictures eased by Brenon's perceptive direction. Years later he called her "a great tragedienne who wanted to play Mary Pickford sunbonnet roles."

In many respects, *War Brides* was an auspicious film debut for Alla Nazimova. She gave a moving, intelligent performance in a role completely devoid of glamour, that of a young mother whose

The volatile Herbert Brenon directed Nazimova in *War Brides* (1916), but he got along surprisingly well with the Russian actress. Later, Brenon directed such hit films as *Peter Pan* and the silent version of *Beau Geste*.

through a series of unprotected trenches. Brenon appeared in need of a competent military advisor, and part of the fault lay in poor art direction and the selection of an unsuitable location. Nazimova photographed well in her drab role—the stunning cinematography was by J. Roy Hunt—and was generally restrained in her performance, although some critics noted she was unable to resist her "famous contortions" in the early portion of the film. Charles Bryant repeated his role, with Richard Barthelmess, the child of her English teacher, making his screen debut (other than some work as an extra) as Nazimova's son. Alla was impressed by Barthelmess's promising performance, and predicted he would become an important star.

Financially, *War Brides* was a success despite its early withdrawal from exhibition, returning more than $300,000 in profits to Selznick. Possibly because of its antiwar theme, which was increasingly incompatible with public sentiment, the film was not well liked. While her acting as the agonizing mother was praised, Nazimova disappointed audiences by not living up to the exotic image that reams of publicity had created. Clearly, *War Brides* was a poor choice to introduce her to motion pictures. Selznick did not press her to make a second film, and for a time it appeared her screen career was at an end.

husband and his brothers have been killed in a senseless war. Told by a king that she must bear more children for future wars, she arouses the women to protest and finally kills herself rather than comply with the edict. With the fighting of World War I raging in Europe, *War Brides* came into release just as the United States was swinging toward military preparedness, and its preachy antiwar message resulted in it being eventually withdrawn from distribution.

Although a superior film executed on a liberal budget, *War Brides* was not entirely successful. Only the last half was based on the Wentworth vaudeville sketch, and the first part was padded out with unrelated events and an overabundance of routine movie comedy. The battle scenes were unreal, showing heroic troops fighting uphill

Charles Bryant made his American film debut with Alla Nazimova in Herbert Brenon's *War Brides* (1916).

In January 1917, Nazimova was back on Broadway in 'Ception Shoals, an intensely melodramatic play that hinted at incest between brother and sister. It had been brought to her attention by a brilliant twenty-three-year-old Dartmouth graduate named Walter Wanger, who was trying to gain a foothold in the theatre. The play was ostensibly codirected by Wanger and Charles Bryant, but it was an open secret in theatrical circles that Nazimova did the directing. 'Ception Shoals was moderately successful with a run of thirty-seven performances at the Princess Theatre, after which it had a limited tour in the East. Bryant, Henry Harmon, Edith Speare, and Mitchell Lewis were in the cast. With the entrance of the United States into the war in April, Wanger was commissioned in the Army and assigned to the film branch of George Creel's Committee on Public Information, the official government propaganda agency. He later became a distinguished motion-picture producer (*Queen Christina*, 1933; *Foreign Correspondent*, 1940; *Joan of Arc*, 1948) and husband of actress Joan Bennett.

METRO AND THE GOLDEN YEARS

In the audience at a performance of *'Ception Shoals* was Maxwell Karger, production chief at the East Coast studios of Metro Pictures Corporation. He had a great admiration for the actress, and had watched her false start in films in *War Brides* with dismay. Karger felt that she could be developed into a major box-office attraction with exotic roles in colorful stories laid in imaginative locales. Aware that her stage career was going nowhere at the time, Nazimova was intrigued by Karger's concept, and, after some haggling over terms, signed a handsome contract with Metro. She was to become the most important addition to a growing stable of Metro stars that included Madame Olga Petrova, Ethel Barrymore, Harold Lockwood, May Allison, Mr. and Mrs. Sidney Drew, and the romantic team of Francis X. Bushman and Beverly Bayne.

Her first Metro picture, *Revelation*, released in March 1918, was an enormous hit. In a ridiculous plot, Nazimova plays Joline, a Paris cabaret singer easily identified as a prostitute. She becomes a

Nazimova played a prostitute in Metro's *Revelation* (1918), who reformed after a religious experience and became a Red Cross worker on the battlefields of World War I.

model for an American artist (Charles Bryant), who paints her as Cleopatra, Salome, Sappho, La Bacchante, and other notorious sinners. A religious element enters the story when the artist paints her as the Madonna, and a miracle occurs through the medium of a mystic rosebud planted with sacred rites a thousand years earlier. Joline reforms and abandons her wanton ways, and does charity work among French peasants. When World War I breaks out, she becomes a Red Cross nurse. She saves the life of the artist when she finds him wounded on a battlefield, and they marry.

Exteriors were filmed on location in New Orleans' Vieux Carré, which doubled for the Paris Latin Quarter, and the climax featured an exciting battle in the French trenches. In marked contrast to her depressing role in *War Brides*, Nazimova created an exciting new personality as the sexy Paris grisette transformed into a mature and poised woman by Christian principles. Handsomely mounted on an expensive budget, *Revelation* was well directed by George D. Baker, a onetime newspaper political cartoonist who gave up a promising career as a stage actor and playwright to direct movies for Vitagraph. (In 1924, Baker made a new but less successful version of *Revelation* for M-G-M, with Viola Dana and Monte Blue in the leads.)

In *Toys of Fate* (1918), Nazimova played dual roles—
a gypsy girl and her daughter. Charles Bryant was the
wealthy roué who tried to seduce both mother and
daughter.

Toys of Fate (1918), Nazimova's second film at
Metro, also directed by Baker, had another lurid
and improbable story. Alla played dual roles. She
is seen first as a gypsy girl seduced by a wealthy
roué (Charles Bryant), who deserts her after she
becomes pregnant. She commits suicide, leaving
her child with gypsies. Nazimova is then seen as
the grown daughter twenty years later. A wild
creature intent upon avenging her mother's death,
she meets the same man, who attempts to lure
her into an incestuous situation. There are many
complications of plot, which are resolved in an
artifical happy ending as the girl marries a young
attorney (Irving Cummings) who defends her on
a murder charge. Although panned by the critics
as a poor vehicle for the star, *Toys of Fate* did
well at the box office.

The script for *Toys of Fate* was written by June
Mathis, later the brilliant scenarist of *The Four
Horsemen of the Apocalypse* (and the discoverer
of Rudolph Valentino). Nazimova was much impressed by her intelligence, and a warm personal
friendship sprang up between the two women. At
the actress' insistence, Miss Mathis was assigned

to write the screenplays of Nazimova's next several films at Metro.

After the completion of *Toys of Fate*, Nazimova was persuaded by Arthur Hopkins to do three months of Ibsen repertory at the Plymouth Theatre in New York. She opened on March 11, 1918, with the first American performance of *The Wild Duck*, and followed with revivals of *Hedda Gabler* and *A Doll's House*. Stimulated by her newfound screen popularity with *Revelation*, which was just coming into release, the plays attracted sell-out audiences and drew rave reviews from the critics. She had marvelous support from Lionel Atwill (particularly in his sensitive portrayal of Torvald Helmer in *A Doll's House*), Dodson Mitchell, Roland Young, George Probert, and Charles Bryant. The Ibsen plays at the Plymouth were her last appearances in the theater for five years.

Partly because of the virulent influenza epidemic that struck hard in the East during the early winter of 1918, Metro was gradually shifting production from New York to its West Coast studios. In June, shortly after the close of the Ibsen cycle, the Nazimova unit was moved to California. Alla was entranced with the climate, and soon purchased a lavish Spanish villa at 8150 Sunset Boulevard for $50,000. Set on three-and-a-half acres of land, it was surrounded by tropical plants, fir trees, and tall cedars. Her home quickly became the social center of a select group of friends and visiting celebrities.

Her director, George D. Baker, had elected to remain in New York, and while she had got along well with him, Nazimova thought his work unimaginative. She was more comfortable with Albert Capellani, a bearded Frenchman with exquisite manners, whom Metro assigned to direct her in *Eye For Eye* (1918). Capellani had spent twelve years as an actor and director with Pathé in France. He was invalided out of the French Army after becoming seriously ill from exposure during the Battle of Soissons, and, with film production curtailed in France by the war, had continued his career in the United States.

Capellani soon became known as a "woman's director," and did well with a series of romantic dramas starring Clara Kimball Young for Selznick. He was something of an individualist, and a strong critic of what he called "factory methods" of film-

Albert Capellani, a pioneer of the French cinema, was best known for his skills as a woman's director. He was responsible for several of Nazimova's most popular films, including *Out of the Fog, Eye For Eye,* and *The Red Lantern.*

making, believing motion pictures should be constructed with care and originality. Capellani liked working with Alla, and later called her "one of the rare intelligent actresses of the American screen." He got along equally well with June Mathis, with whom he collaborated on several Nazimova scripts.

Eye For Eye cast Alla as another exotic adventuress, this time as a tempestuous native girl named Hassouna, who falls in love with an officer of the French Foreign Legion (Charles Bryant). The plot was simply beyond belief, and was cluttered with a half-dozen story lines. Hassouna is

Nazimova was a native adventuress in *Eye For Eye* (1918), who fell in love with Charles Bryant (right), an officer of the French Foreign Legion. Sally Crute is the shocked woman at left.

outcast by her tribe and sold into slavery, from which she escapes to become a dancer in a café frequented by cutthroats. She follows her lover to France, where he has married a stuffy society girl (Sally Crute), and in vengeance tries to seduce the officer's son (Donald Gallaher). From this morass comes a happy ending, although it is apparent the twain can never meet for the white millionaire and his illiterate native wife! A highlight of the film was the terrifying sword dance in the Algerian café, which Alla performed with skill, showing little concern for the razor-sharp blades flashing about her head. Although panned by critics, *Eye For Eye* had an exotic appeal for audiences and made a lot of money. In addition to Bryant, a large cast included E. L. Fernandez (superb as an evil Bedouin chief) and the child actress Miriam Battista.

Near the end of World War I, Nazimova contributed her services to *A Woman of France* (1918), a five-minute film made to stimulate the sale of Liberty Bonds. She played a Paris underground agent who is killed by the Germans for smuggling military information to the French troops. It was one of thirty-six propaganda movies made in behalf of the war effort by major studios with such stars as Mary Pickford, Charlie Chaplin, Lillian Gish, Douglas Fairbanks, Sr. William S. Hart, Mae Murray, Charles Ray, Wallace Reid, and others participating. These films were made available by the government to theaters without charge.

Fearful she was being typecast as a Theda Bara vamp, Nazimova persuaded Metro to buy H. Austin Adams's somber play, *'Ception Shoals*, which she had done on Broadway in 1917, as her next vehicle. Retitled *Out of the Fog* (1919), it was a smash hit and was described by the New York *Times* as "a work of exceptional merit." Nazimova again played dual roles of a mother and daughter, far removed from the lurid characters of her first three Metro films. The story centered around a twisted lighthousekeeper (Henry Harmon) whose sister is compromised by a worthless man. Unable to accept this transgression, he forces her to a despairing suicide as she leaps from the lighthouse during a wild storm. Later, her daughter is subjected to the same senseless bigotry when she tries to escape from her uncle's iron will to marry a young man (Charles Bryant).

Profiting from Capellani's sensitive direction, Nazimova brought strength and conviction to a restrained performance, and *Out of the Fog* was a great personal triumph for the actress. Her versatility was reflected in the physical and emotional believability that she brought to two differing roles, and, although forty-years old at the time, was thoroughly convincing as a sixteen-year-old girl. Much of *Out of the Fog* was shot on location at Gloucester Point Light in Massachusetts, and there were many scenes of fishermen off the Great Banks, all beautifully photographed by Eugene Gaudio. Henry Harmon, repeating his stage role, was excellent as the relentless Job Coffin.

In *The Red Lantern* (1919), a melodrama set in China during the Boxer Rebellion, Nazimova returned to her exotic adventuresses. A mélange of romance and adventure in a colorful locale, it was her most popular motion picture. For the third time within five successive films, Alla again played dual roles—as Mahlee, daughter of a yellow mother and a white father, and as the aristocratic Blanche Sackville, daughter of Mahlee's English father and his white wife. There was a delicate similarity to her playing of the two contrasting roles that hinted they were half-sisters. Nazimova's

The Red Lantern (1919), Nazimova's biggest picture, gave her an opportunity to wear the exotic headdresses that she adored.

Red Lantern was rich in a wealth of colorful detail. The temples and bazaars of Peking were authentically re-created by art director Henri Menessier, and Metro's publicity department asserted 800 Chinese extras were used in the film. Nazimova wore magnificent silken robes and heavy Oriental headdresses that accented her exotic beauty. The exciting scenes of the Boxer Rebellion were packed with action, and the visual highlight of *The Red Lantern* was an imaginatively directed sequence in which Mahlee, borne on a palanquin carried by sixteen men, first appears as a pseudogoddess. These scenes, filmed at night before 300 spectators from the press and entertainment world, were exquisitely photographed by Eugene Gaudio. The intricate photographic setups used six cameramen, 575 Chinese lanterns, 95 other pieces of lighting equipment, and a powerful searchlight.

A tired Nazimova rests between scenes in this candid photograph taken on the set of *The Red Lantern* (1919).

stunning performance had moments of great power.

In the confused plot of *The Red Lantern*, Mahlee is torn between the conflicting loyalties of her mixed parentage. She is rejected by both Chinese and English, and embittered when her color bars her from marrying the white man she loves. Mahlee falls into the hands of Sam Wang (Noah Beery), a brutal half-breed revolutionist who exploits her as a Joan of Arc come to lead the Boxer forces. There is a tragic climax in which she is betrayed by her own father; the Rebellion fails, and she takes poison and dies on the ornate throne from which she had inspired the bloody uprising. (Since the Boxer Rebellion was basically anti-foreigner, the premise that two half-breeds could be its trusted leaders was unreal.)

Splendidly directed by Albert Capellani, *The*

Art Director Henri Menessier restored a Peking temple for Nazimova's *The Red Lantern* (1919). A portion of a lavish set is in this dramatic scene.

For a change of pace in her next picture, Nazimova turned to *The Brat* (1919), based on the
Oliver Morosco stage comedy that opened the previous year. The play was a big hit, running fifteen
months on Broadway with a stellar cast that included Maude Fulton, Lewis Stone, and Edmund
Lowe. The screen version, considerably rewritten,
was less successful, being an unconvincing jumble
of comedy, maudlin sentimentality, and even a
touch of melodrama. The name of Charles Bryant
appeared for the first time as coauthor of the
screenplay, sharing credit with June Mathis. In all
probability, Nazimova had as much or more to do
with the writing as Bryant.

The Brat had some similarities to George Bernard Shaw's *Pygmalion*, and told of a writer
(Charles Bryant) who rescues a shabby little
chorus girl from a night court, where she was
facing charges of shoplifting. Seeking to study her
for a novel he has in mind, he takes her home to
his horrified mother, a snobbish fiancée, and a
worthless brother. There is some amusing comedy
as he tries to transform the girl, a product of
slums and orphanages, into a sophisticated young
woman. After a variety of complications, she and
the novelist marry. Nazimova was appealing and
piquant, although at times overly cute with repe-
titious pouting. Unable to decide if it was comedy

Nazimova's leading men in *The Brat* (1919) were
the ever-present Charles Bryant (center) and Darrell
Foss.

or drama, the film was rather dull. (Fox remade *The Brat* in 1931, with John Ford directing and Sally O'Neil in the lead.

The best parts of *The Brat* were the colorful backstage sequences with Alla as a chorus pony— these scenes used a solid glass runway illuminated from below by 500 Kleig lights. Several days were spent in photographing her rabbit dance, in which she wore a ridiculous rabbit costume of gray plush with a baby-bunting hood, long ears, and a furry tail. According to the publicity, the dance was performed to "Anitra's Dance" from the Peer Gynt Suite by Grieg. Another scene showed her as a debutante doing a classical Greek dance to Dvorak's "Humoresque."

Charles Bryant (left), a *Pygmalion*-type professor and writer, is amused at the antics of Nazimova in *The Brat* (1919). Others are Bonnie Hill, Frank Currier, and Amy Van Ness.

Although forty at the time, Nazimova (right) played a Mary Pickford type, with shades of Eliza Doolittle, in *The Brat* (1919). Others in this scene are Amy Van Ness (seated), Bonnie Hill, and Frank Currier.

Albert Capellani had gone back to New York in an ill-fated attempt to establish his own film company, and the direction of *The Brat* was entrusted to Herbert Blaché, a Metro staff director. Blaché, whose real name was Blaché-Bolton, was an Englishman who spelled and pronounced his name the French way. In 1907, he married Alice Guy, the pioneer French woman-film director, and three days later they left for New York to establish an American unit for Leon Gaumont's company.

Herbert Blaché, an Englishman who made his reputation in early French films, directed Nazimova in *The Brat* and *Stronger Than Death*. He was the husband of the pioneer woman director, Alice Guy Blaché.

In 1910, she became head of the Solax Company, while Blaché built up a moderate reputation as a director of such stars as Mary Miles Minter, Madame Olga Petrova, and Ethel Barrymore. After *The Brat*, Blaché was assigned to Nazimova's next picture, *Stronger Than Death* (1920). For some now obscure reason, he was taken off the film, or resigned, and it was completed by Charles Bryant, who received codirector credit. In all likelihood, Alla did as much of the directing as Bryant.

Stronger Than Death was a theatrical tearjerker cut in the popular Nazimova pattern. Alla played a French dancer adventuring in British East India. She develops a weak heart, and is told by a doctor that she will die if she dances again. She falls in love with an army officer (Charles Bryant), but his stiff-upper-lipped father, the regimental colonel (Charles K. French), forbids them to marry. When a native uprising breaks out, Alla delays an

Exhibitors gave away thousands of cards with Nazimova's photograph and autograph to advertise *The Brat* (1919).

attack upon the garrison by dancing for the rebels in a moonlit Brahma temple until help arrives. Instead of dying, she is miraculously cured, proving love is stronger than death! The old colonel relents, and the lovers are married. The reviews were excellent, with Henry Harmon again stealing the show as an old native.

Nazimova's pictures both contributed to and helped alleviate the financial difficulties that were plaguing Metro in 1919. Since its organization four years earlier by a group of independent exchange owners, the company had led a precarious existence. Unlike its major competitors, Metro owned no theaters and was forced to rely upon small exhibitors for bookings. Deprived of the virtually guaranteed audiences of the big theater circuits and their centralized publicity resources, Metro had barely managed to keep its financial head above water. With many theaters closed down by a nationwide influenza epidemic and fuel shortages, the company's situation became desperate in early 1919.

Metro had initially depended upon a small group of independent producers for its pictures, and most of these were cheaply made (sometimes for as little as $15,000) and of poor quality. Production was soon stablized under the guidance of Maxwell Karger, an aggressive personality who had once been a violinist in the Metropolitan Opera Company orchestra. Karger upgraded the Metro output and substantially increased budgets, particularly for the Nazimova productions. In addition to Alla, he brought such popular favorites as Bert Lytell, Viola Dana, and Alice Lake into the studio. Other Karger recruits did not fare so well, and the German actress Emmy Wehlen and stage stars Emily Stevens, Hale Hamilton, and Edith Taliaferro never seemed to catch on with screen audiences.

While Nazimova's films were among Metro's top money-makers, the margin of profit was limited by heavy production costs. *The Red Lantern* and *Stronger Than Death* had been the most expensive pictures in the company's brief history. Had Metro access to its own theaters, particularly the showcases of the larger cities, the income potentials would have been enormous. (The Nazimova films were too sophisticated for small towns and rural areas, and tended to do less well there.) Alla was

Nazimova coolly holds a gun on Herbert Prior in this
scene from *Stronger Than Death* (1920), a drama of
native uprisings in India.

an excellent draw in most foreign countries, especially in Europe. To complicate its financial
situation, Metro lacked distribution facilities of
its own outside the United States, and sold off
the foreign rights for a lump sum in each country.
Income from such sources was on occasion as low
as $50,000 for the company's entire annual output.

In January 1920, Metro Pictures Corporation
was sold outright to the Loew's theater chain for
$3,100,000. The sale was mutually beneficial, giv-
ing Loew's, Inc. the films it desperately needed
for its theaters, and providing Metro with major

showcases and volume sales for its product. With
subsequent mergers within the next four years,
the company would soon become the powerful
Metro-Goldwyn-Mayer. Marcus H. Loew sent word
that quality and quantity were both to be increased, and henceforth no Metro film would cost
less than $200,000. While this was mostly pub-
licity blarney, there was a substantial upgrading
in Metro's production budgets.

In 1919, Nazimova had signed a new contract
with Metro that tied her to the company through
1921. She was to have her own unit, a substantial

boost in salary to $13,000 weekly, and a small share of the domestic profits of her pictures. A more important concession was the right to select her director, writer, and cast, although Metro retained final approval on stories. She told Karger that *Stronger Than Death* would be the last of her exotic adventuresses, and that henceforth she would play more modern roles in dramatic settings. There were published reports that she would do Ibsen's *Hedda Gabler* in movies, but the film never materialized.

THE TURNING POINT

In 1920, Nazimova did three successive films

that were incredibly bad; all were severely panned by the critics. Her fans were disappointed, and she ranked fourth—after Mary Pickford, Norma Talmadge, and Pearl White—in an annual popularity contest conducted by a fan magazine. She dropped to twentieth the following year. In all of these films she played unsympathetic roles, and she was criticized for being too theatrical in her acting.

In *The Heart of a Child*, her last picture under the old contract, Alla was a cockney girl of the London slums who ruthlessly used a series of men to get ahead, finally becoming the unhappy wife of an equally unhappy English lord who thinks she is all innocence. *Madame Peacock*, the best of the trio, was about an ambitious actress who de-

In *The Heart of a Child* (1920), Nazimova was a cockney girl who schemed to marry a wealthy English lord, Charles Bryant (left).

serts her husband and baby. She becomes internationally famous, but is a cold, self-centered, temperamental woman living only for public adulation. The day comes when a young actress takes the spotlight away from her. She learns the newcomer is her own daughter, and in a totally unconvincing climax goes home after an absence of twenty years to find her forgiving husband (George Probert) willing to take her back. *Billions*, based on an obscure French farce, cast Nazimova as a Russian princess who tries to make a young poet forget the fortune he has inherited. It was thoroughly confusing and chopped up by some absurd dream sequences through which Alla moved like an automaton.

By then in complete charge of Metro production, Maxwell Karger was spending much of his time shuttling between the Hollywood and New York studios, and he was no longer able to give any personal attention to the Nazimova unit. Although she liked and respected Karger, Alla enjoyed the virtual autonomy that she had acquired over her pictures. Since *The Brat*, her scripts had been credited exclusively to Charles Bryant, but it was no secret that she played an important role in their preparation. For the first time, her name appeared on the screen as a scenarist on *Madame Peacock*. Alla also took an active interest in the costuming and art direction of her films, and the publicity for *The Brat* pointedly stressed that Madame Nazimova had collaborated with the veteran art director, M. P. Staulcup, in designing the lavish theater set for the picture.

The choice of her new director, whether made by Nazimova herself or by Metro, surprised Hollywood. Beginning with *The Heart of a Child*, she was directed by Ray C. Smallwood, who until that time had been head of the photographic department at Metro. He had directed only one other film, *Best of Luck* (1920), an inconsequential comedy-drama with Jack Holt and Kathryn Adams. Smallwood was only thirty-two years of age, and before joining Metro had been a cameraman for Universal and the Thomas H. Ince companies. He had directed some of the action sequences for Nazimova's *The Red Lantern*, and had supervised the intricate photographic problems of that film. The selection of Smallwood, inexperienced and without stature, clearly indicated that Nazimova planned to do most of the directing.

As it turned out, Smallwood's contributions to the Nazimova films were far from negligible. She accepted many of his ideas and suggestions, and his knowledge of photography and the technical side of filmmaking were invaluable. Significantly, the New York *Times*, calling the direction of *The Heart of a Child* "extraordinarily good," praised its strong sense of photographic values. Smallwood then directed Alla's next three films—*Madame Peacock*, *Billions*, and *Camille*. He left Metro after the completion of *Camille* in 1921, and the following year directed three cheaply made independent pictures, after which he was unable to get further assignments except for a few short subjects. Many in Hollywood at the time felt Smallwood had promise as a director, but that Nazimova's increasing domination over all aspects of production deprived him of any real opportunity to display his talents. The mediocrity of the Nazimova pictures undoubtedly brought his career to a premature end. (Smallwood died of cancer in 1964, leaving his widow, the silent-screen actress Ethel Grandin.)

In a virulent attack in its June 1921 issue, *Motion Picture* magazine placed the blame for her sharp decline in popularity squarely upon the actress. Asserting the great Nazimova had become "too self-conscious of her greatness and thought she knew more than her directors," the magazine said she was ruining her reputation. "Whether she tries to write her own plays, and tries to direct them, and whether she is too great to accept suggestions from her 'inferiors,' such as scriptwriters, directors, managers, makeup men, technical directors, etc., is something that nobody knows except herself. But one big fact remains—Nazimova is now quite *passé*!"

The article went on to cut her production of *Billions* to ribbons, saying that its characters "do not exist except in Keystone farces. She forgot her art entirely when she drew this character. In fact, the whole story is impossible, and Nazimova played it impossibly. And not only was Nazimova bad, but nearly everyone else in the cast was bad." It criticized her odd makeup that made her look as though she was wearing a false face—a dead white face with jet black lipstick! *Motion Picture* concluded, "Nazimova should do all her future pictures in long-shots. This is the only way in which she can make us remember the Nazimova of old."

Earlier, in November 1920, following the disappointing premiere of *Billions*, Metro announced that henceforth Madame Nazimova would appear only in lavish picturizations of famous classics of literature and the theatre. Although giving no figures, a blast of studio publicity assured exhibitors that budgets for her films would be the highest in Metro history. Moreover, she was to have Hollywood's most popular male stars as her leading men. The new policy was to be inaugurated with Pierre Louy's fantasy of the sex goddess, *Aphrodite*, and Alla was reported to be thinking of doing Shakespeare's *Hamlet* (a not inconceivable possibility for several actresses, including Asta Nielsen, had already tried their hand at the Melancholy Dane)!

Behind the announcement lay a bitter disagreement between the company and its star. Metro felt her increasing domination over all aspects of production had resulted in strange, unpopular films that pleased no one but herself. She was accused of being insensitive to the commercial requirements of filmmaking and interested only in creating artistic *succès d'estimes*. Nazimova blamed Metro for the poor vehicles she was forced to accept, and complained that her films were too hurriedly made. She proposed to Maxwell Karger that she do fewer and more expensive pictures, each based upon a well-known novel or play, under her *complete* supervision. Madame hinted that if Metro was not interested in prestige pictures in keeping with her reputation, she would set up her own company for another distributor. For its part, Metro was not yet ready to part company with the Russian actress, nor was it willing to give her the carté blanche she demanded.

There were concessions on both sides, and in the end Nazimova got most of what she wanted. She agreed to Karger's stipulation that a top screenwriter of Metro's choice should prepare the scenarios—there were to be no more Bryant-Nazimova script collaborations. She also agreed, probably with reluctance, to accept popular film actors as her leading men, which Karger felt would enhance the box office; she was not anxious to have attention taken away from her. Charles Bryant had

appeared opposite her in virtually all of her pictures. While a competent actor, he had not caught on as a leading man. Metro had made no attempt to use him in films with other stars. Significantly, he was given no publicity buildup, and his name was mentioned only casually in newspaper and fan magazine articles about his "wife." In turn, Metro agreed to substantially increase budgets, reduce the frequency of her films, and give her complete "artistic control" over all aspects of production. Nazimova was also to receive screen credit as the producer of her pictures. It was a decision that Karger soon had cause to bitterly regret.

Although the rights to the Louys property had already been purchased, Metro announced two months later that *Aphrodite* was "not suited to the requirements of Madame Nazimova," and instead she would do a new version of Alexandre Dumas's *Camille*. Only four years earlier, in 1917, there had been two unsuccessful versions of the Dumas classic—one with Clara Kimball Young and another with Theda Bara—and Karger worried that it was too soon for another *Camille*. Whatever fears he may have had were soon justified as the film moved through a stormy production period, and by the time of its release in September 1921, Nazimova and Metro had parted company for good.

Rudolph Valentino was Armand to Nazimova's *Camille* in the 1921 version of the Dumas drama. Valentino's penciled eyebrows and slicked-down hair were matched by Alla's frequently bizarre makeup.

Camille met a mixed critical reception. It was hailed by some reviewers as a work of art, and roundly panned by others as worthless trivia. It was most frequently described as "bizarre," and criticized for a strange combination of advanced techniques, old-fashioned acting styles, and a slow pace that left audiences confused. Some critics thought *Camille* ahead of its time and said it would come to be recognized as a classic, a prediction that never materialized.

Except for the script, which was by June Mathis, *Camille* was more than ever a misguided Nazimova tour de force. Ray C. Smallwood was credited with the direction, although Nazimova was the director in fact. She was content to rely upon Smallwood and an excellent cameraman, Rudolph J. Bergquist, for technical guidance, but the dramatic content was wholly of her own devising. The glaring faults of *Camille* provoked another attack upon her, this time by the influential *Photoplay* magazine. "What has happened to the great actress, the splendid genius, the incomparable artiste?", it asked in an open letter.

"With Metro you have the choice of everything, the pick of everything. You have been favored in every way, to the exclusion of everything and everyone else. You have had all the money for yourself and for productions you could ask. . . . You have insisted on selecting, casting, practically directing, cutting, and titling your own pictures. In the opinion of many who have worked with you, you have tried to do too much. Either you have feared to trust anyone else, or you have decided that you are more efficient in every line than anyone else. Or both. Perhaps you have come, unfortunately, to that place where you believe the whispering chorus that says, 'The Queen can do no wrong!' "

Nazimova gave an uneven performance as the ill-fated Marguerite Gautier, alternating between a cold, sexless aloofness and an almost animal sensuousness. In her scenes with her lover in a secluded country retreat, she overdid a pouting coquetry completely out of character with a mature Parisian courtesan. (Alla answered her critics by saying this was how Camille, searching for the love that had been denied her as a young girl, would have behaved.) She was especially poignant in the deathbed scene, which was played with great tenderness and surprising restraint. Alla wore beautiful gowns and jewelry, but was handicapped by what one reviewer called "a Fiji Island makeup."

Carlyle Blackwell had been considered for the role of Armand, but Nazimova thought him unsuitable. The part eventually went to the intense young Latin, Rudolph Valentino, a protégé of June Mathis, who had talked Metro into giving him the male lead in Rex Ingram's *The Four Horsemen of the Apocalypse* (1921). It was released while the Nazimova film was still in production, and his smoldering sex appeal as the Ibáñez hero made him an overnight sensation. Lacking Ingram's sensitive guidance, he gave a heavy-handed performance in *Camille* that was fraught with eyeball rolling, flaring nostrils, and passionate heavy breathing. Valentino's unprecedented popularity was to assure the commercial

Rudolph Valentino soared to overnight fame as the intense young Argentinian in Rex Ingram's *The Four Horsemen of the Apocalypse* (1921). Here he is seen in the uniform of a French poilu for the World War I sequences.

success of *Camille*, and later, at the height of his career, it was reissued to strong financial returns. (What Madame Nazimova thought of Metro's revised posters advertising Valentino as the star of *Camille*, and relegating her to the supporting cast, is unrecorded.) In later years, Alla would claim to have given him his first big break in Hollywood, conveniently forgetting that *The Four Horsemen of the Apocalypse* had been completed months earlier.

Valentino was probably no stranger to Nazimova at the time he was engaged for *Camille*. Some friends insist he first met her in 1916, when she was making films in New York and he was a professional ballroom dancer. (An unsubstantiated report is that Alla put up the money to bail him out of a New York jail after he was arrested, along with a prostitute, in an investigation of a case involving attempted blackmail. The charges were apparently dropped, and Valentino always maintained his innocence.) Earlier, he had been involved in a sensational divorce case that culminated in a prominent society woman, Bianca De Saulles, shooting her former husband. Valentino was in love with her, although it is doubtful that she seriously reciprocated his affection. The actor admitted in court that he helped set De Saulles up in an assignation with Bonnie Sawyer, Valentino's dancing partner, so that Mrs. De Saulles could get evidence for her divorce. In later years the legend grew that the beautiful Bianca had killed her husband because of her infatuation for Valentino, although the shooting took place eleven months after the divorce. Nazimova apparently believed the story and snubbed him when they first met on the Metro lot, but tactfully forgot it when he went to work on *Camille*.

For more than a year Nazimova had been under the domination of Natacha Rambova, a striking young woman of glacial beauty who designed the sets and costumes of *Billions* and *Camille*. The stepdaughter of the wealthy cosmetics manufacturer, Richard Hudnut, she had spent much of her life in Europe, where she became a dancer with Theodore Kosloff's ballet troupe. She met Nazimova in California in 1919, and the two women soon became intimate friends. A talented if erratic designer, Miss Rambova did much work on the aborted *Aphrodite*, and then was given a free hand for *Camille*. Her bizarre and ornate sets overwhelmed both players and the drama, and were an unbelievable pastiche of conflicting styles that the chronic bad taste of the 1920s found acceptable. Her costumes, accented by the garish makeup she also devised—Valentino had slicked-down hair and penciled eyebrows—were equally distracting.

Natacha Rambova's influence upon Nazimova had grown progressively stronger, and the actress sought her opinions on both professional and personal matters. A blunt and often difficult person, Natacha was not the actual director of Alla's films, as was widely reported, but many of her ideas found their way into the finished pictures. It is possible that Miss Rambova suggested Valentino for the role of Armand, although most sources say June Mathis touted him to Nazimova. For his part, Valentino was delighted to be near Natacha. He had fallen in love with the cold, willowy young woman, although for some time she took scant notice of him. She was flattered when Rudy, to gain her attention, sought her advice on his acting, clothes, and personal problems. At first, Nazimova teased him about his infatuation for "the human iceberg," and thought the courtship amusing. Later, when the romance became serious and marriage between Valentino and Miss Rambova appeared imminent, she tried to prevent it.

Metro officials were dismayed by the oddities of *Camille*, and soon after its completion and before any public showings, it was quietly announced that Madame Nazimova had left the studio. No explanations were made, and with a fortune tied up in the costly film, Metro took care not to imply any dissatisfaction with *Camille*. The break between the company and its star had been in the making for two years, and dated from the time Alla began to dominate the production of her films. Nazimova was unwilling to accept Karger's ultimatum that she relinquish control over her pictures, and the contract was terminated by mutual consent on April 20, 1921.

ALLA: THE COMPLEX CHARACTER

Despite a succession of poor films, her personal popularity was largely intact. A continuous pub-

Valentino fell madly in love with Natacha Rambova, stepdaughter of cosmetics king Richard Hudnut. She designed the sets and costumes for several of Nazimova's films, and was a confidant of the Russian actress.

After they were married, Natacha Rambova designed more eye-catching clothing for Rudolph Valentino than the traditional English tweed that he wore in this 1922 portrait.

and forgotten. Her friends and coworkers are unanimous in characterizing Nazimova as a kind and compassionate woman. "She was a very sweet and understanding person," says Charles J. Van Enger, her cameraman on *A Doll's House* and *Salome*. Director Robert Florey, a frequent visitor in her home, called Alla "a gentle woman . . . temperamental only with interfering producers and people who didn't know their business. She was not easily angered, and I never saw her mad at anyone." As the legend of her temperament grew, she became concerned and after leaving Metro persuaded a few fan magazines to publish, somewhat reluctantly, more favorable interviews and articles.

Often impulsively generous, Nazimova gave away valuable books, paintings, and art objects that friends chanced to admire, and she was an easy touch for loans seldom repaid. She liked to have attractive, intelligent, young people about her, and on Sundays her elegant swimming pool, illuminated at night by underwater lights, was crowded with promising Hollywood ingenues, leading men, and other aspiring talents. When she could, Alla helped them in their careers.

Her open houses on Sunday afternoons attracted

licity campaign by Metro had fostered the image of Nazimova as a temperamental artiste whose private life was in keeping with the exotic characters she portrayed on the screen. The public was intrigued when she was described as a queen holding court, and pictured as always the center of attention at a party or the weekend soirees at her home. There was considerable truth in this, for she loved the limelight and never ceased to be the *grande dame* and the relentless actress, delighting in acting out the scenes of her childhood in Russia and early hardships in America. To her, this regal role, leavened by her piquant sense of humor, was simply one of the perquisites of stardom.

The myth of Nazimova's absorbing temperament was largely an invention of Metro's publicity writers. To be sure, there were occasional rages born of frustration, but they were quickly over

Nazimova's Sunday afternoon poolside parties at her home in the early 1920s drew many Hollywood celebrities. Seated in wet bathing suits are, left to right, Patsy Ruth Miller, Virginia Fox, Lois Wilson, and Charles Bryant. Standing are Robert Florey, Gloria Hope, Edna Murphy, Nazimova, Mildred Davis, and Clara Horton.

many European film personalities who came to work in the United States in the 1920s, as well as other visiting foreign celebrities—Feodor Chaliapin, Abel Gance, Nikita Balieff, Elenora Duse, Michael Fokine, Anna Pavlova. Except for an occasional glass of champagne, Nazimova did not drink, and ate sparingly, although there was always a buffet of caviar and Russian delicacies for her guests, as well as vodka and other liquors hard to get during Prohibition. Her gatherings were informal, and Alla, dressed in the black Chinese silk pajamas designed for her by Natacha Rambova, was a vivacious hostess. New films from abroad, which she considered more innovative than their Hollywood counterparts, were shown in a special projection room; there were impromptu musicales with Alla playing Russian melodies on the violin or piano, or performing the Oriental dances that she studied with native teachers. She enjoyed costume balls, and at one appeared in a large diaper and baby's lace cap to represent the New Year! Books were a special passion, and in the midst of a gay party she would read Dreiser or Walpole, her favorite authors, without missing a word of the conversation around her.

The complex character of Nazimova's love life was a source of uneasiness among film industry leaders, particularly after the disastrous publicity of the Roscoe (Fatty) Arbuckle and William Desmond Taylor scandals of the early 1920s. Although the subject was never mentioned in newspapers or fan magazines, her preference for gracious, attractive young women was widely known in blasé Hollywood, and her intimates at various times included several minor actresses. Alla's peculiar relationship with Charles Bryant caused much speculation, and many felt their pretense of marriage over a dozen years was only a public cover for her lesbian attachments. She was heterosexual to a considerable extent, however, and in 1921 had a brief but passionate affair with a young film technician half her age.

Charles Bryant did not interfere with Alla's unconventional private life, and seemed unconcerned at what went on about him. Described as "a placid, peace-loving fellow," he was a pleasant if quiet host, and if the noise of the balalaikas grew too loud, he would simply retire to his room with a bottle of Scotch. From the time he first met her

in late 1911 to their separation in 1924, Bryant had no professional activities outside of his association with Nazimova, and his career was completely subordinated to hers. He was her leading man in virtually all of her plays and motion pictures and in vaudeville. Despite the prominence that these roles brought him, he made no effort, whether by choice or at Alla's insistence, to appear opposite other prominent actresses. He was credited with writing and directing several of her films, but Nazimova's domination kept his contributions to a minimum. Bryant was also her business manager for a time, and was paid the usual ten percent agent's commission on her earnings.

ON HER OWN: *A DOLL'S HOUSE, SALOME*

With the termination of her Metro contract, Nazimova formed her own company in mid-1921, and space was rented at the Robert A. Brunton Studios on Melrose Avenue. First National, an exhibitors combine that had made her an attractive offer one year earlier, was no longer interested. She eventually signed a distribution contract with Allied Producers and Distributors Corporation, a subsidiary of United Artists (which also handled independent productions of Jack Pickford, Charles Ray, J. Stuart Blackton, Max Linder, and others). Because of her declining box-office value, United Artists would not finance her pictures. While some of the money came from a downtown Los Angeles bank at a high rate of interest, she was forced to risk her personal fortune in the venture. At the time, she had considerable savings despite her lavish style of living. Nazimova's contract at Metro had been one of the most lucrative in Hollywood, bringing her in excess of $250,000 annually—then a top figure for salaried performers. She was paid $65,000 per picture in weekly installments of $13,000, plus a bonus if shooting went over five weeks.

In a flurry of publicity, Nazimova announced that she would appear only in films based on famous plays or stories with classic themes. Wisely, as it turned out, she decided to do Ibsen's *A Doll's House*, her resounding stage success, as her first independent production. Alla told the press she had long wanted to play Nora Helmer in movies, but that Metro would not buy the costly rights, and emotionally recalled what the play had meant in her life. She repeated a story, frequently told to interviewers, of how Madame Helena Modjeska had come backstage during a 1907 performance of *A Doll's House* in New York. The great Polish actress, then sixty-three, had thrown her arms around Alla and exclaimed, "I came, I saw Nazimova, and I was conquered!" Alla declared it had been "the happiest night of my life."

Nazimova, whimsically using the pseudonym of "Peter M. Winters" (a ploy on her name, which means "of the winter" in Russian), fashioned a script remarkably faithful to Ibsen's play. Charles Bryant was nominally the director, with Natacha Rambova doing the sets and costumes. Production got off to a bad start. Wallace Beery had been assigned to play Torvald, but after a few days both Nazimova and Beery were unhappy with his work. To complicate matters, she thought her camera-

A Doll's House (1922) gave Nazimova the opportunity to bring a favorite Ibsen heroine, the tortured Nora Helmer, to the screen in a sensitive performance.

man was photographing her badly, and discharged him. A week's costly shooting was scrapped, and Alan Hale was brought in to replace Beery. Her new cameraman, Charles J. Van Enger, was recommended by Beery, whom Van Enger had photographed in *The Last of the Mohicans* (1920). Alla screened several of Van Enger's pictures, including some he had done with director Maurice Tourneur, and was impressed with his work. (*A Doll's House* was the first picture made with the superior new Mitchell camera.)

Van Enger describes the direction of *A Doll's House* (and the subsequent *Salome*) as a joint effort of Nazimova and Charles Bryant. "Nazimova and Bryant, together with myself, would talk over each scene," he says. "She knew nothing about photography, but had perfect confidence in my judgment. We never had a retake for photographic reasons on either picture. It was a very close and cooperative company, and no one's suggestions were ever discarded until they were thoroughly discussed." Others on the set say Alla did the actual directing, and was most insistent upon her own ideas, whether practical or not, and that Bryant had little to do beyond calling, "Lights! Camera! Action!", and, "Cut" (Robert Florey, then writing for a French fan magazine, describes Bryant as "the last man I would choose to direct Ibsen, and the first to do a picture about an English cricket match!")

While Alla valued her opinions on artistic matters, there is nothing to substantiate the reports that Natacha Rambova was the actual director of *Camille, A Doll's House*, and *Salome*. Yet, they seem to be part of the growing Valentino legend. Charles Van Enger says Miss Rambova's designs for the sets were carefully gone over by Nazimova, Bryant, and himself. At times, it was necessary to modify them to meet the requirements of the camera, and Van Enger found Natacha very cooperative and helpful about making such changes, not once showing any sign of resentment. After the designs were approved by Nazimova, Miss Rambova personally supervised the construction of the sets.

Van Enger has nothing but praise for Nazimova. "She was a very sweet and understanding person, appreciative of the smallest things . . . one of the finest women that I ever worked for," he says. "I

Alan Hale gave an uneven performance of the obtuse Torvald Helmer in *A Doll's House* (1922). Wallace Beery was originally cast in the role but withdrew after a week's shooting.

was warned that she was difficult, but she never was—at least not with me or anyone that I know of. It was only a few days until we would sit on the floor of her dressing room and swap stories. After making over 250 pictures, I only know that the two films I did with Nazimova were the most pleasant of all."

A Doll's House had been brought to the screen three times earlier, first by Thanhouser as a 1911 one-reeler. Dorothy Phillips, William Stowell, and Lon Chaney had the leads in Universal's shallow version of 1917, which was directed by Joseph DeGrasse on a slim budget. The following year, Elsie Ferguson, newly recruited to films from the Broadway stage, starred in Maurice Tourneur's more elaborate picturization of the Ibsen play for Paramount-Artclass. All were failures, sharing a common fault of being extremely slow moving, although Miss Ferguson was praised by reviewers for her performance as Nora Helmer (and inevitably compared with Nazimova).

Ibsen's controversial drama, first presented in 1879 (the year of Alla's birth) had become a classic expression of the theme of women's rights. It concerned a doll-like child-wife of an ambitious and self-centered banker who believes that a husband's every wish and whim should be as law to his wife. Unknown to him, she had earlier forged a note to get money to pay for medical care to save his life during a serious illness. She is exposed, and while no charges are brought, her illusions about her husband are shattered when he turns against her, concerned only for his own career. For the first time she sees him as a selfish hypocrite without any regard for her position in the matter. Realizing that she has been cheated of her rights to self-expression as an individual, she abruptly leaves him to find a life of her own.

Despite the difficulties of transcribing the psychological complexity of Nora Helmer into purely visual terms, and without the probing dialogue, Nazimova made a remarkable film of *A Doll's House*. While remaining faithful to the spirit of the Ibsen classic, she interpolated scenes of the early married life of Torvald and Nora that were only referred to in the play. These additions contributed to character exposition, but were marred by Nazimova's kittenish antics as she played Torvald's "lark" and "squirrel" with cloying cuteness. The New York *Times* called her "a jumping-jack" in these scenes, and other reviewers thought she was "flapperish!" In the later portions of the film, she became more restrained, and gave a stunning performance in the powerful climax. *A Doll's House* had moments of great artistry, and for Nazimova it was clearly a labor of love, reflecting her dedication to Ibsen's troubled heroine. The picture emphasized its Norwegian setting, and many beautiful scenes were enhanced by Charles Van Enger's photography and the authentic sets designed by Natacha Rambova.

The reviews of *A Doll's House* were excellent, and it did much to temporarily restore Nazimova's faltering screen career. There was some carping by critics who compared it to the play—and found fault with Alla's overacting in the early sequences, Alan Hale's rather melodramatic performance as Torvald, and some minor tampering with the ending. The finishing touch to Ibsen's drama was the closing of a door as Nora left home, symbolizing her emancipation. While Nazimova loyally retained the unhappy ending, there was a strong suggestion that Nora would eventually return to her husband and children. Although this inference was read into the film by several critics, Alla vehemently denied such a possibility existed. "Did Nora ever return? Never, never, never!" she declared angrily.

A Doll's House drew mixed reactions from screen audiences. It had an enormous appeal to women, who sympathized with Nora's desire to be something more than a plaything for a man. Yet, many found it old-fashioned for the newfound freedom of the 1920s, when women expressed their independence by bobbing their hair, drinking bathtub gin, and wearing short skirts! The common public criticism of *A Doll's House* was that it was slow moving and depressing. Essentially a celluloid *succès d'estime*, it enjoyed popularity only with more selective and discriminating audiences.

Nazimova's second independent film, *Salome* (1923), based on a play by Oscar Wilde, was a bizarre version of the biblical tale of Saint John the Baptist, who was beheaded when he spurned the passion of the Princess Salome. Designed as a lavish spectacle featuring the famous Dance of the Seven Veils, *Salome* proved a gross disaster that cost Nazimova her fortune and soon brought her Hollywood career to a full stop.

The notion of playing Salome had been germinating in her mind for several years—"Salome is my pet child," she told an interviewer for *Photoplay* magazine. Alla was appalled at the traditional dramatic and operatic heroines played by "great, huge, majestic ladies," and conceived Salome as a trim, fourteen-year old ("otherwise she would have already been married"), pretty, pampered, and heavily guarded by male homosexuals and eunichs. Metro officials had once rejected her suggestion of a Salome film, saying it would not pass the censors.

Nazimova was encouraged to do *Salome* by Natacha Rambova, who saw in the picture an opportunity to showcase her own talents as an art director and costume designer. At her suggestion, the decor and costumes were based on the sensual drawings that the eccentric Aubrey Beardsley had done for a book of the Wilde play twenty-five years earlier. Miss Rambova used only black, white,

silver, and gold in her materials to produce a visually satisfying effect. Nazimova wore several ornate wigs and a stunning headdress of glass bubbles, all freely adapted from the Beardsley illustrations. The costumes of the courtesans were equally lavish, although the hooded uniforms of the temple guards today resemble those of the villains in a Buck Rogers serial. Miss Rambova designed a simple but rather absurd costume for Nazimova that accentuated her boyish figure; one reviewer was unkind enough to compare it to the popular one-piece bathing suit of the twenties.

In contrast to the generally breathtaking costumes and coiffures, the Rambova sets were unimaginative and disappointing. Done in heavy masses and straight lines with an occasional application of a Beardsley effect, they were merely functional at best. Only two basic sets were used—a court banquet hall in the palace of Herod, and an adjoining terrace, where most of the action takes place. The spartan furnishings were confined to a few wispy draperies, some chairs, and a table. Clearly, little money had been expended on sets.

The familiar story, drawn from the fourteenth chapter of Saint Matthew, told of Saint John the Baptist (Jokanaan) being imprisoned in a cistern for condemning Herod for marrying his sister-in-law. The bored young Princess Salome releases Jokanaan, but he rejects her passionate advances and returns to his cell. Herod, lusting after Salome, promises her anything—even half his kingdom—if she will dance for him. She performs the famous Dance of the Seven Veils, and in vengeance for Jokanaan's rejection of her, demands his head on a silver charger. In a horrifying ending she kisses the severed head as the anguished Herod orders her crushed beneath the shields of his soldiers.

Salome drew a generally adverse response from the critics, with the *New Republic* calling it "a production of unimaginable stupidity!" Many reviewers were clearly confused by the film, and took refuge in praise for Charles Van Enger's artistic photography and Natacha Rambova's stylized sets and costumes. While likened to a Keystone comedy by one critic, *Salome* also had its passionate supporters, who saw in it the *avant-garde* of free expression in motion pictures. With some justification, others saw influences of the exciting German films of the postwar era. Essentially a team effort of Nazimova, Miss Rambova, Van Enger, and Bryant (who was credited with the direction), *Salome* was nonetheless hailed by some for its highly *personal* quality!

As far as the public was concerned, the major disappointment of the slow-moving *Salome* was its failure to live up to its lurid publicity and advertising. United Artists sold it as an orgy of sex and sin, promising "the decadent lusts of the ages!" The much-heralded Dance of the Seven Veils (done to the Richard Strauss score) proved extremely tame, with Alla flittering about like a freshman in classical Greek dancing. There was none of the nudity that was broadly hinted at in posters and advertisements. For what purported to be a passionate portrayal of one of the world's great sinners, Nazimova's Salome was sexless and a product of her own lesbian psyche.

The best thing that can be said of Nazimova's performance is that it is clinically interesting, particularly when viewed in her concept of Salome as a headstrong fourteen-year old. Although a mature woman of forty-three at the time, she physically looked and acted the part, and her use of body movement, although occasionally overdone, heightens the impression of a very young girl. She moves gracefully in a balletlike portrayal, continuously rising to her toes, swinging on the bars of Jokanaan's cagelike cell, or arching her beautiful neck. The petulance is overemphasized, and is simply a middle-aged woman's idea of how a spoiled fourteen-year old girl would behave when displeased. She is fine and intense in more dramatic moments, particularly the confrontation with Herod to demand Jokanaan's head, and in the final guilt-ridden climax.

The others in the cast are less than adequate. Nigel De Brulier, as Jokanaan, is seen only briefly, and looks old enough to be Salome's grandfather. He is so emaciated that his ribs stand out (perhaps a realistic look at a man who has been imprisoned for months), and there is nothing physically about him to incite Salome's passion. Mitchell Lewis as Herod is something out of Mack Sennett in his scenes of drooling passion over Salome's dull dance. Some of the other characters play obvious homosexuals with such an abundance of embarrassing clichés as to be ludicrous.

DECLINE AND FALL IN HOLLYWOOD

Nazimova's film career had been plunging downward for three years, and despite the support of a coterie of faithful fans, *A Doll's House* and *Salome* were both box-office failures. Her fortune was dissipated on the ill-fated ventures, and plans for a third independent production, *The World's Illusion*, were scrapped and the property sold to director Rex Ingram. Neither Alla nor Bryant, who was ostensibly her manager, had any business acumen, and they made the mistake of trying to personally handle many complex legal and financial details. Nor was there any attempt at economy —money was ladled out in huge sums, and production on both films had dawdled along at a snail's pace.

Nazimova was soon at odds with United Artists, and she blamed the company for a poor job of exploitation and selling. (She felt her pictures were neglected in favor of those of the United Artists' owners, Mary Pickford, Douglas Fairbanks, Sr., Charlie Chaplin, and D. W. Griffith.) Alla was particularly bitter at a company executive, Hiram S. Abrams, and later there was a long controversy over accounting of income and distribution costs that threatened to erupt into the courts. In the end she received only a fraction of what she considered was due her. For some reason, both *A Doll's House* and *Salome* had a limited exhibition abroad, which should have been a principal market, although Nazimova made a hurried trip to England in the spring of 1923 to attend the London opening of *Salome*.

The Nazimova-Rambova relationship cooled appreciably after Natacha's marriage to Rudolph Valentino, which Alla had tried to discourage. On May 12, 1922, she left (along with actor Douglas Gerrard and cameraman Paul Ivano) on a wedding party to Mexicali, Mexico, where the glamorous couple were married the next day by the local mayor. Valentino's interlocutory decree of divorce from Jean Acker (also at one time a Nazimova intimate) was not final, and he was jailed when he returned to California a few days later. A nightmare of publicity on the bigamy charges followed, and upon the advice of Valentino's attorneys Miss Rambova hurriedly left for New York.

At a sensational trial held three weeks later, a

parade of witnesses testified that Rudy and Natacha had never shared a bedroom during their brief stay in Mexico—indeed, Valentino had slept on a cot on a bungalow porch, or shared a room with male friends! A physician told the court that Miss Rambova had been ill, and he had suggested she sleep alone until her health improved. One of the last witnesses was Alla Nazimova, nervous and distraught but still capable of making a dramatic entrance, who confirmed the earlier testimony. Under questioning, it developed that she had been in hiding from process servers, and had been found, swathed in veils, boarding a train for New York. (Alla, still a Russian citizen, was fearful the publicity might bring about her deportation as an undesirable alien.) Valentino, whose first marriage to Jean Acker had lasted only a few hours before she slammed the bedroom door in his face, was freed of bigamy charges. He and Natacha did not go through a second ceremony until March 14, 1923.

By the time *Salome* was completed, Nazimova's financial situation had become critical, and she decided to do a play on Broadway, her first in nearly five years. Rather than accept one of the tempting offers that established producers were dangling before her, she scraped together enough money to produce *Dagmar*, an adaptation of a Hungarian play by Ferencz Heczeg, which opened at the Selwyn Theatre on January 22, 1923. Charles Bryant was ostensibly the director, and also appeared to good effect as a paranoid killer. Nazimova played a Russian countess, a nymphomaniac who toyed with a series of men and was finally murdered by a jealous lover. Wearing beautiful gowns and appealing negligees, she gave a sensuous performance as the smouldering vamp. The New York critics, as always, found her exciting but the play less so. *Dagmar* had a respectable run of fifty-six performances (not bad by 1923 standards) and toured briefly, which gave her a modest and much-needed profit. Others in the cast were Gilbert Emery and a promising young actress named Greta Cooper.

In Hollywood, the failure of *A Doll's House* and *Salome* labeled Nazimova as box-office poison. Her squabbles with United Artists did not help her standing with film executives, and efforts to negotiate a contract at a major studio were fruit-

less. For a time she did not realize the seriousness of her situation, and continued to demand a high salary and autonomy over cast, director, and script.

Alla's financial troubles worsened, and, after a trip to Europe to exploit *Salome*, she decided to return to vaudeville. She opened at the Palace Theatre in New York on October 31, 1923, as the headliner in *The Unknown Lady*, a playlet by George Middleton. Her leading man was Herbert Heyes, an early silent-screen hero. The Catholic Church was outraged by the bold theme of the plot—a married man arranges an assignation with a prostitute (Nazimova) in a hotel room to gain evidence for a divorce action—and charged it made a mockery of New York divorce laws. After two performances, Edward F. Albee, head of the Keith-Proctor vaudeville circuit, cancelled the booking and paid off her $15,000 contract calling for five weeks' work. Albee was quoted as saying Nazimova was "very gracious" about the matter, as well she might be.

The uproar over *The Unknown Lady* took a new turn with New York actors protesting what they felt was arbitrary censorship by Catholic diocese officials. A great many leading performers signed a petition asking that it be allowed to continue. Albee responded that he had not been aware of the licentious content of the playlet when it was booked, to which author Middleton pointed out that it had previously played eight weeks on the Keith circuit under the title of *Collusion* without objection. Middleton also observed that the Palace had advertised the sketch as "sensational" and "dramatic dynamite!" Judge Ben B. Lindsey of Denver, the eccentric advocate of free love, got into the act by writing Nazimova a letter praising *The Unknown Lady* for sharply criticizing outmoded divorce statutes. The storm in a teapot, a publicity bonanza to Nazimova, crested when the touring French Grand Guignol Players invited her to include *The Unknown Lady* in its repertory just opening in New York, but she gave only a week's performances.

In mid-1924, after months of idleness, Nazimova finally signed a two-picture contract with Edwin Carewe, an independent producer-director (*The Bad Man; The Girl of the Golden West*) releasing through First National. She was desperately in need of money, and her salary was only a fraction of what she had earned at Metro a few years earlier. Alla's first film for Carewe was *Madonna of the Streets* (1924), a tearjerker in which she played a role reminiscent of her halcyon days. Milton Sills was a preacher in London's Limehouse who inherits a fortune, and Nazimova was a golddigger who entices him into marriage. She leaves him when he gives his money to the poor. In a ludicrous ending, they are reunited years later when he discovers her in a mission for fallen women.

Madonna of the Streets was hampered by the broad comedy of Wallace Beery and Tom Kennedy, and by slangy Hollywood colloquialisms in the titles. The settings of London's Chinatown were not authentic and looked more like the New York Bowery. Alla was generally praised by the critics, but several noticed she used too much

Edwin Carewe brought Nazimova back to the screen in *Madonna of the Streets* (1924), in which she played a golddigger who enticed a Limehouse minister into marriage.

makeup and did not look good in close-ups. She was distressed when First National's advertising and publicity emphasized the fast-rising Milton Sills, whom it was promoting as a major star. The picture opened to surprisingly strong business in the Christmas season of 1924. (*Madonna of the Streets* was remade as a talkie by Columbia in 1930, with Evelyn Brent and Robert Ames in the leads.)

Soon after the Carewe film was completed, Nazimova signed with the faltering Vitagraph Company for *The Redeeming Sin* (1925), a heavy-handed drama of the Paris Latin Quarter. The absurd plot combined features of *Revelation* and and *The Brat*, and had Alla as a wicked Apache dancer in a Montmartre night club. She falls in love with an aristocratic young sculptor (Carl Miller), reforms and educates herself to be a lady, hoping to win him in marriage. When she sees him with another woman (who turns out to be his sister), she flies into a jealous rage and sends the leader of a cutthroat gang of thieves (Lou Tellegen) to frame him in a jewelry robbery. Everything is eventually set right as love wins out, and there is a happy ending.

Nazimova was embarrassed by the shoddiness of *The Redeeming Sin*. "It is not the kind of film I like to do, nor the kind of part I like to play—but I need the money," she told Robert Florey when he came to visit her at the studio. The cheap sets were all wrong, and the Parisian atmosphere was caricatured by the archaic direction of the veteran J. Stuart Blackton. One of the founders of Vitagraph around the turn of the century, Blackton had once been a top director. He had deserted the company during a financial crisis in 1917, returning several years later after an abortive attempt at independent production. His technique was hopelessly old-fashioned, Florey thought.

"Alla did what she was told, and no more," Florey recalls. "Her heart was not in *The Redeeming Sin*. She was not temperamental, and no longer seemed to care what happened." Surprisingly, Alla did not object, at least publicly, when Blackton asked her to do a burlesque of the Dance of the Seven Veils in the night-club scene, using a grinning jack-o'lantern pumpkin as the severed head of Saint John the Baptist! *The Redeeming Sin* was roundly panned by the critics, and she was

Nazimova shows a flash of thigh in a shabby bedroom scene in *Madonna of the Streets* (1924).

A gag photo made on the set of *The Redeeming Sin* (1925) just before Nazimova did her burlesque of the Dance of the Seven Veils in *Salome*. Otis Harlan is at left, and Robert Florey stands just behind him.

again criticized for overdoing the quick, catlike movements that had become her trademark.

For *My Son* (1925), her second picture under the Edwin Carewe contract, Nazimova made an abrupt change from the flashy and unreal characters she had been playing. In this drama of a New England fishing village, she was a widowed mother who saved her weakling son (Jack Pickford) from marriage with a sophisticated flapper (Constance Bennett). It was pure hokum, but done with taste and understanding, and Nazimova gave a beautifully restrained, low-key performance. Eschewing the pouting and the coquettishness that might have been expected of her, she was warm and gentle in the scenes of her late-blooming love for a Portuguese fisherman (Ian Keith). The picture was moderately received, and *Photoplay* magazine commented that "after a career of strange pretensions and exotic posings, Alla does her best acting in this simple offering." Jack Pickford, whose career was also in decline, won praise as the son.

Much of Alla's success in *My Son* lay in the intelligent direction by Edwin Carewe. Of Indian descent—his mother was a full-blooded Chickasaw —he could be impatient and autocratic on the set, and Hollywood expected a clash of temperaments. To everyone's surprise, he got along well with Nazimova from the very start, and they came to have a great mutual respect for each other. Carewe had sold her on the mother role in *My Son*, frankly pointing out that she was at a crossroads in her career and must take a new direction if she was to survive, either on the stage or the screen. Carewe was planning to direct a play, *The Heaven Tappers*, and he and Alla had many long talks about it. The venture failed in openings in San Francisco and Chicago the following year, and did not reach Broadway. Carewe was soon emotionally involved with the beautiful young Mexican actress, Dolores Del Rio, and guided her career for several years, although they never married.

My Son was Nazimova's last appearance in motion pictures for fifteen years. It was an extremely trying time for her, and she was beset by frustrating professional, financial, and personal problems. Alla was a washed-up Hollywood star, and she was not yet ready to accept the few offers of supporting roles at little money that came her way. In desperation, she again returned to vaudeville in April

Nazimova played a more mature and restrained character as the mother in Edwin Carewe's *My Son* (1925). Charlie Murray holds the stricken Jack Pickford, with Ian Keith at right.

1926, her first work in more than a year. Her old play, *That Sort*, a failure in its original presentation in 1914, was cut down into a sketch, and she opened it at the Palace Theatre of New York on April 20. The critics thought it very talky and old-fashioned. She toured *That Sort*, off and on, for several months, and never failed to delight audiences with her poise and charm. The money, reported to be $2,000 a week, was a godsend. There was continual talk of a new play, or an Ibsen revival, but they never seemed to materialize.

The losses on *A Doll's House* and *Salome* had wiped out her fortune, and as always she found it difficult to economize. The cost of maintaining her lavish home on Sunset Boulevard was heavy, and in addition she had taken an expensive apartment at 34 West 49th Street in New York. She was considering selling the Hollywood property when a group of promoters approached her to turn it into a hotel. In exchange for a lease, she became a stockholder in a new company, and was also paid a monthly sum. As part of the deal, she was to have an apartment above the garage for her lifetime use. Twenty-five villas were built around the pool, and the fabled Garden of Allah opened on January 9, 1927. (Alla was distressed that the promoters added an *h* to her name to give the hotel

an exciting title.) Beset by heavy debts, the company quickly failed, and Nazimova lost all that she had put into the venture. However, she continued to maintain her apartment there for several years.

The Garden of Allah passed through a series of owners and various transformations, and in 1959 was razed to make way for an office building housing the Lytton Loan and Savings Company. In its thirty-two years existence, the Garden was to be the home, at one time or another, of Hollywood's major stars, directors, and writers, and many visiting celebrities stayed there. In the 1930s it was the center of a writers' colony transplanted from New York, presided over by the alcoholic humorist Robert Benchley, that included F. Scott Fitzgerald, Marc Connelly, John O'Hara, George S. Kaufman, Dorothy Parker, Ernest Hemingway, and others. Some of the stars who lived there were John Barrymore, Tallulah Bankhead, the Marx Brothers, Ginger Rogers, Humphrey Bogart, Lauren Bacall, Katharine Hepburn, Lila Lee, and Ronald Colman. The Garden of Allah was the scene of many marathon drinking parties, extramarital assignations, and domestic battles that gave it an international reputation.[6]

In the early 1920s, Nazimova's lavish Hollywood home was hidden among lush tropical plants and cedar trees. Later, it was converted into the famed Garden of Allah Hotel, which housed many film celebrities and a colony of eccentric writers.

6. For a detailed account of the history of the Garden of Allah, see Sheilah Graham's *The Garden of Allah* (New York: Crown Publishers, 1970).

Nazimova's fourteen-year affair with Charles Bryant ended in 1925 when she moved out of their 49th Street apartment to a suite at the Hotel Chatham. The newspapers and magazines carried rumors of impending divorce, but she denied it. In July 1926, Alla returned to Hollywood after a three-month trip abroad, and through her secretary, Jean Adams, announced that she had divorced Bryant in Paris. No details were given, nor could alert reporters find any leads in France.

A month later Bryant married Marjorie Gilhooley, a twenty-three-old society girl from a well-to-do New Jersey family. In his application for a marriage license, Bryant stated that he was single. A New York newspaper hinted that Nazimova's tale of a divorce in Paris was a fabrication. A local district attorney then called Bryant to his office and had him swear under oath that he was not, nor had he ever been, married to Alla Nazimova! Two days later, a tearful Alla admitted the deception to a writer for the New York *Times* by saying that Bryant "did not commit perjury." She accused newspapermen of hounding her, and was much disturbed for fear the scandal would affect her application for United States citizenship. Later, she said she had contemplated suicide, but had been talked out of it by film producer Paul Bern (who was to become a suicide himself after the failure of his marriage to the screen sexpot Jean Harlow). Nazimova blamed the press for "assuming that she and Bryant were married, but offered no explanations as to why they had never bothered to deny it. A story that circulated later said Bryant and Nazimova had not married because Paul Orleneff had refused her a divorce, which raised the question of whether she and Orleneff were actually married. While she had also never troubled to deny newspaper references to her as Madame Paul Orleneff during the early days in New York, it remained doubtful that she and her Russian mentor had gone through a marriage ceremony.

Although many felt Charles Bryant's professional career had been ruined by Nazimova's domination during their fourteen-year association, he was able to make a new start as an actor. For the next dozen years he appeared in many Broadway plays, and some of his better roles were: as King Charles II in *And So to Bed* (1927) and in *The Lady Refuses* (1933); *Richard of Bordeaux* (1934);

The Distaff Side. (1934); and *Forbidden Melody* (1936). He tried unsuccessfully to be a producer in 1927 with the ill-fated play, *The Right to Kill*, which lasted seven performances and lost a considerable amount of money. His last appearance was as the apoplectic father in *Yes, My Darling Daughter* (1937), in which he displayed a delightful gift for comedy. Bryant made no attempt to return to motion pictures, either as an actor or director. He was in retirement until his death, at sixty-seven, on August 7, 1948. He died in a Mount Kisco (New York) hospital after suffering a heart attack at his home. As for Paul Orleneff, he died in Russia in 1932 after spending his later years doing eccentric characters in popular plays; at one time he traveled about Russia putting on plays for peasant workers at the collective farms or large factories.

Except for her vaudeville appearances, Nazimova was inactive for three years after the completion of *My Son*. She was intent upon returning to Broadway, but could not find a vehicle that pleased her. In 1926, she claimed to have rejected thirty-two plays sent to her by New York managers. A. H. Woods offered her the sensational role of Mother Goddam in John Colton's shocker, *The Shanghai Gesture*. The part, that of a Manchu princess reduced to operating a brothel, was tailor-made for Nazimova, but she piously protested that she could not play a character with such a sacrilegious name! (The role went to the aging Mrs. Leslie Carter, who was fired before the play reached Broadway and was replaced by Florence Reed.) There were occasional film offers, mostly for supporting roles. Cecil B. DeMille called Nazimova to play Mary Magdalene in *The King of Kings* (1927), for which she would have been superb. Alla angrily declined when DeMille asked her to take a screen test, and the part went to Jacqueline Logan.

RETURN TO BROADWAY

A turning point came in June 1927, when Nazimova went to London to appear at the Coliseum in *A Woman of the Earth*, a dramatic sketch by Edgar Allan Woolf, in which she played a gypsy murderess. She performed to standing room only as the British critics nostalgically took her in their arms. There was a spate of useful publicity when she was threatened with kidnapping on three occasions by an anonymous telephone caller. Alla soon returned to America, announced to shipboard reporters that "I am through with the movies," and toured *A Woman of the Earth* in vaudeville.

In April 1928, it was announced that Madame Nazimova would be a guest artist with Eva Le Gallienne's Civic Repertory Theatre. Two years earlier Miss Le Gallienne, a distinguished actress only then in her mid-twenties, had nursed to reality her dream of a repertory company presenting the classics. She obtained the Fourteenth Street Theater, an ancient playhouse constructed in 1866, and after a shaky start had succeeded with the plays of Shakespeare, Ibsen, Schnitzler, Molière, Chekov, Giraudoux, Goldine, and others. The admission ranged from 35¢ to $1.50. Her guest stars were guaranteed a twenty-week season, and included such illustrious performers as Jacob Ben-Ami, Paul Leyssac, Beatrice Terry, and Joseph Schildkraut. Among the many aspiring young actors and actresses to be trained there were Josephine Hutchinson, John Garfield, Burgess Meredith, Howard Da Silva, Arnold Moss, and J. Edward Bromberg.

Nazimova's first appearance with the Civic Repertory Theatre was in Anton Chekov's *The Cherry Orchard*, which opened on October 15, 1928. Miss Le Gallienne directed, and a fine cast included Josephine Hutchinson, J. Edward Bromberg, Walter Beck, and Donald Cameron. A drama of a family of improvident Russian aristocrats who lose everything in a changing social order, it was an ideal vehicle for Alla's comeback. There were rave reviews from the critics, and virtually all of her sixty-three performances drew capacity crowds. The success of *The Cherry Orchard* gave her much-needed confidence, and for the first time since her Hollywood fiasco she found happiness.

In February 1929, she made her second and final appearance for the Civic Repertory Theatre, this time in Leonid Andreyev's little-known *Katerina*. Despite the Le Gallienne staging, it was disappointing, and only nineteen performances were given. The rather silly plot concerned a jealous husband who takes a shot at his faithful wife when he mistakenly believes she is having an affair with another man. His suspicions drive her to lead an immoral life. Nazimova was supported by Alma Kruger, John Eldredge, J. Edward Bromberg, and Robert H. Gordon.

The Civic Repertory Theatre engagements led to a lucrative contract with the prestigious Theatre Guild, and Nazimova was starred in Ivan Turgenev's somber play, *A Month in the Country*. It opened on March 17, 1930, to rave reviews and ran seventy-one performances. Directed by the brilliant young Rouben Mamoulian, the play featured Dudley Digges, Alexander Kirkland, and the enormously talented Katharine Hepburn.

To many, the high point of Nazimova's entire career was her stunning performance as Christine in Eugene O'Neill's *Mourning Becomes Electra*, which overwhelmed an opening night audience on October 26, 1931. A combination of three plays that O'Neill first began in 1926, it ran six hours, and was an intense drama of love, hate, passion, and murder. Nazimova played an adulterous mother who has a passionate affair with a much younger man, which leads to revenge and murder. It was a difficult role made believable by Alla's highly disciplined performance, in which there

Rosalind Russell (right), surprises her mother, Katina Paxinou, in a passionate embrace with her father, Raymond Massey, as he returns from the Civil War in the film version of Eugene O'Neill's *Mourning Becomes Electra* (1947). Though considerably edited down from the original stage performance with Nazimova as the mother, many of the aspects of direction, ironically including the foreign accent of the New England mother, were adopted for the film.

was little trace of the distracting posing and body movements. Critics praised her velvety voice, and years later those who saw her would recall the tremendous impact of her measured speeches. She shared acting honors with Alice Brady, who was magnificent as the vengeful daughter Lavinia.

Mourning Becomes Electra was born out of months of difficult and lengthy rehearsals. O'Neill was continuously at the theater, and although he complained that both the characterizations by Miss Brady and Nazimova were entirely different from the way he had written them, he was more than willing to accept their brilliant concepts of the roles. He got along well with Alla, whom he admired, despite his concern at a Russian actress— still with a trace of her Crimean accent—playing a New England matron. (In the 1947 movie of *Mourning Becomes Electra*, Katina Paxinou played the part with a Greek accent.) O'Neill was even more concerned with Alice Brady's interpretation of Lavinia, and constantly reminded her not to put a shred of sentimentality into the part. They had a good rapport, although O'Neill had been much disappointed when his original choice, Ann Harding, declined the role to make movies in Hollywood.

The director of *Mourning Becomes · Electra*, Philip Moeller, was a rather strange and eccentric individual, but extremely gifted in stagecraft. Alla did not totally approve of his approach to the play, and found his methods of direction trying at times, but she unreservedly placed herself in his hands. *Mourning Becomes Electra* ran 150 performances in New York, and Alla toured with it to major cities. Although not every theatergoer's cup of tea, it was unquestionably a milestone in American drama.

Nazimova then played the patient Chinese wife, O-Lan, in Owen and Donald Davis's disappointing dramatization of Pearl S. Buck's best-selling novel, *The Good Earth*, which the Theatre Guild premiered on October 17, 1932. With her striking features, she was physically just right for the role, and gave a beautifully shaded performance. The critics commented on how youthful she looked in the first act—she was then fifty-three—and the thoroughly believable way in which she aged to her poignant death as a sick, old woman. Claude Rains was Wang Lung, the ambitious peasant farmer who becomes a great landowner, and others in the large cast were Jessie Ralph, Sydney Greenstreet, and Henry Travers. Philip Moeller again directed, and Alla was shocked when he confessed at the first rehearsal that, in the interests of a completely fresh approach, he had read neither the book nor the playscript! *The Good Earth* was not a success. It ran only fifty-six performances in New York, and had a brief tour to Chicago and several Eastern cities. When M-G-M brought *The Good Earth* to the screen in 1937, the Viennese actress Luise Rainer won an Academy Award for her performance as a more fragile O-Lan.

Alla's only Broadway play in 1933 was *Doctor Monica*, an oddball drama with just three characters, all women. She played a lady physician who is recovering from surgery that will permit her to bear children—again quite a feat of acting for a woman in her middle fifties! *Doctor Monica* was a disaster, and lasted only sixteen performances. Her fellow victims in the cast were Gale Sondergaard and Beatrice de Neergaard.

Nazimova was absent from Broadway in 1934, although several offers came her way, all of which she rejected. She was extremely disappointed when the lead in Eugene O'Neill's new play, *Days Without End*, for which she was a major contender, went to Selena Royle. She made a few guest appearances at summer theaters, and did occasional teaching at the acting school established in connection with the Westport Country Playhouse. Alla had lost money in the stock market crash of 1929, and her financial situation was poor, despite her fees from the Theatre Guild.

On February 18, 1935, she opened in the Guild's production of *The Simpleton of the Unexpected Isles*. George Bernard Shaw's unappreciated allegory cast Alla as the exotic priestess of an imaginary country, which was used as a background for a satire on British Colonialism. The play was much too talky for New York tastes, and closed with a heavy financial loss after forty performances. A good cast included Romney Brent, Lawrence Grossmith, Alma Lloyd, Leon Janney, and McKay Morris.

Alla had long wanted to play the tragic Mrs. Alving in Henrik Ibsen's *Ghosts*, a role made famous by Elenora Duse. The opportunity came when Robert Henderson, promoter of the Drama

Festival at the University of Michigan at Ann Arbor, invited her as guest star. The results were so successful, and her performance so spectacular, that she and Henderson joined forces to give it a professional presentation on Broadway. Alla raised part of the money on the strength of her name, and *Ghosts* opened at the Empire Theatre on December 12, 1935. Staged by Nazimova, it was a critical success, and reviewers were lavish with praise for her Mrs. Alving. Others in the cast were Ona Munson, McKay Morris, Harry Ellerbe, and Raymond O'Brien. First presented in 1881, the Ibsen masterpiece was a drama of the effects of heredity, profligacy, and disease, and even in the 1930s was considered shocking. For most of the following year, after a run of forty-five performances in New York, Nazimova toured *Ghosts* from coast to coast. It was particularly well received in California, and she wept when old friends from Hollywood came backstage to congratulate her on opening night in Los Angeles. She missed her first performance in thirty-five years in Kansas City when an abscessed tooth made it impossible for her to talk.

Encouraged by the success of *Ghosts*, Nazimova then revived *Hedda Gabler,* apparently forgetting an earlier assertion that she was too old for the part. It premiered at the Longacre Theatre in New York on November 16, 1936, with McKay Morris, Harry Ellerbe, and Viola Frayne in support. She had come full circle in her career—it was almost thirty years to the day since her sensational American debut in *Hedda Gabler* in 1906. Following a month on Broadway, she toured the play throughout the United States, and in some cities alternated it in repertory with *Ghosts*.

The Ibsen tours of 1935-37 were to be virtually her last work in the American theatre. In 1938, Alla went to Hollywood looking for work, but was depressed by the changes that had taken place there. She stayed at the Garden of Allah, kept mostly to herself, and a few old friends who called were shocked by her appearance. Paramount signed her as a drama coach, and she gave acting lessons to Frances Farmer, Olympe Bradna, and other starlets. A flurry of publicity announced that Nazimova would be "technical director" for a new film version of her old stage hit, *Zaza*, with Isa Miranda, a young Italian actress whom Paramount

hoped to make into another Marlene Dietrich. Alla began to coach her in the role, but after a few weeks Miss Miranda was replaced by Claudette Colbert. Director George Cukor, a great admirer of Madame Nazimova, says that she was not involved in the production of *Zaza* to any appreciable extent.

Later in 1938, Alla returned to New York, where she underwent major surgery. Her health improved remarkably, and she was finally signed as star of *The Mother*, a play by Karel Capek (of *R.U.R.* fame), which opened on Broadway on April 25, 1939. A dreary drama of a woman who has sacrificed four sons to a war and is faced with losing yet another, it lasted only four performances. *The Mother* was roasted by the critics, who were mild in their praise of Alla. Most of their plaudits went to an interesting young newcomer named Montgomery Clift.

THE BITTER YEARS

By 1940, Nazimova's finances were in critical shape, and she again sought work in Hollywood, eager to accept even small roles. Although past sixty, she was still a fascinating personality, and with good grooming and stylish clothes could appear quite beautiful. Unfortunately, Alla was not always attentive to her looks, and at times appeared quite drab. Robert Florey, seeing her for the first time in two years, was struck by how much she had aged. "I suddenly realized that the glamorous Nazimova of *Salome* had become a little old lady," he says. Alla had always been nearsighted, and had to put on a pair of eyeglasses with thick lens to recognize her old cameraman, Charles J. Van Enger, when he greeted her on the M-G-M lot.

Through the influence of friends, Nazimova was signed to appear with Norma Shearer and Robert Taylor in Mervyn LeRoy's *Escape* (1940) for Metro-Goldwyn-Mayer. She played a famous actress who is thrown into a concentration camp—obviously in Germany, although the country was not specifically identified—for political activities against the state. Her American son (Taylor) comes searching for her, and the rest of the film is devoted to a hair-raising attempt to smuggle her to safety in a coffin. Alla had only a few scenes—

Nazimova (left) was ravishingly beautiful as the
mother in her screen comeback in Mervyn LeRoy's
Escape (1940). Others in this scene are (left to right)
Felix Bressart, Robert Taylor, and Norma Shearer.

some of her part was left on the cutting-room floor
when the film ran too long—but she did them well
and with great sincerity and professionalism. It
was the first opportunity for motion-picture audiences to hear her lovely voice with its Russian-
flavored accent. She looked extremely beautiful
in the scenes outside the concentration camp.
Escape was a dramatic indictment of the Nazis,
and one of the first in a growing flood of propaganda pictures designed to prepare the United
States for entrance into the war in Europe. (At
M-G-M she could not dispel the memory of an

embarrassing interview with the late Irving G.
Thalberg some years earlier, when the brilliant
young M-G-M executive had bitterly denounced
her for having once snubbed him at a dinner
party.)

Soon after the completion of *Escape*, Rouben
Mamoulian, who had directed her in *A Month in
the Country* on Broadway, called her to play the
role of the mother in 20th Century-Fox's remake
of the old Valentino hit, *Blood and Sand* (1941).
It was a tiny part, that of a scrubwoman whose
son becomes a famous Spanish matador. Her per-

Nazimova was in her sixties when she appeared in the
bit role of the mother in Rouben Mamoulian's 1941
remake of the old Valentino hit, *Blood and Sand*.

formance was not as effective as in *Escape*, and
many felt Mamoulian let her overact. The picture
itself was a failure, slow moving and handicapped
by tired clichés and unbelievable dialogue. Tyrone
Power was stilted in Valentino's role, and Linda
Darnell miscast as the mousy wife. Only Rita Hayworth, in the Nita Naldi part as the sophisticated
vamp, gave the film any vitality. The major assets
of *Blood and Sand* were its beautiful sets and the
exquisite color photography (which won an Academy Award for cameramen Ernest Palmer and Ray
Rennahan).

No further offers were forthcoming, however.
She moved to a small house at the beach, which
she shared with a companion. (Most of Alla's
property at Port Chester had been sold years before, although she retained a small cottage near
the main gate; this was also sold as her income
declined.) World War II was in progress, and
many old friends from Europe, refugees from the
Nazi-occupied countries, came to visit. Her older
sister, Nina Lewton (Leventon), who worked in
the foreign-language department at M-G-M, lived
nearby. Alla's nephew, Val Lewton, a producer at
RKO Radio, was just beginning to attract attention with his brilliant, low-budget horror dramas,
but she thought he was wasting his time with such
things as *The Cat People*.

Nazimova (right) in costume for *In Our Time* (1944), walks to the set with the promising Warner Brothers starlet, Nancy Coleman.

Nazimova (left) had a striking beauty in her role as the patrician mother of *In Our Time* (1944). Nancy Coleman and Michael Chekov also appeared.

In 1944, Nazimova appeared in Warner Brothers' *In Our Time*, an old-fashioned Chekovian drama of the Polish nobility before World War I. The New York *Times* noted that Alla "plays a fine patrician mother in her very best *Cherry Orchard* style." Paul Henreid and Ida Lupino had the leads, and Vincent Sherman directed. Kenneth G. Lawrence, then a young G.I. touring the Warner Brothers Studio, was tremendously impressed when he met Nazimova. "Mainly, I remember her deep, almost musical voice, her thick accent, and those flashing, luminous eyes! She seemed charged with some kind of electricity which had no human foundation," Lawrence recalls. "I also remember that she said it was stage work, not movies, that gave her any satisfaction of accomplishment."

Nazimova then did a bit as an aging noble-woman in *The Bridge of San Luis Rey* (1944), which Benedict J. Bogeaus produced on a low budget for United Artists release. The plot of this clumsy film bore little resemblance to Thornton Wilder's powerful novel. Nazimova's role as the lonely and eccentric Marquessa de Montemayor —a key character in the book— was emasculated,

As the aging Countess in a clumsy film version of Thornton Wilder's popular play, *The Bridge of San Luis Rey* (1944), Nazimova looked drawn and tired. Francis Lederer and Joan Lorring share this scene.

Warner Brothers' *In Our Time* (1944), a drama of a decaying family of Polish nobility, had Chekovian overtones. From left to right are Ida Lupino, Nancy Coleman, Alla Nazimova, Michael Chekov, and Paul Henreid.

Nazimova's last screen appearance was in a bit from David O. Selznick's *Since You Went Away* (1944). A large cast included, from left to right, Shirley Temple, Jackie Moran, Joseph Cotten, Jennifer Jones, Nazimova, Keenan Wynn, and Claudette Colbert. Monty Woolley is in the foreground.

and she had only a few scenes. Unhelped by Rowland V. Lee's pedestrian direction, Alla's performance lacked vigor and definition. The major fault of *The Bridge of San Luis Rey* lay in an epic bit of miscasting, that of Lynn Bari to play the tempestuous young actress (a role taken in M-G-M's sensitive silent of 1929 by the fiery Lili Damita). Miss Bari tried hard, but her performance was a farce. Others in a cast of distinguished performers wasted on the inept film were Louis Calhern, Francis Lederer, Blanche Yurka, Akim Tamiroff, Joan Lorring, and Donald Woods.

Alla Nazimova's final appearance in motion pictures was in a cameo bit as, of all things, a Polish-American lady welder in a shipyard, in *Since You Went Away* (1944). The film was a maudlin drama of emotional hardships on the home front during World War II, produced by David O. Selznick. The tiny part was unworthy of her—she had only a single scene—and was a demeaning and depressing conclusion to a brilliant career. Alla looked old and tired. At the time, there were stories (probably emanating from the studio publicity department) that Selznick had made a part for her in *Since You Went Away* because she was broke and needed money, and as a gesture of appreciation for what she had done for Lewis J. Selznick by starring in *War Brides* in 1916.

There was both optimism and a sense of regret in an interview that she gave on the set of *Since You Went Away*. "I have a terrific interest in life and what's to come," she told reporters. "You won't catch me sitting around looking down at my middle. It gives you a double chin to look down. I've always looked up."

"I've reached the heights," she added, "but it's been a puny success. I could have done so much more with my life had I devoted it to the service of others. I know that now."

During her last months Nazimova lived in an apartment on Havenhurst Drive, just a stone's throw from the Garden of Allah. Her health declined steadily, and she had cardiac and circulatory disorders. On June 30, 1945, she suffered an attack of coronary thrombosis and was taken to the Good Samaritan Hospital of Los Angeles, where she died on July 13. Only a few old friends came to the services. Actor John Beal read a poem and spoke a few words of eulogy.

Nazimova was sixty-six when she died. Alexander Kirkland, with whom she had appeared in *A Month in the Country*, recalled: "It seems a brief span for a woman whom her friends thought of as eternal. But then she once said, 'My heart was born in a deep shadow, and I can never stay out in the sun very long, because it blinds me.' "[7]

7. Alexander Kirkland, "The Woman From Yalta," *Theatre Arts* (December 1949), p. 95.

3

Edwin S. Porter:
Motion Picture Pioneer

EDWIN S. Porter, the first outstanding figure in motion-picture production, is virtually unknown today.

His fame rests largely upon an archaic twelve-minute drama, *The Great Train Robbery*, that he directed and photographed for the Edison Company in 1903. This revolutionary film, with its crude, probing grasp of cinematic principles, assured the future of the motion-picture industry in its critical transition from peep show to nickelodeon.

Porter's other significant contributions to the screen—essentially the fundamental foundation upon which film production is based—have been generally minimized in screen history. The restoration of paper prints of his earliest movies in the mid-1960s have belatedly made possible an objective evaluation of his talents. His creative influence, of pygmy stature beside his contemporary D. W. Griffith, was nevertheless substantial, and extended to Griffith himself (whom Porter started as a movie actor), and to such great names as Eisenstein, Pudovkin, von Stroheim, King Vidor, and perhaps Walt Disney.

He is unquestionably the father of the story film, and is credited with the first comprehensive application of the principles of editing to build

and heighten suspense, the introduction of social values in motion-picture content, the early use of visual effects by imaginative trick photography, and important technological improvements through his many inventions. He developed a classic projector, the Simplex, and experimented with sound, color, and three-dimensional pictures. With Adolph Zukor he founded Famous Players, precursor of the gigantic Paramount complex, and directed the first American feature-length films.

Porter's career in motion-picture production spanned less than twenty years, ending soon after Griffith opened new horizons with *The Birth of a Nation* in 1915. When he died a quarter of a century later, alone and forgotten in a Manhattan hotel room, his passing went unnoticed by metropolitan newspapers and rated only a brief paragraph in most film trade journals. Yet, few men have been of such importance to the motion picture.

BEGINNINGS: TOURING THE MOVIES

Edwin Stanton Porter was born on April 21, 1870, at Connellsville, Pennsylvania, where his father was a moderately successful merchant. At fourteen he left school, which he disliked, and was successively a railway news butcher, a signpainter, a plumber, and finally a telegrapher, a trade that he followed for several years.

In his spare time Porter repaired clocks, was an exhibition ice skater, and sold tickets in a Pittsburgh theater managed by his brother. He next tried tailoring as a custom cutter, but lost his savings in a shop of his own. His brother, who had become advance man for the Washburn and Huntington Circus, gave him a job posting bills, but Porter soon threw it up to be a stagehand with a traveling comic-opera company.

At twenty-two, after a severe bout with pneumonia, Porter went to work for the Cramps Machine Shop, which had a contract to install elec-

trical equipment in *The New York*, a huge cruiser under construction in the Philadelphia Navy Yard. Because of his familiarity with the ship, he was soon induced to enlist in the Navy, and was placed in charge of the electrical department of *The New York*. His mechanical abilities impressed his superiors, and he was assigned to aid Rear Admiral Bradley Allen Fiske, the Navy's gunnery genius, in perfecting the Fiske electrical rangefinder.

On June 5, 1893, while on leave at Cumberland, Maryland, Porter married Caroline Ridinger, daughter of an architect of Somerset, Pennsylvania. There were no children born of the marriage.

Porter's first experience with the embryo motion picture came in the spring of 1896 soon after his discharge from a three-year hitch in the Navy. Not without some misgivings, for he had turned down a job in the promising young automobile industry, he became a mechanic for Raff and Gammon, a firm that marketed the Edison Vitascope. Among Porter's first assignments was to assist in the installation and operation of this crude projector at the historic first New York showing of projected motion pictures at Koster and Bial's Music Hall on April 23, 1896. He worked most of that summer in Thomas A. Edison's laboratories in West Orange, New Jersey, where he found the great inventor strangely pessimistic about the commercial future of motion pictures.

Although Porter at first professed to share Edison's opinion that movies, then limited largely to peep shows, were a passing novelty, he sensed an opportunity to make money. Porter had made the acquaintance of Harry Daniels, a vaudeville ventriloquist and itinerant patent-medicine salesman, who suggested they organize a traveling show with motion pictures as the principal attraction. The two partners bought a Projectorscope, a temperamental machine manufactured by Kuhn and Webster's International Film Company, and about four dozen strips of film, mostly Edison scenics. As part of the deal, Porter was granted a franchise to sell the Projectorscope in the British West Indies.

In his colorful but not always accurate history of the early film industry, *A Million and One Nights*, Terry Ramsaye has painted a fanciful account of the Porter-Daniels tour to Jamaica and Central America that incorporates more fiction than fact. According to Ramsaye, Porter passed

One of the few portraits of Edwin S. Porter.

himself off as Thomas A. Edison, *Jr.*, son of the distinguished inventor, and charmed the President of Costa Rica out of a free pass on the state railway.

There is also a dubious account of an embroglio with authorities that landed Porter in jail when he failed to announce the beginning of the performance by igniting three aerial bombs on the plaza of San Jose, as required by law. For this oversight, he was fined $21.55. Another questionable tale, which probably originated in Harry Daniels's fertile imagination, asserted Porter accepted $10 from a wealthy coffee planter for an introduction to Annabelle, the seductive star of *The Butterfly Dance*, one of the archaic films that Porter cranked out on the Projectorscope each evening. The hoodwinked victim was crushed to find she existed only in a can of film.

After a stopover in the West Indies, where he failed to sell a single machine, Porter was back in New York in the spring of 1897. The tour had been a dismal financial failure. Kuhn and Webster, from whom he had purchased the Projectorscope, were then making advertising films that were shown nightly on a large screen atop the Pepper Building at 34th and Broadway. Porter was employed as projectionist, and each evening from dusk to midnight ground off the films in a tiny, stifling garret that served as a projection booth. The translucent screen allowed the picture to be seen in front, though projected from the rear. These commercial films—for such clients as Haig and Haig Scotch Whisky and Pabst's Milwaukee Beer—were interlaced with short bits of news pictures and scenic travelogues. This promising venture ended when Porter was arrested and fined for blocking traffic as Herald Square became congested with enraptured spectators.

Porter and Daniels then toured Quebec and Nova Scotia for several months, showing films for the famous Wormwood Dog and Monkey Show, an elaborate patent-medicine operation. From the Lumière Brothers of France they obtained pictures of Queen Victoria's Jubilee Celebration in London, which were a sensation with the Canadian audiences.

On his return to New York, Porter was hired as projectionist at the celebrated Eden Musée, a waxworks museum that was experimenting with the use of motion pictures as backgrounds for its wax figures of famous personalities. The films were eventually to become more popular than the waxworks, and the Eden Musée installed a large auditorium where only the best movies were shown. It was here that Porter first saw and was undoubtedly much impressed by the inventive films of Georges Méliès, the French artist and magician.

In 1898, while still at the Eden Musée, Porter developed a projector that he asserted was capable of producing a brighter and steadier picture. It became known as the Beadnell Projector, and was named after Porter's partner in its manufacture, William J. Beadnell, who was also the Eden Musée's publicity director. The machines were made by hand at a tiny machine shop in Brooklyn, and several dozen were sold to the Proctor houses, the Percy Williams theater chain, and the Eden Musée, where they replaced the French Lumière projectors. The Beadnell, which was reportedly similar to Edison's exhibition model, has been frequently confused with the Cinematograph and the Edengraph, two precursors of the later Simplex Projector.

With the sale of each Beadnell, Porter would personally train the operator in its use. Among his students was Nicholas Power of the Novelty Theater in Brooklyn, later the inventor of the Cameragraph, one of the best of early projectors. Porter and Beadnell also brought out a custom-built movie camera, but it was not a commercial success. In 1900 a disastrous fire gutted their factory, and Porter sold his interest in the venture to Beadnell. The manufacture of the projector was not resumed.

During the preceding year (1899) Porter began to do free-lance work as a photographer for the Edison Company, beginning a historic association that was to last ten years. He made many short scenics in and around New York, which were used primarily in the Edison Kinetoscope peep shows. Although some work was done on assignment, many of his films were made at his own expense and sold outright to Edison. At the time, the company was purchasing almost a third of its product from free-lance cameramen across the nation.

Porter also photographed various news events, which were shown in the better vaudeville houses. One of the most famous of these early newsreels was *America's Cup Race* (1899) , a series of films of the annual yachting competition popularized by Sir Thomas Lipton. The race was filmed from the referee's boat, and Porter was dismayed to find his camera facing directly into the sun—something never done with conventional still cameras. He continued to crank away, however, and, when his films were developed, Porter was astonished at their beauty. The white sails cast wispy shadows over the rippling waters for a bedazzling effect. He had inadvertently discovered the principle of back-lighting, a major milestone in motion-picture photography. Although offering few scenes of the race itself, *America's Cup Race* was a sensation when shown on Broadway.

EARLY FILMS AT EDISON

Following the destruction of his factory, Porter became a full-time Edison employee. For a short time he worked in the mechanical department, and tried, without success, to design an improved, light-weight camera. At the suggestion of James H. White, Edison's production chief, Porter became a cameraman-director, making both scenics and fictional films. He soon supplanted White (who remained on until 1903 as a director), and was placed in charge of Edison's new glass-enclosed studio at 41 East 21st Street. For several years he personally directed and photographed a substantial portion of Edison's total output.

Porter's early fictional films, mostly crude sketches or reproductions of vaudeville acts, clearly show the influence of Georges Méliès. Porter is said to have examined Méliès's films frame by frame under a high-power microscope in his laboratory. The technical challenge of Méliès's ingenious effects appealed to Porter, and his Edison pictures often employed stop-motion photography, double exposures (made in the camera), matte shots, a crude form of animation, and eventually the split-screen.

His first comedies in 1900 frequently used stop-motion photography. Many—such as *The Mystic Swing*; *Ching Ling Outdone*; *Hooligan Assists the Magician*; and *The Clown and the Alchemist*—centered around a magician and his ability to make persons and objects disappear and reappear at will. Others, such as *Uncle Josh in a Spooky Hotel*, utilized the device of a rube farmer plagued by lively ghosts. One of Porter's earliest dramatic films was *Faust and Marguerite* (1900), loosely based upon the old classic, in which the devil terrifies Marguerite into marriage by invoking demons and skeletons. The characters were dressed in period costumes and appeared in the setting of an old stone castle.

Porter tried to keep his special-effects methods secret, and later bragged in an interview that it took his competitors "two years to figure out how I did it"—a not altogether accurate statement. His interest in trick films persisted throughout his tenure at Edison, although it diminished sharply after 1903, the year that saw the release of his first important pictures: *Life of an American Fireman*; *Uncle Tom's Cabin*; and *The Great Train Robbery*.

Most of Porter's films of 1899-1902 were based on a single simple situation, with characters more aptly described as caricatures. The camera was stationary, and the studio settings varied widely in quality, ranging from an elaborately painted backdrop to nothing more than a dark curtain strung on a wooden rod. Many of these curiosities did little more than illustrate motion.

Porter's comedies were broad one-joke affairs that seldom exceeded three or four scenes. *A Wringing Good Joke* (1900) merely shows a man pulled over on the floor when a mischievous boy ties his chair to the handle of a laundry wringer. *The Finish of Bridget McKeen* (1901) is about a fat lady who blows herself apart when she pours kerosene on a hot stove; the last scene shows her headstone in a cemetery. *Lovers, Coal Box, and Fireplace* (1901) is considerably more sophisticated. A suspicious husband returns home unexpectedly while his wife is entertaining her lover; when the latter hides in the coal bin, a delivery man showers him with a load of coal. *Burlesque Suicide* (1902), probably made for the Kinetoscope, is a silly item of a man who threatens to shoot himself in the head, then puts down the gun, points his finger at the audience, and laughs! In *Photographing a Country Couple* (1901), a photographer invites a young farmer to get under the camera cloth and look through the viewfinder; the curious rube see his fiancée being kissed by the crafty photographer.

While much of his early work at Edison was quite ordinary, Porter was doing some technically advanced things. *Uncle Josh at the Moving Picture Show* (1902) was notable for its use of matte shots and double exposures, made with an optical printer that Porter developed in his laboratory. One of a series of Edison hick comedies, it shows a country bumpkin attending his first movie. He is so overcome by the exciting pictures that he climbs upon the stage to help the embattled heroine, falls through the screen, and winds up fighting with an angry theater manager. By means of a matte process, Porter incorporated two archaic Edison films, *The Black Diamond Express* (1896) and *Parisian Dance* (1897), as well as *Country Couple,* which probably was made expressly for *Uncle Josh.*

Another creative use of matte shots was in the earlier *Martyred Presidents* (1901), released to capitalize on the assassination of President William McKinley. Portraits of three martyred Presidents (Lincoln, Garfield, and McKinley) were inserted into a memorial film tableau. *Love. By the Light of the Moon* (1901) used crude animation to change the expression on the face of a painted moon as two lovers skylark on a park bench.

Porter's most unique scenes of the era were a series of remarkable documentary films showing the Pan-American Exposition at Buffalo, New York, which was lighted by electricity. He made the first panning shot for *Circular Panorama of the Electric Tower* (1901), using a geared camera mount of his own design to rotate the camera horizontally. In a spectacular 360-degree pan, the film shows the entire Exposition grounds. (The following day Porter made an impressive 180-degree panning shot of nearby Niagara Falls.) A companion documentary of the Exposition, *Panorama of the Esplanade by Night* (1901), was the first motion picture to be photographed at night using incandescent light for illumination. To make it Porter adapted a camera to permit a ten-second exposure of each frame. He worked for several hours to get twenty-seven feet of film.

Early in 1901, Porter poked fun at the penchant of Vice-President Theodore Roosevelt for well-publicized, often politically motivated hunting trips. In *Terrible. Teddy, the Grizzly King*, a character identified as "Terrible Teddy," obviously Roosevelt, shoots a tiny bear cub, then viciously

stabs it while the "heroic act" is recorded by a newspaper reporter and photographer. Whether or not Porter originated this idea as a politically incisive satire is not known, nor is Roosevelt's reaction to the film recorded. T. R. was to have his revenge in 1904 when Porter, using an actor (Harry Ellis) made up to resemble the President, shot some scenes in front of the White House for a picture he was doing for use in Lew Dockstader's minstrel show. Suspicious Secret Service agents followed Porter to New York and supposedly confiscated the undeveloped negative. Actually, Porter substituted another roll of negative, which he exposed to light in the agents' presence, while the offending film remained securely locked in his desk. It was never shown publicly, and was destroyed in the Famous Players studio fire of 1915. Roosevelt was amused when Dockstader owned up to the deception years later.

Porter's most elaborate picture of 1902 was *Jack and the Beanstalk,* a version of the old fairy tale that traced the sale of the cow (played by two men in a papier-mâché dummy), the growth of the beanstalk, and Jack's exciting encounter with the giant. Done in the Méliès manner, it was handsomely mounted with impressive sets, and used dissolves, stop-action photography, and a moving camera. Hand-colored prints were sold for $233.75 each. *Jack and the Beanstalk* was an enormous success, and bootleg copies of the film were still being offered for sale ten years later.

Near the end of 1902—probably in late December—Porter spent three days shooting *Life of an American Fireman*, a historic motion picture in which the principles of modern film editing were first applied. By combining and arranging individual shots into a unified scene, he was able to create dramatic intensity, build suspense, and make a more expressive transition to the following scene. The impact upon the audience was enormous.

Life of an American Fireman is essentially a documentary built upon a fictional circumstance—the rescue of a mother and child trapped in a burning house—in which the everyday activities of metropolitan firemen are pictured. It opens with a fire chief asleep at his desk, dreaming of his wife putting their baby to bed (the dream is shown in a circular double exposure on the firehouse wall). The next scene is a close-up of an alarm box and a hand pulling the handle. The alarm rings in the dormitory where firemen are sleeping. A series of scenes follow, building swiftly and suspensefully to the climax—firemen sliding down the pole, the impatient horses being hitched, the engines bursting from the firehouse doors, and the race to the fire. The scene shifts to the upper floor of a burning house, where a desperate mother and child are overcome by smoke. A heroic firefighter rescues the mother, goes back into the doomed building and returns safely with the child.

Much of the effectiveness of *Life of an American Fireman* lay in the construction of Porter's shots after the arrival at the fire. His primitive editing, crude and fleeting as it was, opened a new dimension to the art of the motion picture. Although Porter is universally recognized as the father of the editing concept, some historians think that he stumbled upon it by accident. Sensing that he had made an important discovery, Porter would expand and refine the technique, as did others, in a somewhat pedestrian fashion. Nearly a dozen years would elapse before the significance of intelligent and imaginative editing was fully realized by Griffith and others.

The late Kenneth Macgowan, in that odd compendium of film facts *Behind the Screen*, questions that Porter originally used intercutting in *Life of an American Fireman*. He points out that the paper print filed for copyright does not contain the climactic intercutting, nor does a shot-by-shot description of the film in the Edison catalogue correspond to some existing prints. Macgowan speculated that Porter made a print for copyright purposes from a partially edited negative after hastily and haphazardly splicing together whole scenes. The presumption is that Porter subsequently reedited the negative to produce the dynamic intercutting.

A great many misimpressions about *Life of an American Fireman* have grown up. It is not largely made up of stock shots of firefighters culled from the Edison library, as has been frequently written. Except for possibly two scenes, Porter shot all new film, devoting two days to photographing the fire companies of Orange and Newark, New Jersey, in action. (The interiors were made in a single day at the Edison studio in New York.) The scenes where there is snow on the ground are usually

identified as stock shots, but it should be remembered that Porter was filming in December, a month of frequent snowfalls. Neither is *Life of an American Fireman* an amplification of Edison's *The Still Alarm*, it having preceded the latter film in release by four months. *The Still Alarm*, also directed by Porter, was nothing more than a dreary newsreel picturing various types of firefighting equipment.

The late Georges Sadoul is among several motion-picture historians who called Porter an imitator and a "copyist" and alleged that his films were inspired by Méliès and such pioneer British directors as Robert W. Paul, James Williamson, G. A. Smith, and Cecil Hepworth. The allegations are not entirely without foundation, for Porter was obviously stimulated by these foreign filmmakers, perhaps more by the Englishmen than by Méliès.

Robert W. Paul's *Plucked from the Burning* (1898) is frequently mentioned as an antecedent to *Life of an American Fireman*, but it was just a brief (108 feet) one-scene movie that Porter may never have seen. James Williamson's *Fire!*, released in 1901, has so many similarities to Porter's film that it was unquestionably a direct incentive. Another British picture, Cecil Hepworth's *Rescued by Firemen*, also cited for its influence upon Porter, actually came out four months later. Porter was subsequently accused of borrowing ideas for *The Great Train Robbery* from the English film, *The Robbery of the Mail Coach* (1903). It was not uncommon for filmmakers, both here and abroad, to deliberately duplicate a successful production scene by scene—and even to release it under the same title!

Most of Porter's other films of 1903 had little to distinguish them. He was still making trick pictures—*Little Lillian: Toe Danseuse* (a vaudeville act in which the dancer's costume inexplicably changes five times); *Casey and His Neighbor's Goat* (a forced comedy of a goat eating dynamite and exploding); *The Office Boy's Revenge* (a mischievous office boy ties the furniture together in such a way that it collapses when the boss opens the door).

Many Porter films were mediocre and incredibly ordinary—*Rube and Mandy at Coney Island* was nothing more than two bumpkins eating frankfurters at the famous seaside amusement park, while *Western Stagecoach Hold-Up* was scenes of bandits robbing a stagecoach. *Rock of Ages* pictured two oldsters swinging in a hammock until it breaks and dumps them on the ground. Occasionally, Porter could be more sophisticated, as seen in his charming comedy, *The Gay Shoe Clerk,* in which a lecherous shoe salesman fondles a young girl's ankle and earns a swat from her mother's umbrella.

His documentaries of 1903 were also frequently commonplace—*Orphans in the Surf,* for instance, was just a few shots of children frolicking at the beach. By contrast, *Scenes in an Orphan Asylum* was an excellent study of the daily care given orphaned children in a state home.

UNCLE TOM'S CABIN;
THE GREAT TRAIN ROBBERY

Porter's most vivid film of 1903, aside from *The Great Train Robbery,* was an elaborate version of Harriet Beecher Stowe's antislavery classic, *Uncle Tom's Cabin.* It comprises a prologue and fourteen separate scenes, each uniquely introduced by a lettered title—another Porter first. Essentially a photographed stage play, made with an immobile camera from the perspective of a theater audience, *Uncle Tom's Cabin* displayed none of the inventive editing that marked *Life of an American Fireman.* Nonetheless, it is a fine motion picture of its era, highlighted by Porter's imaginative special effects—a raging thunderstorm with lightning, the explosion of a Mississippi River steamboat, double exposures of painted scenes of the Civil War. It ran an unprecedented length of 1,100 feet. Some recently discovered photographs of an early (c. 1901) Broadway performance of *Uncle Tom's Cabin* are virtually identical with stills from Porter's film, indicating that he openly copied the stage play.

Porter's best-known work, *The Great Train Robbery*—the single motion picture for which he is remembered—was inspired by a commercial film, *A Romance of the Rail,* which Porter shot for Edison in September 1903. It was commissioned by the Lackawanna Railroad to convince the public that its cars were immaculately clean. Marie Murray, an artist's model, played "Phoebe Snow,"

a character used in Lackawanna's national advertising in newspapers and magazines. She is shown enjoying the sights from the platform of the observation car, her spotless white dress unsoiled by soot or cinders. Enlivened by humor—two tramps riding the rods are dressed in tuxedos—*A Romance of the Rail* was loaned free to exhibitors who would show it.

Porter was much impressed with the color and drama of the railroad, and resolved to build a fictional film around this setting. The result was *The Great Train Robbery,* released in December 1903. The story is simple—a train is hijacked by a band of rough men, who are pursued and killed after a desperate battle. *The Great Train Robbery* marked the beginning of the phenomenal and lasting success of the Western film, although it was not the first Western by any means. That distinction belongs to Edison's 1898 vignette, *Cripple Creek Barroom,* and many earlier Westerns included Porter's own *Western Stagecoach Hold-Up* filmed in 1903.

Porter said later that he undertook *The Great Train Robbery* after becoming concerned that audiences were tiring of dreary scenics and commonplace novelties that dominated the screen. He consciously planned *The Great Train Robbery* as, by 1903 standards, an elaborate and spectacular film for use in nickelodeons. It ran nearly twelve minutes, cost perhaps $600 to produce, and was based upon a semblance of a written scenario—in reality a little more than the detailed notes that Porter put down before actual shooting began. The cast of forty was headed by Marie Murray and four vaudeville performers: Frank Hanaway, George Barnes, A. C. Abadie, and Max Aronson. Aronson would later become celebrated as G. M. "Broncho Billy" Anderson, the screen's first cowboy star. Porter had given him his first movie job in Edison's *The Messenger Boy's Mistake* in 1902.

Supposedly set in the Far West, *The Great Train Robbery* was actually shot on location near Dover in Essex County, New Jersey—again using the Lackawanna Railroad—and at the Edison studio in Manhattan. It is a skillfully made picture with strong visual values, although utilizing few innovations in technique. It is not edited with any particular flair—there is no intercutting but follows a free-flowing, closely knit narrative that

Bandits hold a gun on the engineer in Edwin S. Por-
er's pioneer nickelodeon drama, *The Great Train
Robbery* (1903).

builds to a logical and suspenseful climax, ending
with the famous bit of trickery in which the outlaw leader (George Barnes), shown in close-up,
takes aim and fires a pistol point-blank at the audience. (Edison also sold prints in which this scene
was used to open the picture.) Porter twice used
matte shots to good effect—the arrival of the train
as seen through the windows of the station, and
the countryside rushing by in the doorway of the
moving baggage car (which quickens the pace of
the scene).

The Great Train Robbery, with its succession
of exciting incidents, was a sensation, and for many
years was a staple feature in theaters both here
and abroad. Edison sold hundreds of prints of the
740-foot film for $111, which were shown over and
over until they disintegrated from use. *The Great
Train Robbery* was frequently the opening attraction of new nickelodeons, providing the prototype
for projected motion pictures with mass-audience
appeal. Thousands of these shabby store-theaters
came into existence between 1904 and 1907, sound-
ing the death knell of the peep shows. *The Great
Train Robbery* not only revolutionized film production, but assured the success of a new form of
exhibition that became the basis of the gigantic
motion-picture industry.

STYLE AND SOCIAL VALUES

To meet the demands of the burgeoning nickelodeons, Edison's competitors brought out a flood of longer dramas and comedies with increasingly complex plots. Curiously, Porter was content to plod along, making hundreds of films in the next few years that, with a few notable exceptions, showed little improvement over his early days at Edison. He continued to spend much time in the studio shop and laboratory, experimenting and tinkering with his inventions.

Porter's important films of 1904 were *Parsifal*, an elaborate version of Wagner's opera, and *The Ex-Convict*, which introduced a primitive form of contrasting editing. Each picture was made up of eight separate sections or scenes introduced by a title. *Parsifal* had beautiful sets and authentic costumes, but Porter permitted his cast to overact with grossly exaggerated gestures. Edison planned to use phonograph records of the opera to acccompany the film, but it is doubtful that this was actually done because of mechanical problems of synchronization. At any rate, *Parsifal* was soon withdrawn from distribution after the copyright owners of the opera sued Edison for using the work without permission.

The Ex-Convict, an extremely popular film, described the difficulties of an ex-convict in getting work to support his starving family. He saves a wealthy woman from being run down by an automobile. When he is caught burglarizing her home, she prevails upon her father, a wealthy manufacturer, to give him a decent job rather than having him arrested. Porter used intelligent editing to contrast the poverty-stricken home and the luxurious mansion. *The Ex-Convict* was one of the screen's earliest attempts to interpret social injustice.

Despite the superiority of *Parsifal* and *The Ex-Convict*, Porter's other efforts of 1904 were largely commonplace. *The European Rest Cure*, which incorporated stock travel shots, was a humorous account of an old man who goes abroad for a rest cure and has a series of incredible, exhausting adventures. Porter again used stop-motion photography in this picture, as he did in many other insignificant comedies and novelties that year. A few of Porter's 1904 titles: *Capture of the Yegg Bank Burglars* (in which an officer dresses as a

woman and traps and kills four bank robbers); *Casey's Frightful Dream*; *The Cop Fools the Sergeant*; *Nervy Nat Kisses the Bride*; *City Hall to Harlem in 15 Seconds Via the Subway Route*; *Life of an American Policeman*; and *Rube Couple at a County Fair* (a hick farmer tries to elude his wife at a county fair to see a girlie show). Porter was also still making scenic documentaries, such things as *Elephants Shooting the Chutes at Luna Park*.

The Kleptomaniac, in which Porter introduced parallel editing, was his finest film of 1905. Probably more significant than its advanced construction was the marked extension of social awareness that Porter had first exhibited in *The Ex-Convict* the previous year. An eleven-part picture, *The Kleptomaniac* contrasted the treatment given two women—one rich, one poor—who are caught stealing. The rich woman, aided by her money, prestige, and an attorney, is freed as a victim of kleptomania, while the penniless mother is sent to prison for stealing a loaf of bread to feed two starving children. Porter ended the film with a symbolical scene of Justice, blindfolded, her scales tipped by the weight of gold.

Two other Porter films of 1905, *Seven Ages* and *White Caps*, were of more than passing interest. *Seven Ages* was a series of short scenes, each introduced by a title and depicting a stage in life—infancy, school days, old age, and so forth. Porter made it to experiment with interesting new photographic techniques. There was a greater use of reflected light, increased light intensities, and side lighting—plus the shadowy technique of "Rembrandt lighting" for which Cecil B. DeMille took credit years later. An eighth segment, *Lovers*, was filmed at the same time, but was released as a separate picture. Its content was scarcely more than a young couple, in Civil War costumes, caressing and kissing.

White Caps is notable for its social values—a group of white-hooded men seek out a wife-beater, tar and feather him, and ride him out of town on a rail. The film condones mob law, glorifies the Ku Klux Klan (although it was not identified by name), and contains some explicit violence. As with Griffith's *The Birth of a Nation* ten years later, an essentially brutal vengeance is disguised as the means to an end.

Porter also brought out a parody of *The Great*

Train Robbery in 1905, in which the famous film was remade almost—but not quite—scene for scene with all the characters played by *children*! Aptly entitled *The Little Train Robbery*, it had child bandits rob a toy train, take the loot to a wooded hideaway to divide, and be captured by uniformed child police officers. Another Porter novelty was to have scrambled movable letters arrange themselves to form the titles of *How Jones Lost His Roll* (1905), a technique now widely used by home-movie enthusiasts.

Porter was unable to abandon his trick films for long, and in 1906 he brought out *The Dream of a Rarebit Fiend*, easily the most technologically advanced picture made to that time. Obviously influenced by Méliès, it depicted the nightmare of a man who wolfs down ale and a Welsh rarebit before going to bed. The dreamer is tormented by devils who drum a lively rhythm on his head, his shoes steal out of the room, and the furniture dances about and inexplicably vanishes. His bed sails out of the window, carrying him high about the familiar Manhattan skyline; after some dizzying acrobatics, he is caught in a whirlwind and falls through the roof of his own house, landing awake in his bed. To create the fanciful dream, Porter combined imaginative editing with stop-motion photography, matte shots, dissolves, double exposures, and a remarkably fluid camera. Said to have cost only $350, *The Dream of a Rarebit Fiend* earned more than $30,000 for Edison.

By 1907, in addition to supervising all Edison production, Porter was personally directing, photographing, and editing a substantial portion of the company's product. Some films were made by Will S. Rising, an early Edison actor, and Frank G. Kugler, a German-born director and photographer who Americanized his name to Kirby during World War I. Porter was given two new assistants, J. Searle Dawley and Gilbert P. Hamilton. The latter, hired as an assistant cameraman and laboratory aide, did not remain long and soon left to become a director at other studios, and was replaced by cameraman Otto Brautigan. Dawley was to be associated with Porter, off and on, for more than ten years, and would become one of the more important early screen directors.

J. SEARLE DAWLEY, FIRST COLLABORATOR

A native of Colorado, J. Searle Dawley had wangled a job at seventeen as an actor with the popular Lewis Morrison Stock Company, which specialized in elaborate costume dramas (*Faust*; *Richelieu*; *Frederick the Great*). Later, after a brief stint in vaudeville as a dramatic monologist, Dawley joined the Spooner Stock Company of Brooklyn as actor and director. He soon turned to writing, and by 1907 had authored fifteen moderately successful plays.

Porter may have realized his own shortcomings in the dramatic aspects of film production, and probably hired Dawley to complement his own technical know-how. Another story is that it was Edison officials who felt Porter needed dramatic guidance and experience in acting techniques, and insisted that he bring someone with stage experience into the company. From the start, Porter and Dawley hit it off well, although the two men were completely unalike. Porter was stout and florid—Adolph Zukor once described him as resembling a brewmaster—quiet, fascinated by mechanics and engineering, and lacking in literary pretensions. By contrast, Dawley was thin and peppery, sharp-featured, scholarly, disinterested in the mechanical side of filmmaking, and possessed of an intuitive sense of drama. Both are invariably described as kind, considerate, compassionate gentlemen.

For several months Porter and Dawley functioned as a team, although Dawley was ostensibly Porter's assistant. In effect, they were codirectors, Dawley coaching the actors and endlessly attentive to dramatic detail, Porter handling the photography and technical aspects. Porter quickly came to rely heavily upon Dawley, and throughout their association at Edison and later at Famous Players never ceased to seek his advice and counsel.

His apprenticeship under Porter completed, Dawley was made a full-fledged director, and during the next six years turned out over 350 films for Edison, mostly one- and two-reelers. Although handicapped by a fondness for saccharine and overemotional scenes, he became an able director, later best known for his comedy-dramas with Marguerite Clark. To the end of his screen career Dawley was unable to shake the influence of his stage training.

His pictures, while well acted and marked by attention to detail, lacked a visual acuity, and Dawley never seemed to fully comprehend the uses to which a camera could be put.

Porter tended to reserve for himself the films in which action or trick effects predominated, while assigning Dawley to what he called the "emotional" pictures. This policy deprived both men of a much-needed opportunity to broaden their talents. After Porter's departure from Edison in 1909, Dawley attempted several pictures with only moderate success. His best film of this genre was an elaborate version of *The Charge of the Light Brigade* (1912), shot on location at Fort Russell, Wyoming.

In 1907, an out-of-work young actor who called himself Lawrence Griffith, later better known by his real name of David Wark Griffith, tried to sell Porter a script based on the opera *La Tosca*. Porter did not buy the scenario, but, impressed by Griffith's rugged good looks, hired him to play a mountaineer in *Rescued From an Eagle's Nest*. Porter later cast him in several other Edison films, but Griffith soon moved to Biograph, where he began his directorial career the following year with *The Adventures of Dollie*. Porter later recalled that Griffith "took direction from me very well."

Rescued From an Eagle's Nest was one of those periodic Porter movies that attracted attention through its novelty. The story centered around efforts to rescue a baby seized by a giant eagle and deposited in its nest on a towering mountainside. Porter delighted in this type of challenge, and spent days with his art director, Richard Murphy, in devising ways of making a mechanical eagle, strung on piano wires, swoop down and carry off the child. Dawley apparently had a hand in the making of *Rescued From an Eagle's Nest*, and in an interview in *The Moving Picture World* in 1914 claimed to have directed the film. It is likely that he handled the dramatic portions, while Porter supervised the technical details and photography.

Another Porter novelty, *The Teddy Bears* (1907), used stop-motion photography to animate seven teddy bears, graduated in size, in a series of amusing antics. Porter worked twelve hours a day for a week to get ninety feet of film. *The Teddy Bears* was a popular box-office hit that brought

millions of children into the theaters. It was still being booked by Edison as late as 1914.

A reevaluation of Porter's early work has been made possible by the painstaking efforts of Kemp R. Niver to restore the paper print collection of early movies in the Library of Congress to modern, safety-film stock. This remarkable ten-year project, completed in the late 1960s, won Niver a special Academy Award for technological achievement. He recovered over 3,000 pictures of 1894-1912, including several hundred of the Edison Company. It is no longer possible to determine with certainty all that Porter personally directed. Through diligent sleuthing in old records, Niver has been able to identify many of Porter's films, while other Edisons of the era can only be presumed to be Porter's work.

As yet, no exhaustive study of this mass of film has been made. An objective review by a talented investigator, possibly as the subject of a doctoral dissertation, may well provide a completely new look at early motion-picture history. Niver's own studies have elicited many new facts—for example, some techniques attributed to Griffith and others were used earlier by Porter. A cursory reevaluation of some of Porter's better-known pictures does not bear out statements of many film historians who based their information on published accounts rather than personal viewing. For instance, *Uncle Tom's Cabin* appears to be a more superior film than originally thought, while *Life of an American Fireman* does not have as much of the inventive editing with which it has been credited.

During his last three years at Edison, Porter functioned increasingly in a supervisory capacity, devoting more of his time to administrative duties and laboratory experiments. He had helped design Edison's new $100,000 studio at 2826 Decatur Street in the Bronx, which opened in 1907, and spent much effort in improving its technical facilities. About 1908 he began to work closely with Frank Cannock, inventor of the Edengraph, on a new projector that eventually became the famous Simplex. Porter personally financed research in talking pictures at a small machine shop in Manhattan, although Edison's engineers were still struggling with the problems of synchronization at the Menlo Park laboratories. With all these multiple activities, Porter continued to direct as many as a half-dozen films each month. His best pictures of 1908-09 were *Nero and the Burning of Rome*, a spectacle inspired by *Quo Vadis*; a new version of *Faust*; *Hansel and Gretel*, another lavish fairy tale with many beautiful special effects; two films of social protest, *The Strike* and *Capital Versus Labor*; *The Pony Express*; *The Star of Bethlehem*; *On the Western Frontier*; *A Cup of Tea and She*; and *Pocahontas*.

THE BREAK WITH EDISON

Porter was increasingly dissatisfied at Edison. He was critical of the company's role as a ringleader in the Motion Picture Patents Company, whose vicious practices in trying to suppress certain independents were bringing Edison much unfavorable publicity. His attitude did not endear him to Frank L. Dyer, the Edison attorney who masterminded the patents war, and who was quite influential in the company's top management. Porter tried without success to persuade Edison to establish a scenario department to develop new ideas. While some films were returning their cost a hundred times over, production budgets were skimpy. Studio pay scales were notoriously low, and except for Ben Wilson, Mary Fuller, Miriam Nesbitt, and a few others, Porter was unable to build and hold a stable of promising players. He was particularly distressed when Maurice Costello left for a much better-paying job at Vitagraph. The Edison Company began to lose ground, and was soon overshadowed by the more aggressive Biograph and Vitagraph companies. Burdened by penuriousness, shoddy treatment of employees, and the bitter heritage of the patents war, Edison deteriorated steadily, but did not finally go out of existence until 1918.

Porter abruptly resigned from Edison in November 1909, and announced plans to enter independent production. Although he recommended that J. Searle Dawley succeed him as production chief, the job went to Horace G. Plimpton, a one-time carpet salesman and protégé of Frank L. Dyer, who had been working at Edison as a director-cameraman for several months. While the internal dissension at Edison must have been a factor in his departure, Porter intimated that he left the

company simply to make more money. "All about me I saw men, many with no experience in motion pictures, reaping a fortune overnight," he said later. "I wanted a share of those rewards."

With Joseph W. Engel, a nickelodeon operator, Porter set up Defender Pictures Company. The studio was located on the second floor of a loft building on the west side of Eleventh Avenue, between 41st and 42nd Streets. Arthur Miller, later the brilliant cinematographer of *How Green Was My Valley* (1941) and *The Song of Bernadette* (1943), then in this teens, was Porter's first employee—a combination handyman and assistant cameraman.

Four months were spent in fixing up the studio, which contained a well-equipped laboratory and was illuminated by banks of the new Cooper-Hewitt mercury-vapor lamps. Defender's first picture, *Russia—Country of Depression*, did not go into production until April 1910. It was a somber drama of the Russia Revolution, and despite some action scenes (filmed on Staten Island) was not successful. Porter followed it with *Too Many Girls*, a broad comedy of shenanigans in a girls' finishing school, which proved more popular. Other Defender titles included: *The White Red Man*; *Sherlock Holmes, Jr.*; and *Castles in the Air*. These inconsequential one-reelers were released weekly through Carl Laemmle's Motion Picture Distributor and Sales Company.

For some reason Defender abruptly folded at the end of 1910 after less than eight months of production. Porter, Engel, and William H. Swanson then organized Rex Film Company, using financing largely supplied by Carl Laemmle. Swanson, a tough and aggressive Chicago exchange operator, was a partner in several Laemmle ventures, and a major figure in the bitter struggle with the patents trust. Despite his alignment with the independents, Porter was singularly free of any harassment by the Motion Picture Patents Company, possibly because of many industry friendships born in the Edison days. Porter had refused when the trust offered to license the Defender product. He was able to shoot on location, mostly at Staten Island, without any of the savage attacks by gangs of hired bullies sent to plague many independents, nor was any attempt ever made to sabotage his studio or place spies on his payroll.

The Rex unit took over the old Cameraphone Studio on Eleventh Avenue near 43rd Street, where Porter had been conducting some talking-picture experiments. Arthur Miller went along with the new company, and was much impressed with the revolutionary arc-light equipment that Porter had installed.

Porter inaugurated the Rex program with *A Heroine of '76* (1911), a story of Revolutionary War patriotism in which an innkeeper's daughter sacrifices her life to save George Washington from assassination. Lois Weber, later one of Hollywood's few women directors, was the star, and the role of Washington was taken by her husband, Phillips Smalley, a well-known stage actor. It was an auspicious beginning for the company, although *The Moving Picture World* suggested that Porter was operating on a slim budget: ". . . the company wisely restricted its initial outlay to what was really necessary without starving the picture," it said. "The scenery and photographic facilities are adequate, and it is really astonishing what highly attractive films you can make with comparatively simple accessories, and quite a limited company of performers."

The Rex Company was only moderately successful. Most of its early pictures teamed Lois Weber and Phillips Smalley, and the talented couple soon assumed increased production responsibilities. Smalley did much of the directing—Porter relied on him, as he had on Dawley at Edison, for assistance in handling the actors—while Miss Weber wrote scripts and later did the editing. Some of the Rex films were: *The End of the Circle; Love's Four Stone Walls; The Price of Money; The Strength of the Weak;* and *Through Flaming Gates.* Porter continued to make occasional trick films at Rex, and one of the most unusual was *By the Light of the Moon* (1911), which was done entirely in silhouette.

Arthur Miller said that Porter would leave the set without provocation and disappear into the laboratory or dark room to work on some special effect. While he was gone, the actors would discuss various ways to do the scene; when Porter returned he would listen attentively to their suggestions, and frequently accepted their ideas. "Porter was a director by necessity," Miller recalled, "but he never had the ego to make a *great* direc-

tor. He was soft-spoken, kindly, and completely unselfish, but he always answered a question as briefly as possible. It was his way of making a person think for himself."

When Porter was at Rex, he always developed the film of the day's shooting before going home. "He never thought of himself of just a director," Miller said, "but as a manufacturer of motion pictures, able to personally handle every phase of filmmaking from turning the crank of the camera to printing and toning the final positive. His life was devoted to movies, and he did more to create the motion picture business than those who invented the camera."

Porter may have left many of the production duties at Rex to the Smalleys because of his preoccupation with another project, the introduction of his Simplex Projector. This finely designed, precision machine was a joint effort of Porter and Frank Cannock, a Scotsman who at one time had been an engineer with the Singer Sewing Machine Company. Cannock had already designed two improved projectors while employed as chief projectionist at the Eden Musée, the Edengraph and the Cinematograph, which were commercially unsuccessful because of high manufacturing costs.

The Simplex had many new improvements, including the first completely enclosed mechanism with center frame bearings, a new style of sliding gate, and a means of adjusting the revolving shutter during operation. The Simplex also enabled greater precision focusing through an improved method of lens mounting. No basic changes were made in the Porter-Cannock Simplex for more than fifteen years, and it was universally recognized as the finest projector on the market.

Despite its superiority, the Simplex did not immediately get into mass production. During part of the time that he and Cannock were experimenting with it, Cannock was employed as a plant superintendent for George Kleine, a manufacturer of stereoptical equipment (and later a distributor of American and foreign-made films). Kleine brought suit against Cannock, charging that the Simplex had been developed while the latter was in Kleine's employ. However, the patents were in Porter's name, with a half-interest assigned to Cannock, and the suit was eventually dropped. The first Simplex projectors were manufactured by a small machine shop, the Multi-Speed Shutter Company, which made shutters for still cameras, and that Porter had often employed to build his inventions.

ADOLPH ZUKOR AND FAMOUS PLAYERS

One of Porter's early visitors to the Rex Studio was Adolph Zukor, the diminutive manager of the Comedy Theater nickelodeon, to whom he had been introduced by Carl Laemmle. A Hungarian immigrant, Zukor had spent several years in the fur business before becoming an official of the Marcus Loew theater chain. Zukor talked vaguely of getting into film distribution, and urged Porter to follow the lead of French and Italian producers by turning out longer pictures. But Porter doubted that exhibitors would buy anything over two reels.

Early in 1912, Frank Brockless, an American engaged in distributing films abroad, attended a London showing of *Queen Elizabeth*, a four-reel spectacle that Louis Mercanton had directed in Paris with the celebrated Sarah Bernhardt in the title role. Because of its length, the picture had failed to find a buyer for the United States. Brockless was impressed by the film's handsome mounting and the box-office potentials of the Bernhardt

Sarah Bernhardt, the celebrated French actress, was the star of *Queen Elizabeth*, a spectacular four-reel feature that Edwin S. Porter and Adolph Zukor imported into the United States in 1912.

name, and wired Joseph W. Engel, urging him to purchase the American rights for Rex. Porter was lukewarm to the proposal, but finally instructed Engel to take an option on *Queen Elizabeth*, apparently with the idea of selling it outright to a distributor. Remembering Zukor's enthusiasm for longer films, he suggested that Engel approach the little Hungarian to buy it.

There are several conflicting versions of how *Queen Elizabeth* was brought to the United States. One is that Zukor paid $40,000 to Mercanton for the American rights *before* the film went into production. Another places the price at $35,000, and says Zukor snapped up the film without haggling on the strength of a single telephone call from Engel. Terry Ramsaye, in *A Million and One Nights*, asserts Zukor gave $18,000 for it.

What actually happened is that Zukor, sensing an opportunity to make money, persuaded Porter and Engel to join him in an entirely new company, the Engadine Amusement Corporation. Using financing supplied by the Irving Trust Company of New York, it bought the American rights to *Queen Elizabeth* for $35,000, of which $18,000 was paid down in cash. The original intention was to use the picture as the first release of a new distributing organization that would specialize in top-quality foreign features.

At this point Zukor's fertile mind evolved the concept of "famous players in famous plays," using the pick of Broadway stars in screen versions of classic stage properties and current hits. Engadine's interest in *Queen Elizabeth* would be assigned to a dynamic new company, Famous Players Film Company, and shown at advanced admissions after an extensive publicity campaign. Thereafter, the company would both produce and distribute only features of four reels or more, each with a leading stage personality, whom Zukor proposed to lure with handsome salaries—up to $10,000 per picture.

In retrospect, Zukor appears to have established Famous Players with deceptive ease, despite the precarious financing problems of the first year. The Irving Trust Company, along with some of Zukor's former associates in the Loew theaters, supplied most of the money. To gain entrée into the rarified Broadway circles, he charmed impresario Daniel Frohman, then suffering from a run of flop plays, into the new company—much to the

"The Divine Sarah" was sixty-eight years of age and hobbling about on a wooden leg when she played the lead in *Queen Elizabeth* in 1912.

dismay of Frohman's brother Charles. Alexander (Al) Lichtman, an aggressive young film salesman then in his early twenties, was named sales manager, and sent on the road with the Bernhardt film. He eventually wrote more than $80,000 in contracts for *Queen Elizabeth*, giving the infant company a nice profit.

Over a heavy dinner at Reisenweber's Restaurant, Zukor induced Porter to become director-general of the new studio, as well as treasurer of the corporation. In addition to supervising all production, Porter would personally direct the more important films. For his efforts he was to receive a block of Famous Players stock and an attractive salary. The conservative Porter had doubts that Zukor could sign up the caliber of Broadway stars that he sought, and told him he needed "a fellow like Griffith—someone with stage experience." Porter was not miffed when Zukor gently admitted that Griffith had rejected his offer of $50,000 a year to leave Biograph and work for Famous Players. Ironically, Griffith had suggested Porter for the job!

Porter sold his interest in Rex Film Company, with considerable relief, to his partner, William L. Swanson. He had not been happy nor particularly successful as an independent producer, disliking the burdensome administrative details and prob-

lems of distribution. Lois Weber and Phillips Smalley took over the production reins at Rex, and remained for two years, when Allan Dwan joined the company as producer-director, bringing with him the rising young Wallace Reid as star. Rex was eventually absorbed into Universal. B. P. Schulberg, Porter's enterprising publicity director at Rex, also moved over to Famous Players, and eventually became head of Paramount's West Coast studio.

If Porter had any intention of spending months to build a new studio and search for properties—as he had done with both Defender and Rex—Zukor quickly dispelled such notions. Porter was aghast when Zukor, without consulting him, announced a first year's program of forty-two pictures—eventually cut to twenty-one—with the initial release within sixty days! Porter had no studio, no script, and no star, although Daniel Frohman was busy trying to line up several Broadway luminaries.

For its first production Famous Players selected Alexandre Dumas's perennial classic, *The Count of Monte Cristo*, with the aging matinee idol James O'Neill (father of playwright Eugene O'Neill) in the lead. Over a period of thirty years O'Neill had played the vengeful Edmond Dantes more than 4,000 times in a popular stage version. Frohman inticed him with a deal that called for twenty percent of the profits of the film.

Albert A. Kaufman, Zukor's brother-in-law, was dickering for a three-story building on 26th Street for use as a studio, but it was not immediately available. Porter hastily put *The Count of Monte Cristo* into production in rented quarters at the Crystal Studio in New York. The script was by Porter and his assistant, Joseph A. Golden. In addition to directing, Porter personally did the photography and editing. The four-reel film was completed in less than two weeks at a cost of $13,400, to which prints and distribution expense added another $14,000.

Zukor's troubles worsened. Except for *Queen Elizabeth*, the Motion Picture Patents Company had declined to license any other Famous Players product, although Porter was using a Pathé camera. Apprehensive of sabotage, Zukor ordered the Crystal Studio closely guarded. Probably at the trust's instigation, Selig Pictures rushed through a three-reel version of *The Count of Monte Cristo*, starring Hobart Bosworth, at its California studio. It was hurriedly edited and released without advance publicity.

Rather than compete with the inferior Selig film, Zukor decided to shelve *The Count of Monte Cristo*, and it was not put on the market until the following year. As it turned out, the O'Neill picture was mediocre, and would have been a disastrous debut for Famous Players. Despite Porter's careful photography, O'Neill's age was painfully apparent—he was sixty-five at the time—and his exaggerated acting style was ill suited to the screen. The settings were unreal, and the Chateau d'If was nothing more than a crudely painted backdrop of light canvas that frequently rippled in the drafts of the shabby Crystal Studio. In spite of its lukewarm reception, *The Count of Monte Cristo* eventually grossed $45,539.32, of which O'Neill received $3,813.32.

Meanwhile, Famous Players moved into its own studio at 213 West 26th Street, between Seventh and Eighth Avenues, occupying the two top floors of a building that once served as the Ninth Regiment Armory. The old drill area on the top floor was 100 by 200 feet, and was illuminated by a few skylights and banks of Cooper-Hewitt lights. Part of the space was cut up into tiny offices and a carpenter shop, over which a cutting room and projection booth, reached by a ladder, were built. The floor below contained a laboratory, dressing rooms, and a costume department.

After six months of frustrating delay, Famous Players was finally launched with a smash hit, a picturization of Sir Anthony Hope's *The Prisoner of Zenda* (1913), which had just closed a long run on Broadway. The star, James K. Hackett, a reigning matinee idol then in his middle forties, was a flamboyant character known for his heavy drinking. He lived in a grand style, and was always in need of money. Frohman had overcome Hackett's disdain for the movies with a handsome fee of $1,250 a week. The actor's second wife, Beatrice Beckley, whom he married after divorcing the beautiful English actress Mary Mannering, was signed to play Princess Flavia.

Porter's first few days with Hackett were extremely difficult. Unused to the mechanical limitations imposed by the camera, Hackett would step out of range or inopportunely turn away, and then refuse to do retakes. Production came to a standstill when he declined to do the climactic moat scene in the studio tank. Hackett was finally persuaded to swim the moat, not once but four times, after Porter and Kaufman got him drunk on a fifth of whiskey.

Porter remained patient with his temperamental star, although he frequently disappeared into the darkroom to cool his temper, and Hackett soon began to take a genuine interest in the film. Unlike James O'Neill, he soon recognized that the screen required a more restrained acting style, and he asked Porter to reshoot the earlier scenes in which he overacted. A month was required to complete *The Prisoner of Zenda*, and by that time the two men had acquired a mutual respect for each other.

Handsomely mounted at a cost of nearly $50,000, and enlivened with many action sequences, *The Prisoner of Zenda* was a huge success. Porter was praised for his direction and photography (which made Hackett look years younger), and for the beautifully executed split-screen effects that enabled Hackett to play the dual roles of King Rudolf and his look-alike British cousin, Rudolf Rassendyll. An invitational premiere, attended by an audience of New York bluebloods, featured an announcement by Frohman that Famous Players had settled its differences with the patents trust.

The success of *The Prisoner of Zenda* enabled Frohman to sign many Broadway stars to appear in Famous Players films—Minnie Maddern Fiske, Lily Langtry, Arnold Daly, Robert Edeson, Henrietta Crosman, Cecilia Loftus, and the young John Barrymore. It was evident that Porter could not personally direct a slate of twenty-one pictures, much less the fifty-two that Zukor envisioned for the second season. He brought in his old associate from Edison, J. Searle Dawley, whose dramatic talents fitted in well with the famous stage personalities who came to the 26th Street studio. Once again, he and Dawley worked as a team, as codirectors, and on occasion Porter was simply the cameraman while Dawley directed. It was a flexible arrangement that enabled Porter to handle his multiple duties efficiently. Most of the Famous Players features took less than three weeks to shoot, and a week or so to edit.

Somewhat to his own surprise, Porter got along well with most of the Broadway stars at Famous Players. He was much opposed to the hiring of Minnie Maddern Fiske, then in her early fifties, and behind her back referred to her as "the old lady." But with Dawley's help he extracted a good, although not sensational, performance from her in *Tess of the D'Urbervilles* (1913), some of which was shot at her country home in upstate New York.

Porter was even more upset when Frohman signed the legendary Lily Langtry, the British beauty whose admirers included Judge Roy Bean of Texas. "The Jersey Lily" was then in her sixties, quite plump, and completely unsuited for the heroine of *His Neighbor's Wife* (1913). Por-ter warned Zukor that she would not photograph well, but Zukor was determined to go ahead, saying "the public wants to see Lily Langtry." *His Neighbor's Wife* turned out to be incredibly bad, and although the picture made money, it disappointed an army of Langtry fans who knew her only by reputation. Porter was right—she did photograph badly—but he found her a charming, still beautiful woman.

One of the Broadway greats whom Frohman lured to Famous Players was the distinguished playwright and director, the near-legendary David Belasco. Frohman had bought the rights to Belasco's stunning stage success, *A Good Little Devil*, which included his services as consultant on the

After a stint on Broadway, Mary Pickford returned to films as the blind girl in *A Good Little Devil* (1913), directed by Edwin S. Porter. It was a role she had created on the stage for David Belasco.

script and direction. As part of the deal, the original Broadway cast, including Mary Pickford, was to appear in the film version.

A Good Little Devil went badly from the start. Belasco, assisted by J. Searle Dawley, was originally slated to direct. After appearing in a prologue that introduced the leading characters, Belasco withdrew from any real participation in the film. Porter, who was doing the photography, assumed the direction, although Dawley appears to have directed some scenes, either by himself or in co-operation with Porter. The finished product, credited exclusively to Porter, clearly showed the influence of too many cooks. *A Good Little Devil* was a dull and static picture, incredibly slow

moving. At Dawley's insistence, it had been filmed exactly as it was presented on the stage, with the players mouthing the full text of their lines—an absurdity for a silent motion picture.

Miss Pickford, with the enormous appeal of her radiant personality, was the best thing in *A Good Little Devil*, and Zukor immediately sensed her potentials as a star. She was already well known to movie audiences from her appearances for Griffith and others prior to returning to the stage. Before *A Good Little Devil* was shown outside the studio projection room, Zukor signed her to a term contract, but not until after some wrangling over salary. He wisely postponed the release of *A Good Little Devil* for ten months, until Miss

Edwin S. Porter's *A Good Little Devil* (1913) was filled with fairies and fantasies, and did not make much sense. Famous Players held up its release for a year—until after Mary Pickford had scored an enormous hit in other pictures.

MERCY ATTEMPTS SUICIDE WITH A BULLETLESS GUN

MARY PICKFORD IN "CAPRICE"

Caprice (1913), directed by J. Searle Dawley, gave Mary Pickford several opportunities to demonstrate her comic talents.

Pickford had firmly established her popularity with three other films. The first under the new contract was *In the Bishop's Carriage* (1913), a drama of a young woman who enters upon a life of crime, reforms, and becomes a famous actress. Porter and Dawley collaborated on the direction, with Porter doing the photography. The second, *Caprice* (1913), was directly by Dawley alone.

FILMING IN EUROPE AND CALIFORNIA

It was soon apparent that the New York studio could not accommodate the ambitious schedule Zukor had announced, and it was decided to establish a Famous Players studio in California. In November 1913, Porter went west and rented a farmhouse at the intersection of Hollywood and Sunset Boulevards. A rude, open-air stage was built in the yard, along with a shed to store props and scenery. Porter used the kitchen of the house as his office, and other rooms were converted to dressing rooms for the performers and quarters for a secretary and bookkeeper.

The first Famous Players film to be made on the West Coast was Mary Pickford's *Hearts Adrift*, released in January 1914. It was a melodramatic tale of a Spanish girl shipwrecked on a deserted island. Later, a man (Harold Lockwood), another shipwreck victim, joins her; they fall in love and have a child. The man's wife appears with a rescue party, and the Spanish girl throws herself and her child into the sea. Porter both directed and photographed *Hearts Adrift,* incorporating many beautiful shots taken along the Pacific beaches. It was a smash hit, and a great personal triumph for Mary Pickford.

Porter followed *Hearts Adrift* with another enormous Pickford success, *Tess of the Storm Country* (1914), also filmed in California. Mary played a spunky squatter who invokes the wrath of an intolerant community by pretending to be the mother of a child born out of wedlock to another woman. Porter's direction was confused and uneven, weakest in the handling of plot and characterization, and he did not use a single close-up. His photography and special effects were widely praised, particularly the lovely shots of a quiet fishing village and the spectacular re-creation

Porter's photographic compositions for Mary Pickford's *Caprice* (1913) included a setting sun, although the farm set was artificial and obviously constructed within the studio.

Tess of the Storm Country (1914), directed by Edwin S. Porter in California, cast Mary Pickford as a spunky squatter. Harold Lockwood reacted appropriately when Mary pretended to be the mother of a child born out of wedlock.

of a devastating storm. Harold Lockwood was again the leading man. Made at a cost of only $13,000, *Tess* reaped huge profits.

Mary Pickford said later that she and the other actors got little help from Porter. "He knew very little about acting," she recalled in an interview at Pickfair in 1962. "Mr. Porter was more an inventor than a director. He would rush through a scene with the actors, giving them little guidance, and then spend hours trying to get some camera effect. My principal recollection of him is that he was always tinkering with the camera or some piece of machinery. I have always thought that he did not really enjoy directing."

H. Lyman Broening, the first cameraman to be hired by Porter at Famous Players, is another who emphasizes Porter's preoccupation with the technical details of filmmaking. "He often did his own dark room work," Broening says. "When I went to Famous Players in 1913, my fellow cameramen warned that I would not last long—that Porter knew everything about the camera, and was too particular." However, Broening got along well with Porter, and remained at the studio for six years, photographing most of the Marguerite Clark films.

"My first meeting with Edwin S. Porter was at his Rex Studio," Broening recalls. "He was busily engaged in editing one of his pictures. A huge bin contained scenes which were pinned along the edge. Film in those days was highly inflammable, but Porter was nonchalantly smoking a big cigar, apparently oblivious to the danger of fire." Broening got on the Famous Players payroll when he was doing some scenes for an independent picture, Monopol's *The Dead Secret*, which was being made at the F.P. studio. Porter came to the set and watched closely, then offered Broening a job after becoming intrigued at his ability to handle an intricate triple exposure.

Early in 1914, Daniel Frohman persuaded Hugh Ford, the gifted director and designer of such Broadway hits as *The Garden of Allah* and *Bird of Paradise*, to join Famous Players. He believed the Ford name would help lure many stage personalities still hesitant to appear in movies. Ford was genuinely interested in motion pictures, but felt the need for training in film mechanics. He was packed off to Hollywood to observe and learn from Porter. Although totally unalike, the two men soon became close personal friends and worked together as a team until Porter's departure from Famous Players the following year. It was a happy combination of talent, Porter handling the

MERCY DECIDES TO WEAR THE OLD GINGHAM GOWN

MARY PICKFORD IN "CAPRICE"

Although head of production at Famous Players and its principal director, Edwin S. Porter was content to serve as cameraman on *Caprice* (1913). Mary Pickford is at right.

camera and technical details, with Ford concentrating upon the acting, settings, and plot construction. Porter soon came to rely upon Ford, as he had relied earlier upon Dawley, and to a lesser extent upon Phillips Smalley.

Porter and Ford first collaborated on Mary Pickford's *Such a Little Queen* (1914), an improbable tale of a runaway princess who flees from her kingdom to New York, where she finds love with an exiled king (Carlyle Blackwell) in a dreary tenement. The interiors were made at the California studio, and the exteriors were shot later in Manhattan. *Such a Little Queen* was made to measure for Mary Pickford, and was immensely successful. Some if the profits went into a new Famous Players studio on Long Island, which Porter helped to design and equip.

Porter and Ford returned to New York in April 1914, and after a busy month went abroad with plans to film a series of spectacular pictures in England, France, and Italy. Zukor tendered them

After an apprenticeship with D. W. Griffith at Biograph, Mary Pickford blossomed into stardom in a series of popular films directed by Edwin S. Porter.

a farewell banquet at Reisenweber's, with the studio's top executives, directors, and cameramen enjoying the huge steaks. The pair barely made the 5:00 A.M. sailing of the steamship *Kaiser Auguste Victoria*.

At at London press conference Porter and Ford heartened the impoverished British film industry by announcing plans for a Famous Players studio at Islington. They shot considerable footage of the beautiful English countryside and stately castles, some of which was used later in Marguerite Clark's *The Prince and the Pauper* (1915).

In Paris, Porter and Ford hurriedly completed *Monsieur Beaucaire*, Booth Tarkington's swashbuckling novel of a timid barber who gets involved with a Spanish princess. James K. Hackett, who had appeared in an unsuccessful stage version in America, was the star. He was then drinking heavily, and was upset by a lawsuit that threatened to deprive him of a $1,179,383 inheritance from an obscure niece whom he had barely known. *Monsieur Beaucaire* was enhanced by Porter's beautiful photography of the Normandy country. For some reason, it does not appear to have been widely shown in the United States.

In July, Porter and Ford continued on to Rome and began production on a lavish film, *The Eternal City*, produced at a cost of more than $100,000. Based on Hall Caine's popular novel, it concerned a courtier, the mistress of the Prime Minister of Italy, who tries to take the blame when a young man with whom she has fallen in love kills her seducer. The picture starred Pauline Frederick, whom Zukor signed after she scored a huge success as Potiphar's wife in the Broadway biblical spectacle, *Joseph and His Brethern*. Porter's camera captured the beautiful Castle Saint Angelo, the Villa d'Este gardens, the Appian Way, and many other Roman landmarks. He and Ford also filmed the impressive processions of the Pope's Jubilee Year, as well as political disorders that broke out at the Coliseum. These scenes were later woven into the plot.

Before *The Eternal City* was completed, World War I exploded in Europe, and the Vatican hastily withdrew permission for further filming in the area. When the company attempted to shoot needed scenes with Miss Frederick on the steps of Saint Peter's, the Swiss Guards angrily chased her away. The following day the Italian government suggested that Porter and Ford leave the country, and their visas were revoked. The war brought an end to plans for them to make a series of pictures with Mary Pickford in Europe, each to be set in a different country.

The Eternal City was completed in New York—only a few interiors remained to be filmed—and it was given a lavish premiere at the Astor Theater the following April. It was a critical and box-office success, and made an overnight screen favorite of Pauline Frederick. She signed a handsome contract with Famous Players at a beginning salary of $1,000 a week.

Porter had been away from the New York studios for nearly eight months, first in California and then in Europe, and he returned to find subtle changes in the hierarchy of power had taken place. The production staff had been greatly enlarged, and, in addition to J. Searle Dawley, included such directors as James Kirkwood, Joseph Kaufman, Francis Powers, Frederick A. Thomson, and Oscar Eagle, the latter another recruit from Broadway. Although Porter was ostensibly still in charge of production, he was quickly aware that his authority had diminished. During his absence Zukor and Frohman had shared his duties and seemed reluctant to step aside. Porter began to devote more of his time to the technical operations of the studio, directing only an occasional picture. Earlier in the year his title at Famous Players had been changed (without his knowledge) from director-general to technical director, indicative of his changing responsibilities.

Porter was still dabbling in color and talking pictures, and for more than ten years had been conducting intriguing experiments in three-dimensional movies, using the anaglyph method. The principle did not originate with him, but was first advanced by William Friese-Greene, the ill-fated British pioneer who claimed to have invented motion pictures. The anaglyph method involved the photographing of two pictures of the same scene, taken approximately two-and-a-half inches apart, and then projected simultaneously side by side in the same ratio. The screen was viewed through special eyeglasses worn by the spectators, with one lens tinted red and the other green.

In cooperation with W. E. Waddell, a former Edison associate, Porter made the first practical demonstration of three-dimensional motion pictures. An experimental three-reel film was shown on June 10, 1915, at the Astor Theatre in New York on calibrated projectors specially designed by Porter and Waddell. The first reel was composed of scenes of rural America, followed by dramatic sketches with Marie Doro and John Mason (the latter in bits from *Jim the Penman*), climaxed by 1,000 feet of film of Niagara Falls.

The Porter-Waddell experiments, although novel, were not very successful. Reviewers complained of too many blurred movements, particularly if the actors moved too fast, and of the discomfort of wearing the special glasses. The demonstration film, said reviewer Lynde Denig of *The Moving Picture World*, shimmered like a reflection on a lake, but when applied to commercial motion pictures "could not be practical in its present form without detracting from the plot."

LAST DAYS WITH FAMOUS PLAYERS; THE SIMPLEX

George J. Folsey, later one of Hollywood's finest cinematographers (*Meet Me In St. Louis*, 1944; *The Harvey Girls*, 1945), was a fourteen-year-old office boy at Famous Players in 1915. He remembers Porter as a serious but kindly gentleman who was always deeply absorbed in whatever he happened to be doing at the moment. "He and Hugh Ford had just returned from Europe when I went to work at the 26th Street studio," Folsey recalls. "I remember seeing Mr. Porter in the cutting room with long rolls of film about his neck. Having directed and photographed the film, he was now editing it—and as long as I was there Porter did his own cutting."

Folsey says that Porter, burdened with multiple duties, decided that he needed an assistant cameraman. For some reason he hired a complete novice, a man named Arthur Lane, a down-on-his-luck diamond salesman married to Porter's secretary. It was the first time that the job of assistant cameraman existed at Famous Players, and previously Porter and the other cameramen even carried their own equipment. Lane turned out to be hopeless, Folsey says, and was soon fired. Porter gave his job to another office boy, Joseph Goodrich, who later became one of Paramount's top cinematographers.

Zukor had urged Porter to turn the photography over to others, feeling it was below his position as production chief, but Porter could not bring himself to give up his first love. However, he did bring many other cameramen into the studio—H. Lyman Broening (to whom Folsey became a sixteen-year-old assistant), Hal Young, William C. Marshall, Emmet Williams, and others.

Folsey thinks Porter grew increasingly unhappy at Famous Players. "I remember coming into Mr. Zukor's office to announce a caller," says Folsey. "He was having a bitter argument with Mr. Porter, who was quite agitated. As I entered, Mr. Porter said, 'I haven't any authority here anymore —why, I couldn't fire an office boy!'" Folsey feared that he was the subject of discussion, but soon afterward Porter gave him a $2 weekly increase in salary. (H. Lyman Broening thinks that Porter greatly resented Zukor's policy of placing numerous relatives on the studio payroll regardless of their qualifications.)

The office boy was frequently sent for Porter's lunch or dinner to a Chinese restaurant on 27th Street, always with instructions to bring back several Pittsburgh stogies, a cheap, foul-smelling cigar that Porter enjoyed. (He would also fetch John Barrymore's meals from the plush Castle Cove Restaurant on Seventh Avenue.) Folsey recalls that Porter often worked late into the night in his laboratory or darkroom at the studio. Each evening after dinner the top executives—Zukor, Porter, Frohman, Dawley, Al Kaufman, and sometimes Mary Pickford and her mother—would gather to look at the rushes from the previous day's work, or to discuss production problems. Some of these sessions were held in Frohman's office behind the balcony of the Lyceum Theatre.

The early fiasco with Lily Langtry had convinced Porter that the famous names of Broadway, by and large, would never become leading screen favorites. He and Zukor frequently clashed on this point, and Porter complained that many of the expensive stage properties purchased by the studio —such as A Good Little Devil—were totally unsuited for filming. He believed Famous Players should develop its own stars, younger men and women with fresh personalities and youthful looks,

and pointed out that thousands of dollars in high salaries could be saved. At Porter's insistence, he was permitted to establish a permanent stock company whose members were used in low-budget pictures and in supporting roles in the more expensive films. Some of the initial players included House Peters, Harold Lockwood, Lois Meredith, Elmer Booth, Betty Harte, Peter Lang, Marie Leonhard, Hal Clarendon, Lorraine Huling, and Walter Craven. Only Peters and Lockwood achieved any real success.

However, Porter could not persuade Zukor to abandon his faith in "famous [Broadway] players in famous plays." Despite the lukewarm reception of many stage luminaries, their films did well financially, and Famous Players was realizing profits of $30,000 to $50,000 each on most pictures. Porter and Zukor quarreled over the signing of May Irwin, a stout, elderly comedienne in the Marie Dressler manner, who failed dismally in movies. (Miss Irwin was one of the first actresses to appear in motion pictures—in Edison's The Kiss, with John C. Rice, a ten-second film of 1896 that shocked the nation's clergymen.) Others who did poorly at Famous Players were Maclyn Arbuckle, Carlotta Nilsson, William H. Crane, Gaby Deslys, and Hazel Dawn. Of all the stage performers that Zukor signed, only Marguerite Clark, Pauline Frederick, and William Farnum had any lasting screen success.

After their return from Europe, Porter and Ford collaborated on The Prince and the Pauper (1915), a lavishly mounted version of Mark Twain's popular classic. It was a major hit for Marguerite Clark, Mary Pickford's only rival at the studio, and gave Porter an opportunity to create precise double exposures and split-screen effects for her dual role.

Porter and Ford then codirected four pictures with Pauline Frederick, following her success in The Eternal City with Sold; Zaza; Bella Donna; and Lydia Gilmore. Sold (1915) was a silly thing about a wife who posed nude for an artist to obtain money for her husband's career; their marriage is nearly wrecked when he suspects her of infidelity.

Zaza (1915) was based on David Belasco's hit play, which had starred Mrs. Leslie Carter on Broadway. Miss Frederick took the title role of a

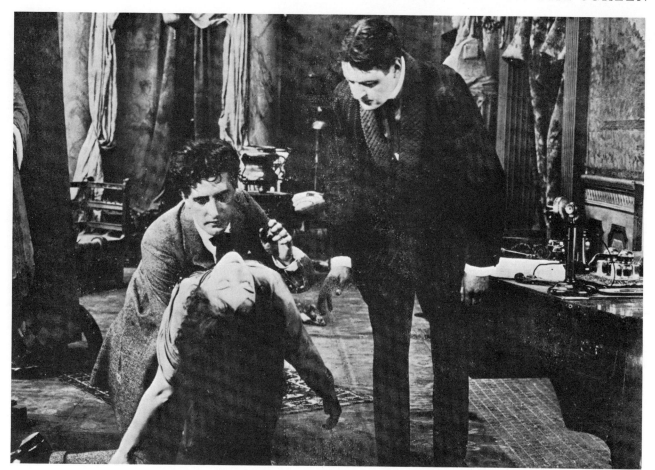

Sold (1915), codirected by Edwin S. Porter and Hugh
Ford, cast Thomas Holding, Pauline Frederick, and
Julian L'Estrange in a drama of marital infidelity.

Paris music-hall singer who falls in love with a
married man and sets out to wreck him. *Bella
Donna* (1915), taken from Robert Hichens's best-
selling novel and a popular play with Nazimova,
was a lurid tale of an unprincipled adventuress
who tries to kill her husband so she can marry a
rich sheik. Porter's last film, *Lydia Gilmore*, was
released early in 1916. It was another tearjerker
in which Pauline Frederick was a doctor's wife
who tried to shield her philandering husband from
a murder charge.

Porter's growing disenchantment with Famous
Players came to a head after the disastrous fire
that gutted the 26th Street studio on September
18, 1915. Much of his experimental work in wide-
screen film was destroyed, and Porter had no heart
to try and rebuild a new studio. When he told
Zukor he wanted out, the company offered to buy
his stock for $800,000. In November 1915, Porter

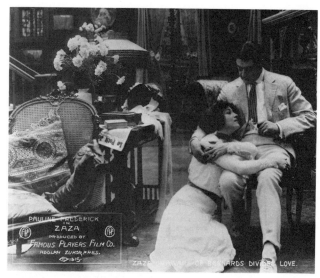

Pauline Frederick and Julian L'Estrange had the leads
in *Zaza* (1915), based on David Belasco's hit play. It
was one of Porter's last films as a director.

left Famous Players, bringing to an end fifteen years as the motion picture's leading director, second only to D. W. Griffith.

He was then free to enjoy his wealth—Porter was reputed to be worth over a million dollars— and to tinker endlessly with his many inventions. He bought an expensive Rolls-Royce and a handsome country home in upstate New York where he could hunt and fish. At the time, he told friends he would never return to film production.

A substantial portion of the proceeds from his Famous Players stock was invested in the Precision Machine Company, which manufactured the Simplex Projector that he and Frank Cannock had invented. This firm was an outgrowth of the Multi-Speed Shutter Company, which manufactured the first Simplex, and was originally financed by James A. Stillman, a New York banker. More than $80,000 was poured into the factory by the time the first Simplex came off the production line.

A few months after his departure from Famous Players, Porter was named president of Precision Machine Company. He was a capable promoter and businessman, and under his direction the firm became the leading manufacturer of motion-picture projectors. In 1917, Porter designed an inexpensive, lightweight 35mm camera, also known as the Simplex. It was intended for sale to exhibitors, who were encouraged to make their own weekly newsreel of local community happenings. However, very few of these cameras were made or sold.

In 1921, Porter and his former associate in 3-D experiments, W. E. Waddell, formed Pordell Projectors, Inc., which was capitalized at $100,000. It manufactured a small projector for still pictures, which could be mounted with an ordinary flashlight, but the device was not successful. Porter's brother, E. M. Porter, served as president of the organization. During the 1920s, Edwin S. Porter resumed his talking-picture experiments—he had worked off and on in trying to solve the problems of synchronization since the *Parsifal* fiasco of 1904 —but again nothing came of his efforts.

Precision Machine Company was merged with other companies in 1925 to form International Projector Company, at which time Porter resigned as president. Later, he invented a pocket-size 16mm movie camera that was manufactured by International. While working on this invention, Porter

Edwin S. Porter in 1922, several years after he gave up directing to devote his time to inventing and perfecting motion-picture equipment.

came to the Paramount studio in Astoria, asking to see a clutch then in use on their cameras. George J. Folsey, by then head of the Photography Department, was aghast to find Porter had been kept waiting in a common reception room of the studio he had helped to establish.

The details of Edwin S. Porter's later years are obscure. He was reported to have lost his fortune in the 1929 stock market crash, although Adolph Zukor seems to doubt this. Other friends, including H. Lyman Broening, think that Porter was able to retain some of his money. Porter became more and more of a recluse as the years went by, conducting his experiments in a small New York machine shop. At one time he was involved in a motion-picture equipment store, and was also reported to have been in the retail coal business for a time. The story that he worked as a salaried mechanic in an appliance shop is questionable.

In his last years Porter lived at the Taft Hotel near Times Square in New York. H. Lyman Broening visited him there about 1940, and found Porter quite feeble after a slight stroke. At the time he was experimenting with a preloaded film magazine for still cameras, and he had been interested in the use of cassettes for home movie cameras as early as the 1920s. In the same year of Broening's visit, Porter told a reporter for the New York *Times* that he rarely went to movies and felt the initiative and excitement had gone out of film-making.

Edwin S. Porter died in New York on April 30, 1941, at the age of seventy-one. Only the New York *Herald-Tribune* noted the passing of this great motion-picture pioneer.

4

Louis Wolheim

BY his own admission, Louis Wolheim was "the ugliest son of a bitch in the world."

His face was his fortune. The mashed nose broken in college football, powerful, massive shoulders, and squinting pig-eyes gave him a brutish appearance. On Broadway and in motion pictures he played killers, wife-beaters, executioners, sadists, prizefighters, stokers, gangsters, and tough soldiers. Yet, he wanted to play romantic leads, and in 1927 was restrained by a court order, sought by a Hollywood producer, from undergoing plastic surgery on his face.

Wolheim's private life, at least in later years, was the antithesis of the rough characters he portrayed on the screen. He was scholarly, soft-spoken, and gentle, and never seen in Hollywood's plush social circles. But it was not always so, for he loved to fight and drink, and once, in front of the Astor Hotel in Times Square, it took four policemen swinging nightsticks to arrest him.

He spoke five languages (including some Yiddish), was a brilliant mathematician, and often said his only ambition was to be a Ph.D. and teach in a quiet university town. He was versed in philosophy and history, worked several years as a mining engineer, and spent his spare time writing plays and poetry. If legend can be believed, he was also a gun runner in the Mexican Revolution of 1910.

Today, Louis Wolheim is best remembered as the war-weary Katczinsky of *All Quiet on the Western Front* (1930), an old soldier who, despite the hard veneer that four years in the trenches of World War I has given him, cannot bear to see a succession of callow young men die in a senseless struggle. In this portrayal, as in most of his roles, there was a tender compassion that overcame his striking homeliness.

CORNELL, MEXICO, AND FIRST BIT ROLES

Louis Robert Wolheim was born in New York City on March 28, 1881. His parents were Jews of Polish-German extraction, and his father, Elias, seems to have followed a variety of small occupations. Wolheim was an excellent student, fascinated by mathematics and languages, and in 1903 received a Bachelor of Science degree from City College of New York. Part of his tuition was earned by prizefighting, but he gave it up when his parents objected.

Wolheim moved on to Cornell University at Ithaca, New York, where he played football, and was graduated in 1906 with a degree in Mechanical Engineering. He worked briefly for a Manhattan engineering firm, but was fired when he walked into the office smoking a cigarette. Wolheim then returned to Ithaca, where he remained for four years. He did some graduate work at Cornell in

For a chronic villain, Louis Wolheim was positively pleasant in this 1930 portrait.

once before in a prizefight, and in the absence of proper surgical care remained mashed to his face —the source of his ultimate fame and fortune!

Another Cornell alumnus recalls Wolheim as "something of a bum" in his Ithaca days, a heavy drinker always ready for a brawl. Yet another terms him an *agent provocateur* who loved to stir up trouble. He remembers Wolheim as the ringleader of a riot that erupted after a Cornell football victory. Dozens of undergraduates swarmed downtown, built a huge bonfire in the middle of State Street, and mixed it up with the police. Wolheim, grinning fiendishly, was content to direct the fray from the safety of a telephone pole, shouting encouragement and battle orders.

Wolheim was uncomfortable in university circles, and preferred to associate with the newspapermen, prizefighters, traveling salesmen, and passing actors who frequented the Dutch Kitchen bar of the Ithaca Hotel. His tutoring was also done there, over several steins of strong beer, but with great efficiency. "I still remember what clear, effective, and understandable explanations of physics were put out by Lou Wolheim," said Francis W. Parker, Jr., one of his students. The evening usually ended with Wolheim thoroughly drunk, telling fanciful tales of an imaginary childhood in Russia or Germany—which probably accounts for some sources listing his birthplace in one of those countries. His favorite story was of how he trudged through the snows of Siberia with a cask of vodka on one shoulder and a side of bear meat on the other, for which reason he acquired the physique of a gorilla!

One of the Cornell students whom Wolheim tutored was the scion of a wealthy Castillian family, and he proposed they go to Mexico to seek a lost gold mine. During an interview while appearing on Broadway as a Mexican general in *The Broken Wing* in 1920, the actor spun a lurid yarn of his experiences south of the border. While looking for the gold mine (which they never found), Wolheim and his companion were captured by bandits and held for $100,000 ransom—or so Wolheim said—but the pair managed to escape. Another version is that his friend was tortured and killed by the outlaws. At any rate, Wolheim decided to remain in Mexico, and he got a job as an engineer for an American mining company.

The Mexican Revolution then intervened, and

1906-07, possibly with the intention of getting a Ph.D., but mostly he worked as a tutor for lagging students and as a clerk at the cigar counter of the Ithaca Hotel. For a short time he taught at Cornell Preparatory School.

A growing legend about Wolheim's Ithaca days has sprung up, and it is difficult to separate fact from fiction. Although he played on Cornell's Big Red football teams of 1904-05, he was not the star fullback, as has often been written, but a substitute second-stringer. "Wollie was sent in just to frighten the opponents with that ugly face of his," says a former classmate. "He was strong as an ox and had huge shoulders, but he wasn't fast enough to be a star player."

While trying out for the Cornell team, Wolheim broke his nose in a scrimmage. It had been broken

Wolheim eased into it as a messenger for the insurgent leader, Francisco Madero. Many of the Maderists lived in El Paso, Texas, but had extensive interests in Chihuahua. Wolheim, in need of extra money, was approached to carry cash and messages to the revolutionists. He traveled openly on the railroad, which was controlled by the Diaz government, and pretended to be (or actually was) slightly drunk. The money was sewed into the lining of his coat, which he casually tossed over the back of his seat. Later, he helped the Maderists move 20,000 rounds of ammunition from Chihuahua to a ranch several miles away by concealing it in crates used to ship gasoline. Government spies were everywhere, but Wolheim was never caught.

Although Wolheim did spend more than two years in Mexico (1910-12), it is impossible to say whether the stories of his adventures are true, or are just some of the tales he loved to tell later. Another story, repeated in his obituary in the New York *Times*, but untrue, is that he served in the U.S. Cavalry and was with General John J. "Black Jack" Pershing in the punitive expedition against the bandit chief, Pancho Villa. By that time—1916 —Wolheim was acting in motion pictures in New York.

Late 1912 found Wolheim back in Ithaca, again clerking at the cigar counter of the Ithaca Hotel and tutoring Cornell students on the side—"there was a line the length of Quarry Street when it was learned Wolheim was tutoring again," says a friend. Earlier that year, two pioneer moviemakers, Theodore and Leopold Wharton—later the directors of such celebrated serials as *The Mysteries of Myra* and *Patria*—came to Ithaca to photograph a Cornell sporting event. Impressed by the lush natural surroundings of the area, they returned the following summer (1913) to film dramas and comedies for Essanay. Cornell's professors grew accustomed to seeing the stars, Francis X. Bushman and Beverly Bayne, using a part of the campus as a set. The Whartons were headquartered at Ithaca for five years, off and on, producing independently for release by Pathé and other companies.

Ithaca townspeople and Cornell students were occasionally recruited as extras for mob scenes. Wolheim, short of money, made his screen debut as an Indian in a Wharton film shot on July 9, 1914. Over the next year he appeared as an extra

in several other pictures, and played his first bit as a policeman in *The Warning*, a Wharton effort released in November 1914. It was his first identifiable screen role.

LIONEL BARRYMORE AND BROADWAY

The real impetus to Wolheim's acting career came from Lionel Barrymore, who was in Ithaca to appear as the villain in a Pearl White serial, *The Romance of Elaine*. There are several stories of their first meeting. One is that Barrymore encountered him in a bar, and intrigued by Wolheim's massive build, challenged him to a wrestling match. Legend has it that they struggled on the barroom floor for hours before declaring the bout a draw! A more likely story is that Barrymore, buying cigars from Wolheim at the Ithaca Hotel, was struck by his ugliness and urged him to try acting. As Barrymore told a friend, S. E. Hunkin: "I used to stand and look in complete wonderment at that face and say to myself, 'What a fortune here, if he could only act!' " (Wolheim himself, in a curious interview published in *Theatre* magazine in 1926, asserted he first met Barrymore in a bar on the Mexican border in 1910.)

The Ithaca days were the beginning of a lifelong friendship between Lionel Barrymore and Louis Wolheim. Attracted by each other's bohemian wit and intelligence, they spent much time together. Many Cornellians remember Barrymore as somewhat reticent and a bit surly, and given to playing the piano alone in his hotel suite for hours at a time. *The Romance of Elaine* was finished in May 1915, and Barrymore returned to Manhattan. A few months later, Wolheim—after playing several bit parts in the Whartons' comedy series, *The New Adventures of J. Rufus Wallingford*—left Ithaca for New York, where Barrymore kept a promise to get him work as an actor. He was an extra in several films that Barrymore made at a Fort Lee, New Jersey, studio for Metro release, and was soon playing bit roles, mostly villains, in such Barrymore pictures as *The Brand of Cowardice* (1916) and *The Millionaire's Double* (1917).

Wolheim was often seen as a frequent drinking companion of both Lionel and John Barrymore, and also in a coterie of Russian and Polish friends. He could speak fluent Russian, and until his death had a circle of acquaintances—mostly artists, actors, dancers, and writers—who were refugees from the Bolshevik revolution.

At Ithaca, Wolheim had been earning $30 a week, and for a time in New York his earnings were considerably less. He said later it was an extremely hard time financially for him. He pieced out his acting income with odd jobs, once as a furniture mover, but friends suspect part of his money came from his parents.

His film appearances in 1917-19 were unimportant. In many pictures he was little more than an extra, and often was not credited in the cast. Wolheim appeared with Barrymore in *The End of the Tour* (1917), and through Lionel's influence got a small part in sister Ethel's *The Eternal Mother* (1917). He was the villain who menaced Harold Lockwood in a cheap Western, *The Avenging Trail* (1918), and was a one-eyed pirate who kidnapped Peggy Hyland in *Peg O' the Pirates* (1918). He did two serials, appearing as one of a gang of crooks who tried to gain control of Pearl White's munitions factory in *The House of Hate* (1918). Director Donald MacKenzie, who did much of *The Perils of Pauline*, hired him for *The Carter Case*, a low-budget fifteen-episode chapterplay of 1919, with Herbert Rawlinson and Marguerite Marsh in the leads. He was billed as "Louie" Wolheim.

The Barrymores were urging Wolheim to try the stage, and he began to see all the Broadway plays, using passes supplied by a growing number of actor-friends. He also began voice and acting lessons under a teacher recommended by Lionel, but was an irregular and impatient pupil.

In the spring of 1919, Wolheim tried out for the important role of Gabriello in *The Jest*, which John and Lionel Barrymore were doing for producer Arthur Hopkins. He had a bad case of stage-fright and could not speak above a whisper, and the part went to Walter P. Richmond. The play opened on April 19 to good notices and ran until June 14, when it laid off for the summer due to lack of air-conditioning at the Plymouth Theatre. When *The Jest* reopened on September 19, Wolheim had succeeded Alexander F. Frank in the lesser role of executioner. He did not appear until

the third act, and had only a few words to speak. The part was tailor-made for Wolheim's brutish appearance, and he made the most of a realistic fight scene in which he and Lionel Barrymore slammed each other about the stage.

Wolheim's several months in *The Jest* gave him needed confidence, and Lionel selected him for a small role in his next play, *The Letter of the Law*, a melodrama that opened at the Criterion Theatre on February 23, 1920. It was only moderately successful. Wolheim went unnoticed by the critics, who reserved their praise for Barrymore, Clarence Derwent, Maud Hosford, and Doris Rankin (Lionel's wife at the time).

His first real Broadway success came as a colorful bandit chief in a banana republic in *The Broken Wing*, which premiered at the 48th Street Theatre on November 29, 1920. George Abbott, later the distinguished stage director, Mary Worth, and Inez Plummer had the leads. Wolheim's Mexican adventures paid dividends because he played the role with an authentic accent and much native swagger. In a rather egotistical interview for one with such limited acting experience, he proclaimed that "any actor who goes before the footlights with a dialect that he has not painstakingly studied is cheating his audience as certainly as the unscrupulous gambler cheats his victim with marked cards." The New York run of *The Broken Wing* was followed by an Eastern tour of several weeks. He greatly enjoyed the changing experiences of the road, and was struck by the differences in audiences from city to city.

Wolheim's newfound stage success brought him a good income for the first time in his life, and he began to dress fashionably and live in the better hotels. He was still acting during the day in movies made in and around New York, and while his growing Broadway reputation earned him better film roles, he would still indiscriminately accept very small bit parts.

He appeared in support of Francis X. Bushman and Beverly Bayne in Metro's *A Pair of Cupids* (1918), menaced Harry Morey in Vitagraph's *The Darkest Hour* (1919), and was seen in a lighter role in Metro's *The Belle of the Season* (1919). The latter film, a sophisticated comedy with Emmy Wehlen, had been on the shelf for more than a year, and its release was apparently delayed after the death of its director and co-star, S. Rankin Drew, who was killed in France during World War I. Wolheim's parts as gangsters in two of George Walsh's acrobatic adventures of 1920, *A Manhattan Knight* and *Number 17*, were extremely small. His first significant screen appearance was in John Barrymore's *Dr. Jekyll and Mr. Hyde* (1920) as the proprietor of a low dive that Hyde frequents.

In George Fitzmaurice's *Experience* (1921), a confused morality play in a modern setting, Wolheim played the symbolical role of Crime. An-

other Ithacan, Edna Wheaton, who had won a New York *Daily News* beauty contest, was also in the cast. Richard Barthelmess was the star. There is a glimpse of Wolheim at the climax of D. W. Griffith's *Orphans of the Storm* (1921) as the executioner who straps Lillian Gish into the guillotine. Griffith, to whom he had been introduced by Lionel Barrymore, persuaded Wolheim to do the bit in the familiar drama of the French Revolution. Naked to the waist, Wolheim's brutish appearance gave the scene a terrifying impact, although he was on the screen only a few seconds.

Louis Wolheim played the proprietor of a Limehouse dive frequented by John Barrymore (right), as the evil Mr. Hyde, in Paramount's 1920 version of *Dr. Jekyll and Mr. Hyde*.

He had a good role as one of the villains who stalked John Barrymore in *Sherlock Holmes* (1922), for which location scenes were shot in England. A superb cast included Carol Dempster (in one of her few non-Griffith appearances), William Powell, Roland Young, Reginald Denny, Hedda Hopper, and Gustav von Seyffertitz, who was ideally cast as Holmes's archenemy, Professor Moriarty. Wolheim was little more than an extra in *Determination* (1922), a cheap film starring the aging Maurice Costello.

Wolheim was back on Broadway in *The Fair Circassian*, an incredible turkey that opened on December 6, 1921, and closed after seven performances. Dennis King, Margaret Mower, and comedian Harry Green had the leads. Only a week after its demise—on December 20—Wolheim turned up in the cast of *The Idle Inn*, a play that he and

D. W. Griffith was struck by Wolheim's remarkable ugliness and used him in *Orphans of the Storm* (1921 and *America* (1924). Photo taken on the set of *Drums of Love* in 1927.

Isaac Goldberg had fashioned from a Jewish folktale by Peretz Hirshbein. At the last moment one of the actors had fallen ill, and Wolheim stepped into the part. Arthur Hopkins, with whom Wolheim was to develop a long personal and professional friendship, was the producer. The cast of *The Idle Inn* included a great favorite of the Yiddish theater, Jacob Ben-Ami, and the fast-rising Edward G. Robinson.

The Idle Inn was not Wolheim's first effort as a playwright. Earlier in 1921, he and Edward Delaney Dunn had adapted a successful French play, *La Griffe*, by Henri Bernstein (a paramour of showgirl Peggy Hopkins Joyce). Arthur Hopkins presented it on Broadway as *The Claw*, and it had a long run with Lionel Barrymore in the lead. (Not only was Barrymore's wife, Doris Rankin, in the cast, but it also included Irene Fenwick, eventually to become Lionel's second wife.)

The extent of Wolheim's part in the writing of *The Claw* is now difficult to determine. At the time, Edward Delaney Dunn was a brilliant young Harvard architectural student with a passionate interest in the theatre. He was neglecting his studies to try his hand at writing plays, and was originally commissioned by producer Jake Shubert to adapt *The Claw*. When the play tried out in Boston, Dunn was appalled to find the program credit, "adapted by Louis Wolheim," and no mention of himself. He protested to Shubert, who had sold the rights to Arthur Hopkins, and when *The Claw* opened on Broadway, it carried the credit "adapted by Edward Delaney Dunn and Louis Wolheim." Although Dunn contends he could find no evidence of Wolheim's work, his version was apparently given a rewrite by Wolheim at Hopkins's request. The two collaborators, Wolheim and Dunn, never met personally. (Dunn became a distinguished architect, and authored two books and several plays, including *The Red Robe; Midnight; The End of the World;* and *The Last Waltz.*)

Wolheim continued to write, off and on, but none of his subsequent plays was produced. He even turned out a few movie scenarios, which did not sell, although one, *History Repeats Itself— Even in Rome*, written in collaboration with Philip Hart Dunning, was published in book form in 1930.

Louis Wolheim reached stardom with his stunning performance in Eugene O'Neill's *The Hairy Ape*, which opened at the Provincetown Theatre in Greenwich Village on March 9, 1922. Described by one critic as "a striking dramatic novelty," it told of a paranoid brute who worked as a stoker in the hold of a transatlantic steamship. He becomes involved with a thrill-seeking debutante, and when she finally rejects him, the stoker goes berserk and is killed when he climbs into the cage of a giant gorilla in a zoo.

Wolheim had been introduced to O'Neill by Lionel Barrymore several years earlier. The playwright could not forget Wolheim's striking ugliness, and when he expanded an unpublished short story of 1917 into *The Hairy Ape*, he visualized Wolheim in the role of Yank Smith, the stoker. Because of the significance of the character's physical repulsiveness, O'Neill was apprehensive about approaching Wolheim, and finally sent Charles Light, a director for Arthur Hopkins, to offer him the part. Far from being offended, Wolheim was delighted to accept.

The reviews of *The Hairy Ape* were lukewarm, although a few critics raved about it. Wolheim's performance was highly praised. After its run in Greenwich Village, *The Hairy Ape* moved to Broadway where Carlotta Monterey, soon to be Eugene O'Neill's wife, assumed the feminine lead. She delighted in playing pranks and practical jokes on Wolheim, which he also found amusing. Following its New York run, Wolheim toured with *The Hairy Ape*. It continued to meet a mixed reception, particularly in the smaller towns, and he was annoyed when less sophisticated audiences snickered at the play's bizarre climax.

Wolheim was affected by the depressing part, and he became moody and argumentive, and on several occasions got into fights (usually over imagined criticisms of his acting). Friends felt he was trying to live up to a tough-guy image, and urged him to be less hostile, fearing that with his powerful strength he might seriously injure or perhaps kill someone. Wolheim took their advice, and from that time, a period of great personal stress, he mellowed and became more gentle as the years went by. Recalling the actor in the 1920s, S. E. Hunkin says: "He was not a friendly fellow, and no doubt had many frustrations in his lifetime."

THE CONTRACT WITH HEARST

After his success in *The Hairy Ape*, Wolheim signed a one-year contract with William Randolph Hearst's Cosmopolitan Productions, then based in a Harlem studio and releasing through Paramount and Goldwyn. Hearst admired Wolheim's portrayal of Yank Smith, although he disliked O'Neill's play for its frank language.

The first of the Hearst films, *The Face in the Fog* (1922), reunited Wolheim with Lionel Barrymore, who played Boston Blackie, the reformed thief. It was an action-packed melodrama about Blackie's efforts to help a beautiful Russian noblewoman (Seena Owen) recover some stolen royal jewels. Wolheim was a swarthy revolutionist who had a rousing fight with Barrymore, reminiscent of their fight scene in *The Jest*. Lowell Sherman and Gustav von Seyffertitz were in the cast, and Alan Crosland, a great favorite of both John and Lionel Barrymore, directed. In *The Go-Getter* (1923), Peter B. Kyne's story of a crippled war hero (T. Roy Barnes) determined to make good, Wolheim played a straight character role. Seena Owen was again the girl.

His best part in 1923 was as Kid Hogan, a brutal prizefighter known as "The Hoboken Terror," in Marion Davies's *Little Old New York*, a drama of the first steamboat. In the climactic scene, Wolheim attempted to horsewhip Miss Davies—she was disguised as a young boy—but was given a sound thrashing by the hero (Harrison Ford). He brought many comic touches to the role. *Unseeing Eyes* (1923), partially filmed on location in the Canadian snow country, had Wolheim as "Frozen Face Laird," a vicious trapper who attempts to loot a silver mine owned by a beautiful girl (Seena Owen) and her brother (Walter Miller). He was again given his comeuppance by Lionel Barrymore, a daredevil aviator. The film had many exciting flying scenes. Wolheim described the character he played as "the sort of man who every time he saw a head he wanted to give it a wallop!"

Wolheim was cast in another Lionel Barrymore vehicle for Hearst-Cosmopolitan, *The Enemies of Women* (1923), an overlong version of Vicente Blasco-Ibáñez's novel of the Russian Revolution. Alan Crosland directed many scenes that were later deleted, including all of Wolheim's role. He was seen in two other 1923 films—*Love's Old Sweet Song*, an independent production in which he was a Secret Service agent posing as a tramp to catch a crooked banker, and Metro's *The Last Moment*. In the latter, Wolheim was a maniacal sea captain who shanghaied the hero (Henry Hull) and the heroine (Doris Kenyon). When they tried to escape, Wolheim unleashed an apelike monster called "The Thing" to bring them back, but Hull managed to drown it.

In 1923, Wolheim married Ethel Dane, a talented actress, painter, and sculptress, with whom he had a lasting marriage. Her pet name for the burly actor was "Baby Dear!" There were no children.

Wolheim's next film, *The Uninvited Guest* (1924) was a drama of the South Seas filmed on location in Bermuda. It was one in a series of novelty pictures turned out by J. E. Williamson, a pioneer in underwater photography, and featured many beautiful shots of multicolored fish made in a two-color Technicolor process from a diving bell. Jean Tolley, an unknown who swam well and looked fetching in a grass skirt, and Maurice B. "Lefty" Flynn, a part-time cowboy star, had the leads. Wolheim was a lecherous diver who was crushed to death by a huge octopus.

D. W. Griffith then cast Wolheim as the psychopathic white renegade, Captain Hare, in his Revolutionary War drama, *America* (1924). Lionel Barrymore was the principal villain, the treacherous Captain Walter Butler, and Wolheim was his henchman who incited the Mohawks to massacre white settlers. Few roles offered him such opportunity for unbridled savagery. In the climactic battle he was seen half-naked, in Indian war paint, in scene after scene of bloody violence, including one in which he gouged out the eye of a white captive.

Wolheim worried that his role in *America* was too sadistic, and devoid of any saving grace. "It would seem to me that the villain would be so much more awful to the audience if a contrast of his conduct was made," he told an interviewer. "If they were to portray certain kindly incidents in the life of the villain, he would appear so much worse in his wickedness." He deplored the one-dimensional aspect of Captain Hare, but resignedly said that "in movies there's no time to study the part—I just go out and do what they tell me." Yet, he denied having any theories of acting—"either you can act or you can't."

Louis Wolheim greatly admired D. W. Griffith. In an interview in the New York *Times* (February 3, 1924), he said: "I have a lot of fun working with Mr. Griffith. He has a knack of giving an actor a great deal of scope. The player puts his own individuality into the part, and yet, Mr. Griffith is able to mould the man's impersonation so deftly that the actor is hardly aware of it. In the end Mr. Griffith gains the resources of the actor harnessed to his own ideas or conceptions."

His only other screen appearance in 1924 was in Paramount's *The Story Without a Name*, directed by Irvin V. Willat. It was a lurid melodrama about a young scientist (Antonio Moreno) who invents a "death ray" for the United States Army. Moreno and his sweetheart, Agnes Ayres, are kidnapped by enemy agents (Wolheim and Tyrone Power, Sr.) who want the device, but the couple is conveniently rescued by a Navy submarine. Willat was fascinated by submarines and managed to work one into the plot of several of his pictures. In a publicity tie-in with Paramount while the film was in production, *Photoplay* magazine conducted a contest among readers to select a title. The winner was *Without Warning*, but by that time the picture was so well-publicized as *The Story Without a Name* that Paramount decided to release it under that title.

BACK TO BROADWAY: WHAT PRICE GLORY?

Wolheim's stage work during 1923 was largely confined to touring in *The Hairy Ape*, although he admitted later to tiring of the demanding role. On May 6, 1924, he opened on Broadway in the supporting cast of *Catskill Dutch*, a somber drama of religious hysteria in a small Dutch community in upstate New York during the eighteenth century. Frank McGlynn, who frequently played Abraham Lincoln in both films and on the stage, Kenneth MacKenna, and Minnie Dupree had the leads. *Catskill Dutch* was a flop and closed in a week.

Discouraged by his lagging stage career—Broad-

When Fox made a screen version of *What Price Glory?* in 1926, Louis Wolheim's stage role of Captain Flagg was taken by Victor McLaglen (standing right). Leslie Fenton and Edmund Lowe are doughboys at left.

way producers said he was hard to cast in leads—Wolheim was considering trying his luck in Hollywood when Arthur Hopkins called to offer him the lead in *What Price Glory?*, a new play of World War I by Laurence Stallings and Maxwell Anderson. It was, Hopkins said, the opportunity of a lifetime for Wolheim—and so it proved to be. He gave a superlative performance as Captain Flagg, a hard-boiled Marine officer who accepts the degrading experiences of war with gentle wit and irony.

What Price Glory? opened at the Plymouth Theatre on September 3, 1924, to unanimous critical raves. (Alexander Woollcott, in a paroxysm of enthusiasm, offered to bet Charles MacArthur $500 that it would run for a hundred years.) Laced with salty dialogue and comedy situations, it was built around the endless bickering of two tough Marines, Captain Flagg and Sergeant Quirt (played by William "Stage" Boyd), usually over a woman. *What Price Glory?* was a realistic and derisive look at war, born largely out of Stallings's experiences in France—he had lost a leg in the Argonne—with none of the romantic jingoism that marred many of the Broadway war plays of the early 1920s.

The bitter irony of *What Price Glory,* was best expressed in Wolheim's performance. He had much in common with Captain Flagg—a rough surface that shielded a deep understanding of human nature, intelligence, a basic tenderness, and a frustration derived of deserving more than he received.

What Price Glory? firmly established Wolheim as a gifted actor, rewarding him with the elusive acclaim he had sought in eight discouraging years on the stage and in films. The play would tie him up for most of two years, It ran 299 performances on Broadway, and Wolheim then took it on a triumphant nationwide tour to sellout audiences. He stopped off at Ithaca to renew old acquaintances, and became a frequent speaker before Cornell alumni groups, where he was usually introduced as an ex-Cornell professor of mathematics—an impression he seldom bothered to correct. "Are you sorry you gave up the quiet of a professor's life for this?" he was asked in Chicago. "It's a great life," Wolheim answered. "You never know what you are going to do next. Nothing is determined in advance. No! No professors for me, thank you—not now." But in Cleveland he said, "If it hadn't been for Lionel Barrymore, I would be happy today, teaching mathematics for a couple of thousand a year."

The tour of *What Price Glory?* was punctuated by frequent drinking parties. Wolheim would consume enormous quantities of bootleg liquor, yet always appear cold sober for each performance. An old friend from the Ithaca days entertained the cast one weekend in Cleveland, and he recalls that Wolheim spent most of two days drinking and holding forth in the host's kitchen, conducting philosophical discussions, spinning imaginary tales of his childhood, or acting out bits of plays and films. The group finished off eleven quarts of Scotch smuggled in from Canada, of which Wolheim drank three by himself. "When I saw the play on Monday evening, Wolheim never could have been better," his friend recalls. "Yet, when I went backstage to congratulate him, he wanted to come home with me and resume the party."

In addition to speaking to Cornell alumni clubs, Wolheim became a frequent guest for various drama groups, particularly at the informal luncheons of the New York Drama League. At the latter, in 1925, he attacked radio broadcasting as a threat to the theatre, and said radio was "soulless" and "without personality." The following year, he told the Drama League that producers who sell purity and pander to smugness, complacency, and self-satisfaction were more dangerous than the producers who sell dirt. Yet, in the same speech, he was equally critical of plays with a message, and asserted the theatre should be solely "the home of entertainment and emotional release."

In March 1925, while he was still appearing on Broadway in *What Price Glory?,* Wolheim was signed by Henri Diamant-Berger for a role in *Lover's Island,* starring Hope Hampton and James Kirkwood. The distinguished French director (*The Three Musketeers; Boubouroche*) had established an independent studio, Diamant Films, at Fort Lee, New Jersey, with financing by Jules E. Brulatour, the multimillionaire distributor of Eastman film stock. Part of the deal was that Miss Hampton, Brulatour's ambitious wife, was to star in several features, although the director did others with such performers as Lionel Barrymore, Owen Moore, and a young Constance Bennett.

Lover's Island, which was not released until 1926 (by Associated Exhibitors), was a poor picture, due largely to a confused script and Miss Hampton's noticeable lack of talent. Wolheim played a vengeful sea captain who tracked down the man who raped his daughter. Diamant-Berger was fond of Wolheim, and described him as "a well-educated gentleman, extremely cooperative, and easy to direct." He was impressed by the actor's fluent French and knowledge of French drama and literature, and the two had long discussions between work. Later, Diamant-Berger tried to get Wolheim for another film, but the dates could not be worked out.

In May 1926, Wolheim was engaged to co-star with Billie Burke in *Pardon My Glove,* a new play by Zoë Akins. He portrayed a rough Italian whose financial cunning made him a millionaire. Beset by desire for another man's wife (Miss Burke), he evolves a complicated plan to win her love by ransoming her son from kidnappers that he has hired. Despite a fine cast that included Louis Calhern and Ilka Chase, the play failed miserably in tryouts in Rochester and Cleveland, and was closed before it reached Broadway.

THE HOLLYWOOD YEARS

Early in 1927, Louis Wolheim was brought to Hollywood by Howard Hughes to co-star with William Boyd in *Two Arabian Knights*. The eccentric young millionaire had been dabbling in movies for more than a year, having put $150,000 into *Everybody's Acting*, a gay comedy that his playboy friend, Marshall Neilan, produced and directed for Paramount release with Betty Bronson in the lead. Later, he had been talked into backing *Swell Hogan*, a feature that Ralph Graves, a former leading man for D. W. Griffith (and a comic for Mack Sennett), wrote, produced, directed, and starred in. It was so bad that it was never released.

Despite his reverses with *Swell Hogan*, Hughes set up Caddo Productions, hired a bright young man with an Oxford degree—John W. Considine, Jr.—as production supervisor, and embarked upon a program of high-budgeted features for United Artists' release. *Two Arabian Knights* was the first, and to direct Hughes selected the twenty-nine-year-old Lewis Milestone, who had attracted attention with several bright sophisticated comedy dramas

William Boyd (bottom), later famous as Hopalong Cassidy, and Louis Wolheim were two quarreling A.E.F. buddies in *Two Arabian Knights*.

(*Seven Sinners*, 1925; *The New Klondike*, 1926). The picture was originally planned as a straight drama, but Milestone persuaded Hughes to let him make a comedy of it.

The plot of *Two Arabian Knights* concerned two American doughboys, Wolheim and Boyd, who escape from a German prison camp during World War I, and after a series of misadventures wind up in the Middle East. They fight over a pretty Arabian girl (Mary Astor), as well as with a gang of cutthroats headed by her father. Wolheim brought many amusing and sympathetic moments to a role reminiscent of Captain Flagg in *What Price Glory?* Geared strictly for laughs and liberally sprinked with Rabelaisian humor, *Two Arabian Knights* was a huge success in 1927, although it is largely forgotten today. Milestone received an Academy Award for his direction. The film was the beginning of a close friendship between Milestone and Wolheim that lasted until the latter's death.

Wolheim was then cast as the sadistic Sergeant-Major Buck in *Sorrell and Son* (1927), Herbert Brenon's picturization of Warwick Deeping's depressing novel of a father's selfless devotion to his son. He brought delicate shadings to a completely unsympathetic role as an ex-British Tommy who becomes head porter at an English inn. He tyrannizes the hero (H. B. Warner) before being caught

Wolheim played an American soldier again in Lewis Milestone's World War I comedy, *Two Arabian Knights* (1927).

Louis Wolheim and William Boyd, at left, escapees
from a German prison camp in *Two Arabian Knights*
(1927), bribe their way on a steamer bound for Jaffa.

in a sordid affair with a kitchenmaid. Wolheim's
brutality was contrasted by his fawning attempts
to retain the favor of his employer (Norman
Trevor). Brenon took Wolheim and fifteen other
cast members on a hurried trip to England to
shoot authentic backgrounds for *Sorrell and Son*.
An out-and-out tearjerker, it succeeded through
Brenon's sensitive direction and fine performances
by H. B. Warner, Alice Joyce, Nils Asther, Wolheim, and the ill-fated Mary Nolan.

In United Artists' *Tempest* (1928), a drama of
the Russian Revolution, Wolheim was a comedy
sidekick to John Barrymore. The frail plot was
about an army sergeant (Barrymore) who is sent
to jail for offending a nobleman. Freed by the

revolution, he becomes a power in the new regime
and marries a haughty princess (Camilla Horn)
who once laid the whip to him. Wolheim had
some amusing moments when he evens the score
with an aristocrat (Ullrich Haupt) who had tortured him with lighted cigarettes. Poorly constructed and short on action, *Tempest* was beset
by production problems. It was begun by the brilliant Russian director, Viatchelav Tourjansky, who
was removed by producer Joseph M. Schenck—the
previous year Tourjansky had been fired from a
Tim McCoy Western at M-G-M. Lewis Milestone
then took over, but soon gave up in disgust at the
confused script, and the film was finally completed
by Sam Taylor, best known as a comedy director

In this confrontation scene from *Sorrell and Son* (1927) are, left to right, H. B. Warner. Norman Trevor, Louis Wolheim, and Alice Joyce.

Friends since the days of *The Jest* on Broadway, John Barrymore and Louis Wolheim were reunited as Russian soldiers in *Tempest* (1928).

In *Tempest* (1928), John Barrymore and Louis Wolheim were tossed into jail for offending the Russian nobility.

for Harold Lloyd and Mary Pickford.

The Racket (1928) reunited the triumvirate of *Two Arabian Knights*—Hughes, Milestone, and Wolheim—this time in a tense drama of gang wars and political corruption. Wolheim played Nick Scarsi, a ruthless beer baron engaged in a death struggle with a rival bootlegger. He kills a patrolman, and is in turn shot down by an honest police captain (Thomas Meighan). Marie Prevost scored as a hard-boiled gunmoll who deserts her protector. A classic among early gangster films, due largely to Lewis Milestone's punchy direction, *The Racket* was nominated for an Academy Award as the best picture of the year.

As he had in New York, Wolheim frequented a circle of friends drawn from Hollywood's Russian colony. He was often seen at the Russian Club, near Western Avenue in the 1920s, where

Louis Wolheim (second from left) played a kingpin bootlegger in *The Racket* (1928). George E. Stone, to the right of Wolheim, was an unlikely choice as Wolheim's gangster brother.

excellent vodka was served, and at the home of Ivan Mosjoukine, the Russian matinee idol who was doing a film at Universal, *Surrender* (1927). The group frequently included Nikita Balieff of the Chauve-Souris, Broadway producer Morris Gest, director Dimitri Buchowetzki (*Graustark*; *Valencia*), Lewis Milestone, Lionel Barrymore, Viatchelav Tourjansky and his wife, Nathalie Kovanko and her brother, the actor Boris de Fas, and two French actresses, Arlette Marchal and Ginette Maddie—and generals, dukes, and assorted White Russians, many of whom worked as waiters and doormen in the posh Hollywood restaurants.

In Samuel Goldwyn's *The Awakening* (1928), Wolheim was an evil villain who became a reluctant hero. He played a French Army sergeant known as La Bete (The Beast), who was rejected by an Alsatian peasant girl (Vilma Banky). She falls in love with a German officer (Walter Byron), and enters a convent as a novice after he goes off to fight in World War I. Later, she finds her lover wounded, and it is Wolheim who drives them through shot and shell on the battlefield in a wild ride to safety and a predictable happy ending. Except for the exciting climax, the film was slowly paced and lacked the vivid direction that Victor Fleming usually brought to his pictures. *The Awakening* was one of the first postwar movies to treat the German soldier in sympathetic terms.

Louis Wolheim, Walter Byron, and Vilma Banky in a beautifully photographed scene from Victor Fleming's *The Awakening* (1928).

In Pathé's *The Shady Lady* (1928), Wolheim was again a gangster in a role similar to his Nick Scarsi in *The Racket*. Phyllis Haver was the girl who discovered her boyfriend (Robert Armstrong) was a gunrunner. She helps him in an attempt to outwit a powerful rival (Wolheim), but finally persuades Armstrong to go straight. Some of the picture was filmed in Cuba, and the highlight was an exciting gun battle through the streets of Havana. *The Shady Lady* was shot during the last days of the silent era, and after it was completed, Pathé decided to add a musical score and synchronized sound effects. The ending was redone with dialogue, and Wolheim was revealed to have "an ingratiating voice," as one reviewer put it. He stole the scene as he philosophically accepted defeat and went off to prison.

Wolheim's next, *Wolf Song* (1929), was also a silent to which a musical score, several songs (sung by Lupe Velez), and sound effects were added. A drama of the Spanish Southwest in the 1840s, it suffered from an implausible story about a young trapper (Gary Cooper) who left his Mexican wife when he heard "the wolf song"—the call of wanderlust. No one was particularly surprised when Cooper finally returned to Lupe's obvious charms. Wolheim was a delight as a filthy, profane hunter who loved to drink, fight, and leer at women, al-

Louis Wolheim was ill at ease as the rival of Walter Byron (right) for the hand of Vilma Banky in *The Awakening* (1928).

Wolheim was again a gangster, and the striking
Phyllis Haver his moll, in *The Shady Lady* (1928).

though at times he seemed mildly amused by the
whole proceedings. Victor Fleming, of whom Wolheim was quite fond, was again the director.

In Pathé's *Square Shoulders* (1929), a part-
talkie, Wolheim played a drunken bum whose
family believes he died a hero in the trenches of
France. Years later, he returns home to find his
son, Junior Coghlan, selling newspapers and
headed for delinquency. Without revealing his
identity, Wolheim helps the boy to realize his
ambition to attend military school, but the father
dies at the hands of a petty thief. Although cheaply
made and hampered by a lack of love interest,
Square Shoulders was an entertaining family film.
Wolheim was excellent in a sympathetic role, but

encountered tough competition from a gang of
cute kids, including Junior Coghlan, Anita Louise,
Philippe de Lacy, Johnny Morris, Erich von Stroheim, Jr., and Charles F. Riesner, Jr.

Frozen Justice (1929) was a ludicrous tale of
a half-breed Eskimo girl (played by stage star
Lenore Ulric) who yearns for something better
than the igloo. She runs away to Nome with a sea
captain (Ullrich Haupt) and his sadistic first mate
(Wolheim). Haupt kills Wolheim in a fight over
the girl, but meets death at the hands of her Eskimo spouse (Robert Frazer) seeking revenge.
Miss Ulric, nearing forty, was too sophisticated
and exotic for her role, and added to the unreality
of the film by singing several modern ditties

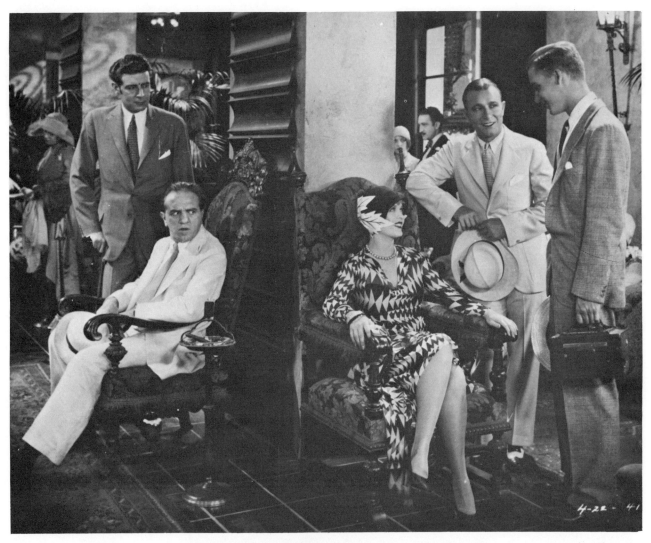

The Shady Lady (1928) was a silent to which a talking sequence was added. In this scene, Wolheim is eavesdropping on Phyllis Haver, Robert Armstrong, and Russell Gleason.

Louis Wolheim and Gary Cooper were two rough trappers in Paramount's *Wolf Song* (1929).

Gary Cooper (left), in a tasteful nude bathing scene
in *Wolf Song* (1929), listens to the bickering of Louis
Wolheim and Constantine Romanoff.

penned by L. Wolfe Gilbert (as well as such old
favorites as "A Bird in a Gilded Cage" and
"Goodbye, Dolly Gray."

Frozen Justice was shot at the Fox studio under
a 100° July sun, and Wolheim and the other actors
sweltered in heavy furs, trying to pretend the gyp-
sum snow was real. The script was much too talky,
and Wolheim and director Allan Dwan sat up most
of one night paring down the excessive dialogue.
Wolheim's villainy was rather ordinary—some critics thought he overacted—and only Dwan's colorful re-creation of Nome in the gold-rush days saved
an otherwise dull picture.

In Samuel Goldwyn's *Condemned* (1929), Wolheim was a murderer confined to Devil's Island.
He helps the hero (Ronald Colman), a convicted
thief, engineer an escape. Ann Harding was the
love interest. Well directed by Wesley Ruggles, it
featured a long chase through the treacherous
jungle as Colman and Wolheim were pursued by
guards. Wolheim was ideally cast, and added a
touch of French accent to his characterization.

M-G-M's *The Ship From Shanghai* (1930) cast
Wolheim as a paranoid steward on a luxury liner
who hated the idle rich. He incites the crew to
mutiny, takes pot-shots at the hero (Conrad Nagel)

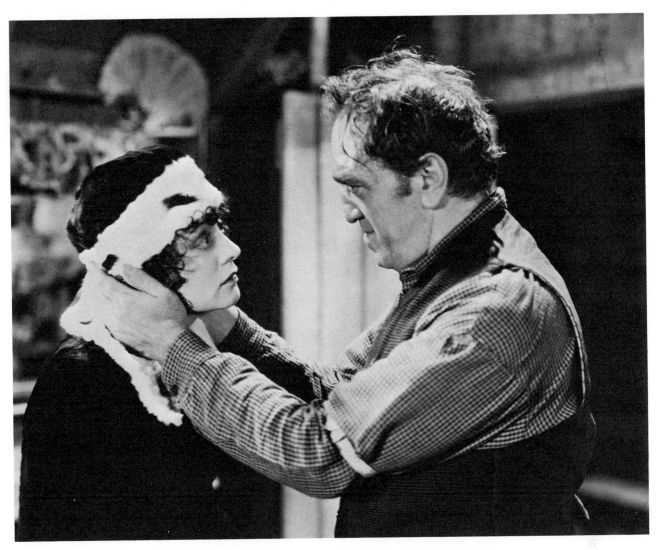

Famed stage star Lenore Ulric was an unlikely Eskimo heroine in Fox's *Frozen Justice* (1929). Wolheim played a sailor who was killed in a fight over the girl.

Louis Wolheim and Ronald Colman escape from Devil's Island in this scene from *Condemned* (1929).

with a pistol, and starves the passengers. Handicapped by some unbelievable dialogue—by John Howard Lawson—the picture had a striking climax when the heroine (Kay Johnson) tells the crazed steward to look into a mirror and see the reason for his rejection. In a scene that recalls *The Hairy Ape*, Wolheim stares into the mirror and realizes the repulsion of his ugliness. He goes berserk and throws himself into the sea. Wolheim seemed uncomfortable in his role and was allowed by director Charles J. Brabin to spend too much time in theatrical leering and skulking about the ship.

ALL QUIET ON THE WESTERN FRONT: THE LAST YEARS

Louis Wolheim's finest screen performance came in Universal's *All Quiet on the Western Front* (1930), a classic film based on Erich Maria Remarque's pacifist novel of a German army decaying in the ravages of defeat. He gave a beautifully low-key portrayal of Militiaman Stanislaus Katczinsky, an old soldier alternately funny with his rough, ironic humor, and touching in a fatherly compassion for the stream of disillusioned youths killed and maimed about him.

After four years in the trenches, Katczinsky can no longer be horrified by the vicious rats that infest the dugout, the feel of a bayonet plunged into a nameless enemy, the maggots of the rotten food, or the cries of the wounded. His flattened nose can sniff the bombardment that is about to commence. He has abandoned any hope of home, and when in the midst of a fierce attack he wishes himself "home," he means only the wretched dugout. He accepts war without question.

Wolheim's disciplined performance was shaded with the right proportions of sentiment, humor, irony, and subdued bitterness, largely conveyed through his expressive face. Although the focus is on the young hero (Lew Ayres), the audience builds a growing sympathy for Kat—from the early scenes when he shepherds the frightened recruits through their first taste of shellfire with derisive jeers, to the final heartbreak of his death in the unforgettable sequence in which Ayres carries the dying Wolheim to a field hospital. The script— by Maxwell Anderson, George Abbott, and Del

Louis Wolheim and Lew Ayres (right) gave stunning performances as the old sergeant and the young soldier in *All Quiet on the Western Front* (1930).

Andrews—gave more comic qualities to Kat than had Remarque's original, but Wolheim integrated them into his performance with measured restraint.

A landmark in the cinema, *All Quiet on the Western Front* was the lasting triumph of its brilliant director, Lewis Milestone, who selected his friend Wolheim for the role of Kat. (Paul Fejos, the Hungarian director, was originally scheduled for the assignment, but was replaced before shooting began, and at one time Erich von Stroheim was considered to direct.) In retrospect, Wolheim would seem the obvious and perhaps only choice for the part, although Carl Laemmle, president of Universal, had mentioned James Murray in an interview at the time the rights to the Remarque novel were purchased. Murray, an unknown who had attracted attention as the bewildered protagonist of King Vidor's *The Crowd* (1928), was a completely illogical choice for Katczinsky.

Lew Ayres, whose sensitive performance in *All Quiet on the Western Front* catapulted him into stardom, has warm memories of Louis Wolheim. "As an actor he was superbly realistic, his personality irreplaceable, unique," Ayres says. "Mr. Wolheim got along very well with everyone, including the young actors of *All Quiet*. His relationship with them was professional, not fatherly or professorial. He was so easy to work with—an understanding, responsive actor."

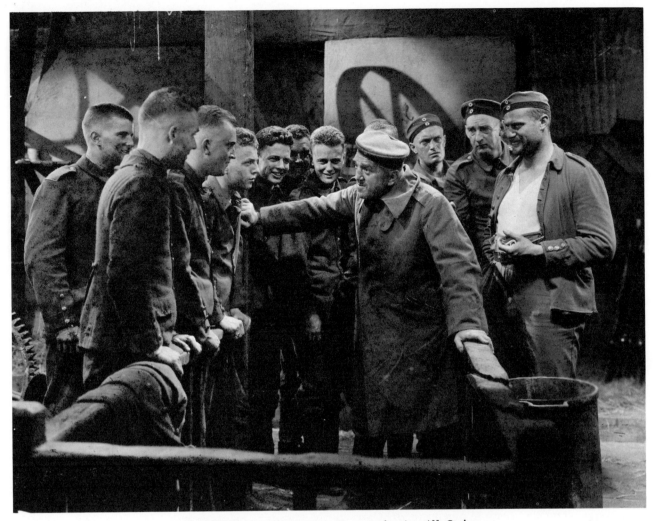

As Militiaman Stanislaus Katczinsky in *All Quiet on the Western Front* (1930), Louis Wolheim gave the portrayal for which he is best remembered. Lew Ayres is at center, with Harold Goodwin, Slim Summerville, and Richard Alexander at right.

Knowing of Ayres's interest in astronomy, Wolheim gave him a rare book on the subject, which Ayres treasured until it was lost in a fire several years later. Ayres remembers that the younger players were in awe of Wolheim's financial prestige—he was making around $4,500 a week, while they were getting a few hundred. Ayres recalls:

He always carried a large sum of cash with him, even in uniform in the trenches on the set, perhaps a thousand or two thousand dollars, saying that he wished to be able to make an immediate purchase of any item that caught his fancy—antiques, objets d'art, etc. He also relished fading all comers in a crap game, usually demolishing the opponents and closing down the game.

Shortly after the completion of *All Quiet on the Western Front*, Wolheim was signed to a one-year contract by William LeBaron, production chief at RKO Radio. The deal specified that Wolheim was to be the star of all films in which he appeared, and that he would be permitted to direct at least one feature.

Wolheim's first at RKO Radio was *Danger*

All the disillusionment of war is etched on the faces of Lew Ayres (left) and Louis Wolheim in *All Quiet on the Western Front* (1930).

Robert Armstrong and Louis Wolheim were rivals in RKO Radio's railroading drama, *Danger Lights* (1930).

Lights (1930), a railroad melodrama filmed in the Natural Vision or Magniscope 3-D process. This system, developed by the Swedish scientist P. John Berggren and financed by early film magnate George K. Spoor (of Essanay Pictures), was more of a wide-screen device utilizing 70mm film, and only gave an illusion of three dimensions. *Danger Lights* played in wide-screen form in only a few large cities, and Spoor claimed later that the Motion Picture Association of America, fearful of the financial involvement for new equipment, pressured RKO Radio into abandoning the 3-D version and releasing it in standard 35mm for most theaters.

Danger Lights, directed by George B. Seitz (whom Wolheim had first met during the Ithaca

days), profited from the novelty of its wide-screen presentations in New York and Chicago, but in conventional width it was less impressive. Many of Seitz's shots, made expressly for 3-D, lost their impact in 35mm, and were boring in their repetitiveness. Wolheim played a railroad superintendent who loses his girl, Jean Arthur, to a young engineer (Robert Armstrong) whom he has rehabilitated after a bout with alcoholism. The finale was a wild ride into Chicago, with Armstrong at the throttle, in an effort to save Wolheim's life after a railroad accident.

The Silver Horde (1930), based on Rex Beach's popular novel, was a red-blooded drama of warfare between two rival salmon fisheries. Director George Archainbaud took the entire company to Alaska, where Leo Tover's cameras caught many breathtaking scenes of natural beauty as well as the annual salmon-spawning run. Wolheim was excellent as the ruthless cannery owner, although he was not well while the film was in production. *The Silver Horde* boasted an exceptional cast— Evelyn Brent, Jean Arthur, Blanche Sweet (fine as a wisecracking dance-hall hostess), Raymond Hatton, Gavin Gordon, and a young Joel McCrea in his first important screen role.

Wolheim made an inauspicious bow as a director with *The Sin Ship* (1931), in which he also starred, his third and last picture under the RKO

Radio contract. He was miscast in a romantic lead opposite Mary Astor, and, as in other pictures in which he undertook a romantic role (*The Awakening; Danger Lights*), he was unbelievable in the love scenes. The absurd plot concerned two crooks (Miss Astor and Ian Keith) posing as missionaries, who reform Wolheim, a hard-bitten sea captain. He becomes deeply religious after falling in love with the girl. There is a mawkish ending in which Miss Astor, inspired by Wolheim's changed life, joins him after Keith is killed by the police. Wolheim's direction of *The Sin Ship* was distinctly pedestrian. Friends felt he was disappointed with the film, and said that he expressed no further desire to direct. His contract with RKO Radio was not renewed.

In M-G-M's *Gentleman's Fate* (1931), his last picture, Wolheim played, of all things, John Gilbert's brother. Gilbert was a snob socialite who discovers his brother and father are rumrunners. He becomes a gangster, loses his girl (Leila Hyams), and is machined-gunned by rival bootleggers. As he dies in Wolheim's arms, Gilbert whispers a campy bit of dialogue: "Get out of the racket, Frank—its no good!" Well directed by Mervyn LeRoy, *Gentleman's Fate* had the requisite fight between Gilbert and Wolheim. Gilbert was still struggling with a voice that did not record well, and was ill at ease. Wolheim was excellent in a dramatic role, but had little to do.

Howard Hughes had bought the Charles MacArthur-Ben Hecht play, *The Front Page*, a smash hit on Broadway, and assigned Lewis Milestone to direct the screen version. Wolheim was anxious to play the role of the tough managing editor of a metropolitan daily, Walter Burns (a character modeled upon the legendary Chicago newspaperman Walter Howey, uncle of screen star Colleen Moore). Hughes thought he was right for the part, but was concerned that Wolheim had been unwell for several weeks and had gained considerable weight. Wolheim went on a diet, and in less than a month lost thirty pounds.

As shooting on *The Front Page* began, it was apparent that Wolheim was seriously ill. On February 4, 1931, he collapsed on the set, and was compelled by his physician, Dr. Roland Cummings, to withdraw from the cast. Adolphe Menjou was hastily called in to replace him.

Wolheim was taken to the Los Angeles Osteopathic Hospital, and two weeks later an exploratory operation for suspected appendicitis disclosed widespread stomach cancer. A second operation was planned to remove the malignancy, but the actor was so weak that it was postponed. He was given blood transfusions, and after a brief rally sank into a coma and died on February 18 without regaining consciousness. His wife was at the bedside. The body was cremated, and simple funeral services were limited to a few select friends.

His death brought eulogies from across the nation, and his obituaries uniformly recalled his striking ugliness and his memorable performance as Katczinsky in *All Quiet on the Western Front*.

Filmographies

100 CIVIL WAR MOTION PICTURES: A SELECTIVE FILMOGRAPHY

1903

Uncle Tom's Cabin.
Edison. Director, Edwin S. Porter. Except for Porter's incredible special effects, this archaic version of Harriet Beecher Stowe's classic looked much as it would have been done by a traveling stock company at the turn of the century.

1908

The Guerrilla.
Biograph. Director, D. W. Griffith. Cast. Arthur Johnson, Harry Myers, Dorothy West, Herbert Yost, Mack Sennett, Harry Salter. In Griffith's first Civil War film, an old slave sacrifices his life to save his mistress from a Confederate renegade.

1909

The Girl Spy.
Kalem. Director, Sidney Olcott. This was the first in Kalem's popular series of Civil War dramas featuring Gene Gauntier as Nan, the Girl Spy, an orphan who became a Confederate agent. Some of the other one-reelers in this series were: *The Girl Spy Before Vicksburg* (1910); *The Love Romance of the Girl Spy* (1910); *Further Adventures of the Girl Spy* (1910); *The Bravest Girl in the World* (1910); *The Little Soldier of '64* (1911); and *A Daughter of the Confederacy* (1913). Jack Clark was usually the leading man.

In Old Kentucky.
Biograph. Director D. W. Griffith. Cast: Henry B. Walthall, Owen Moore, Mary Pickford, Kate Bruce, Mack Sennett, Verner Clarges, William J. Butler. Griffith made an early use of panning the camera in this drama of two brothers who fought on opposite sides in the Civil War.

1910

The Honor of His Family.
Biograph. Director, D. W. Griffith. Cast: Henry B. Walthall, James Kirkwood, W. Chrystie Miller, William J. Butler, Gus Pixley, Verner Clarges. Griffith's Civil War battle scenes showed cavalry maneuvers, exchanges of artillery fire, and hand-to-hand combat between Union and Confederate soldiers.

In the Border States, Or a Little Heroine of the Civil War.
Biograph. Director D. W. Griffith. Cast: Henry B. Walthall, W. Chrystie Miller. Griffith used cross-cutting to good effect in this drama of a strong Southern family.

The House with Closed Shutters.
Biograph. Director D. W. Griffith. Cast: Henry B. Walthall, Dorothy West, Edwin August, Charles West, Grace Henderson. There was an early use of makeup to age the actors in this drama of a family that hid the cowardice of a son.

A Dixie Mother.
Vitagraph. Director, Van Dyke Brooke. Cast: Florence Turner, Carlyle Blackwell, Norma Talmadge, Charles Kent, Mary Maurice.

The Fugitive.
Biograph. Director, D. W. Griffith. Cast: Edwin August, Lucy Cotton, Owen Moore, Joseph Graybill, Lily Cahill, Verner Clarges, Dorothy Davenport, Kate Bruce, Edward Dillon, Dorothy West. Lloyd B. Carleton.

Uncle Tom's Cabin.
Vitagraph. Director, J. Stuart Blackton. Cast: Maurice Costello, Earle Williams, Clara Kimball Young, Norma Talmadge, Julia Arthur, Charles Kent. Thanhouser also brought out *Uncle Tom's Cabin* in 1910 with Frank Crane and Baby Rosemond " (The Thanhouser Kid") in the leads. Vitagraph's version ran thirty minutes, twice the length of the Thanhouser edition.

1911

His Trust.
Biograph. Director, D. W. Griffith. Cast: Wilfred Lucas, Claire McDowell, Mack Sennett, Adele De Garde, Violet Mersereau, Dorothy Bernard, Del Henderson. Griffith originally made this story of a slave's loyalty during trying Civil War times as a two-reeler, but Biograph insisted upon releasing it as two separate pictures.

His Trust Fulfilled.
Biograph. Director, D. W. Griffith. Cast: Wilfred Lucas, Linda Arvidson, Dorothy Bernard, Claire McDowell, Verner Clarges, Gladys Egan, Grace Henderson, Kate Bruce. The sequel to *His Trust*.

Swords and Hearts.
Biograph. Director, D. W. Griffith. Cast: Wilfred Lucas, Dorothy West, Claire McDowell, W. Chrystie Miller, Frank Grandin. A drama of Reconstruction.

The Battle Hymn of the Republic.
Vitagraph. Director, Lawrence Trimble. Cast: Ralph Ince (as Abraham Lincoln), Julia Swayne Gordon. In 1917 Vitagraph reissued this stirring account of the writing of the great Civil War song as propaganda for World War I.

The Battle.
Biograph. Director, D. W. Griffith. Cast: Blanche Sweet, Charles West, Lionel Barrymore, Robert Harron, Donald Crisp, Spottiswoode Aitken. Griffith's most expensive film to date was marked by panoramic Civil War battle sequences.

Lieutenant Grey of the Confederacy.
Selig. Director, Francis Boggs. Cast: Sydney Ayres, Thomas Santschi, Bessie Eyton, Herbert Rawlinson, Frank Richardson, Jane Keckly, Fred W. Huntly, Leonide Watson, Anna Dodge, James Dayton (as

Abraham Lincoln), Alvin Wyckoff (as Ulysses S. Grant).

1912

The Informer.
Biograph. Director, D. W. Griffith. Cast: Henry B. Walthall, Mary Pickford, Walter Miller, W. Chrystie Miller, Harry Carey, Joseph Graybill, Dorothy Gish, Christy Cabanne. Griffith's last Civil War film before leaving Biograph.
    Note: In 1912, Kinemacolor began and subsequently abandoned *The Clansman*, an uncompleted film based on the novel and play by Thomas W. Dixon that ultimately became the basis for D. W. Griffith's great masterpiece of the Civil War and Reconstruction, *The Birth of a Nation*. William Haddock was the director, and the leads were taken by members of the Campbell MacCullough Players, a traveling stock company.

1913

The Battle of Gettysburg.
Broncho-New York Motion Picture Company-Mutual. Director, Thomas H. Ince, assisted by Raymond B. West and Charles Giblyn. Cast: Enid Bennett, Herschel Mayall, Enid Markey, Ann Little, J. Barney Sherry, Frank Borzage, Charles K. French, Walter Edwards. The most significant of Civil War films yet produced, it was the basis on which Thomas H. Ince built his reputation as a producer of imaginative and compelling motion pictures.

Pauline Cushman-The Federal Spy.
Selig. Director, Oscar Eagle. Cast: Winifred Greenwood, Charles Clary, Lafayette McKee, Harry Lonsdale, T. J. Commerford. An exciting account of how the American actress spied for the Union to help General William S. Rosecrans in the Chickamauga campaign.

Shenandoah.
Kalem. Director, Kenean Buel. Cast: Henry Hallam, Alice Hollister, Hal Clements, Robert G. Vignola. A spectacular film dramatizing the famous ride of General Philip Sheridan from Winchester to Cedar Creek to rally his troops.

The Powder Flash of Death.
Universal-Bison. Director, Allan Dwan. Cast: Wallace Reid, Marshall Neilan, Pauline Bush, Jessalyn Van Trump, J. D. Kirkland. Allan Dwan directed several other films set in the Civil War in 1913, all starring Wallace Reid, including: *The Call to Arms*; *Women and War*; and *The Picket Guard*.
    Note: In 1913, Charles Ray began a series of Civil

War dramas for Thomas H. Ince, which culminated in his greatest hit, *The Coward*, two years later. Some of the titles: *The Favorite Son*; *The Sharpshooter*; *The Lost Dispatch*; *The Sinews of War*; *Bread Cast Upon the Waters*; *A Slave's Devotion*; *Soul of the South*; *A Military Judas*.

1914

Fitzhugh's Ride.
Lubin. Director, John E. Ince. Cast: Louise Huff, Edgar Jones, George W. Barnes.

The Fair Rebel.
Biograph-Klaw & Erlanger. Cast: Linda Arvidson, Dorothy Gish, Charles West, Charles Perley, Jack Brammall, Clara T. Bracey, Walter Lewis, Florence Ashbrook, Robert Drouet. Supposedly supervised by D. W. Griffith, this film of the notorious Libby Prison in Richmond was actually the work of David Miles, later production chief at Kinemacolor.

Lincoln the Lover.
Vitagraph. Director, Ralph Ince. Cast: Ralph Ince (Abraham Lincoln), Anita Stewart (Ann Rutledge), E. K. Lincoln, Logan Paul, Johnny Hines. A sensitive telling of the Lincoln-Rutledge romance in New Salem.

The Southerners.
Edison. Directors, Richard Ridgely and John H. Collins. Cast: Mabel Trunnelle, Bigelow Cooper, Allen Crolius, Richard Tucker, Herbert Prior, Julius A. Moods, Jr. Fire swept the Edison Studio at Bedford Park, New York, while this picture was in production, destroying part of the negative and sets.

The Littlest Rebel.
Photoplay Productions. Cast: E. K. Lincoln, Mimi Yvonne, Martin Reagan, William J. Sorrelle, Bert S. Frank. A silent version of the popular play, later made into one of Shirley Temple's top hits.

The Tavern of Tragedy.
Majestic-Mutual. Director, Donald Crisp. Cast: Dorothy Gish, Fred A. Turner, Donald Crisp.

1915

The Birth of a Nation.
Epoch Producing Corporation. Director, D. W. Griffith. Story, Thomas Dixon, Jr. Screenplay, D. W. Griffith, Frank E. Woods, and Thomas Dixon, Jr. Photography, G. W. Bitzer, assisted by Karl H. Brown. Incidental Music, Joseph Carl Breil. Cast: Henry B. Walthall (Ben Cameron, "The Little Colonel"), Lillian Gish (Elsie Stoneman), Mae Marsh (Flora Cameron), Miriam Cooper (Margaret Cameron),

Josephine Crowell (Mrs. Cameron), Spottiswoode Aitken (Dr. Cameron), Ralph Lewis (Hon. Austin Stoneman), George Siegmann (Silas Lynch), Wallace Reid (Jeff, the Blacksmith), Elmer Clifton (Phil Stoneman), Robert Harron (Tod Stoneman), Joseph E. Henabery (Abraham Lincoln), Donald Crisp (Ulysses S. Grant), Howard Gaye (Robert E. Lee), André Beranger (Wade Cameron), Alberta Lee (Mary Todd Lincoln), Mary Alden (Lydia Brown), Maxfield Stanley (Duke Cameron), William Freeman (The Mooning Sentry), Sam de Grasse (Senator Charles Sumner), Walter Long (Gus), Elmo Lincoln ("White-Arm" Joe), Raoul Walsh (John Wilkes Booth), Olga Grey (Laura Keene), Tom Wilson (Negro Servant), Jennie Lee (Mammy), Eugene Pallette, Erich von Stroheim, Violet Wilkey, Madame Sul-te-Wan, William de Vaull. In 1935, M-G-M announced a remake of *The Birth of a Nation*, but the plan was quickly dropped. In 1954, an independent producer named Phil L. Ryan also announced a talking picture remake. Dudley Nichols was mentioned to write the script, and Raoul Walsh to direct. Ryan's project folded up due to objections from black organizations and a lack of financing.

Barbara Frietchie.
Metro. Director, Herbert Blaché. Mary Miles Minter, Anna Q. Nilsson, Guy Coombs, Mrs. Thomas W. Whiffen, Wallace Scott, Myra Brooks, Jack Burns, Frederic Heck, William A. Morse. John Greenleaf Whittier's poem was produced four times on the screen—the 1915 version was the third and best of the lot.

The Coward.
Kay-Bee-Triangle. Director, Reginald H. Barker. Cast: Charles Ray, Frank Keenan, Margaret Gibson, Nick Cogley, Gertrude Claire, Charles K. French. Charles Ray's performance as a fear-obsessed youth who deserted the Confederate Army was intensely dramatic, but audiences liked him best as a country bumpkin in such light comedies as: *The Clodhopper*; *The Hired Man*; *String Beans*; and *The Busher*.

The Heart of Maryland.
Tiffany-Metro. Director, Herbert Brenon. Cast: Mrs. Leslie Carter, William E. Shay, J. Farrell MacDonald, Matt Snyder, Doris Baker, Vivian Reed. The old David Belasco melodrama came to the screen three times at intervals of six years, but never so unconvincingly as with the fifty-three-year-old Mrs. Leslie Carter playing a teenage heroine.

The Warrens of Virginia.
Paramount-Lasky. Director, Cecil B. DeMille. Cast: Blanche Sweet, House Peters, Mabel Van Buren, James Neill, Marjorie Daw, Richard LaReno, Page Peters,

Mildred Harris, Marguerite House, Mrs. Lewis Mc-Cord. DeMille had acted in *The Warrens of Virginia* on Broadway, his brother William wrote the play, and much of it was based on the Civil War experiences of their grandfather.

1916

The Crisis.
Selig. Director, Colin Campbell. Cast: Bessie Eyton, Thomas Santschi, George Fawcett, Marshall Neilan, Matt Snyder, Frank Weed, Cecil Holland, Eugenie Bessesser, Will Machin, Sam D. Drane (as Abraham Lincoln). Selig called *The Crisis*, "A Superfilm of Superfilms," and proudly reported that a command performance at the White House was attended by President Wilson and his Cabinet. Of Sam D. Drane's performance as Abraham Lincoln, Thomas A. Edison said that it preserved the characteristics of the President "in a manner so true to life that it recalls to my mind the Great Emancipator as I knew him."

Her Father's Son.
Paramount-Morosco. Director, William D. Taylor. Cast: Vivian Martin, Alfred Vosburgh, Helen Jerome Eddy, Herbert Standing. Extremely popular on Broadway, Vivian Martin never quite made it in films, but fans enjoyed her as a Confederate belle who spied for the South, sometimes while posing as a young boy.

The Sting of Victory.
Essanay. Director, J. Charles Haydon. Cast: Henry B. Walthall, Anne Leigh, Thomas Commerford, John Lorenz, Antoinette Walker. Henry B. Walthall failed to repeat his success in *The Birth of a Nation* with this mediocre film of a Southern turncoat who tried to redeem himself with good deeds during Reconstruction.

A Rose of the South.
Vitagraph. Director, Paul Scardon. Cast: Antonio Moreno, Peggy Hyland, Gordon Gray, Rose Tapley, Charles Kent, Mary Maurice.

1917

The Little Yank.
Fine Arts-Triangle. Director, George Siegmann. Cast: Dorothy Gish, Frank Bennett, Kate Toncray, Alberta Lee, Fred A. Turner, Hal Wilson, A. D. Sears, Robert Burns. George Siegmann, the Silas Lynch of *The Birth of a Nation*, showed little influence of his association of D. W. Griffith as director of this routine tale of a Yankee girl who loved a Confederate officer.

Those Without Sin.
Paramount-Lasky. Director, Marshall Neilan. Cast: Blanche Sweet, Tom Forman, James Neill, Mabel Van

Buren, Billy Jacobs, Charles Ogle, Dorothy Abril.

Note: In 1917 Benjamin Chapin assembled four of his scholarly short subjects about Abraham Lincoln for showing as The *Lincoln Cycle* at the Globe Theatre on Broadway. Their success led to two compilations, *Children of Democracy* and *Son of Democracy*, which inexplicably failed as feature films.

1918

Madam Who?
Paralta Plays-Hodkinson. Director, Reginald H. Barker. Cast: Bessie Barriscale, Howard Hickman, Joseph J. Dowling, Edward Coxen, David M. Hartford. Another routine Confederate spy story.

Morgan's Raiders.
Universal. Director, Wilfred Lucas. Cast: Violet Mersereau, Edward Burns, Frank Holland, Ben Lyon, Barbara Gilroy. In this film the Kentucky guerrilla must have really had in his mind on the Civil War not to notice his new recruit (Violet Mersereau) was a girl in disguise.

Uncle Tom's Cabin.
Paramount-Lasky. Director, J. Searle Dawley. Cast: Marguerite Clark, Frank Losee, J. W. Johnston, Florence Carpenter, Walter Lewis, Ruby Hoffman, Henry Stanford, Mrs. Priestly Morrison. The petite Miss Clark played both Topsy and Eva in this lighthearted romp through the old Stowe classic.

1919

The Copperhead.
Paramount-Artclass. Director, Charles Maigne. Cast: Lionel Barrymore, Doris Rankin, Richard Carlyle, William P. Carlton, Frank Joyner, Arthur Rankin. Barrymore and his wife, Doris Rankin, re-created their original roles in Augustus Thomas's Broadway hit play of 1918 about an undercover Union agent.

Secret Service.
Paramount-Lasky. Director, Hugh Ford. Cast: Robert Warwick, Wanda Hawley, Theodore Roberts, Raymond Hatton, Irving Cummings, Edythe Chapman.

Hay Foot, Straw Foot.
Paramount-Ince. Director, Jerome Storm. Cast: Charles Ray, Doris Lee, Spottiswoode Aitken, William Conklin, J. P. Lockney. Ray was Ulysses S. Grant Briggs in this comedy about World War I, which had many amusing flashbacks as he imagined himself a Civil War hero.

1920

Held By the Enemy.
Paramount-Lasky. Director, Donald Crisp. Cast: Lewis Stone, Jack Holt, Agnes Ayres, Wanda Hawley, Josephine Crowell.

The Little Shepherd of Kingdom Come.
Goldwyn. Director, Wallace Worsley. Cast: Jack Pickford, Clara Horton, Pauline Starke, Clark Marshall, J. Park Jones. The erratic Jack Pickford, beset by personal problems and an unstable temperament, never took acting or anything else very seriously, and his picturization of John Fox, Jr.'s best-selling novel marked the beginning of a steady decline in his career.

1921

The Highest Law.
Selznick. Director, Ralph Ince. Cast: Ralph Ince (as Abraham Lincoln), Aleen Burr, Margaret Seddon, Robert Agnew, Cecil Crawford. Tad Lincoln, the President's son, was a character in this drama of Lincoln's conflict with Secretary of War Edwin M. Stanton.

The Heart of Maryland.
Vitagraph. Director, Tom Terriss. Cast: Catherine Calvert, Crane Wilbur, William Collier, Jr., Ben Lyon, Henry Hallam, Jane Jennings, Felix Krembs, Bernard Siegel, Warner Richmond, Victoria White, Marguerite Sanchez.

1922

Grandma's Boy.
Associated Exhibitors-Roach. Director, Fred Newmeyer. Cast: Harold Lloyd, Mildred Davis, Noah Young, Anna Townsend, Charles Stevenson, Dick Sutherland. The best part of this modern comedy was the Civil War flashback with Harold Lloyd playing his own grandfather in a Confederate uniform and square-rimmed spectacles. Originally planned as a two-reeler, it was expanded to feature length as the comedian grew more entranced with his story and its comic possibilities.

1924

The Warrens of Virginia.
Fox. Director, Elmer Clifton. Cast: Martha Mansfield, Wilfred Lytell, Rosemary Hill, J. Barney Sherry (as General Lee), Harlan Knight, Frank Andrews, Wilbur J. Fox (as General Grant), Helen Ray Kyle, Robert Andrews, James Turfler. A remake of DeMille's earlier film.

Barbara Frietchie.
Producers Distributing Corporation-Regal. Director, Lambert Hillyer. Cast: Florence Vidor, Edmund Lowe, George A. Billings (as Abraham Lincoln), Charles Delaney, Emmett King, Louis Fitzroy, Joe Bennett. A happy ending in which the star-crossed lovers escaped death and were reunited after the Civil War—insisted upon by producer Thomas H. Ince—lessened the impact of this pedestrian retelling of the familiar story.

Abraham Lincoln.
Associated First National-Rockett. Director, Phil Rosen. Cast: George A. Billings (Abraham Lincoln), Ruth Clifford (Ann Rutledge), William Humphrey (Stephen A. Douglas), Nell Craig (Mary Todd Lincoln), William Moran (John Wilkes Booth), Walter Rogers (Ulysses S. Grant), James Welch (Robert E. Lee), Louise Fazenda, Fred Kohler, Fay McKenzie, Charles K. French, Madge Hunt, Raymond Lee, A. Edward Sutherland, Danny Hoy, Pat Hartigan, Otis Harlan, Mickey Moore, Francis Powers, Earl Schenck, Frances Raymond, Ivy Livingston, Nick Cogley. An artistic and critical success, but a financial failure.

1926

The General.
United Artists. Directors, Clyde Bruckman, Buster Keaton. Cast: Buster Keaton, Marion Mack, Glen Cavender, James Farley, Frederick Vroom, Charles Smith, Mike Donlin, Frank Barnes, Joseph Keaton, Thomas Nawn. *The General* got only a moderate reception when first released in 1926, and it was not until years later that it came to be recognized as one of Keaton's three classic comedies (the other two: *Sherlock, Jr.,* and *Steamboat Bill, Jr.*).

Hands Up.
Paramount. Director, Clarence G. Badger. Cast: Raymond Griffith, Marion Nixon, Virginia Lee Corbin, Montague Love, George A. Billings (as Abraham Lincoln), Noble Johnson (as Sitting Bull), Charles K. French (as Brigham Young), Mack Swain. A Civil War spoof that offended Mormons with its pot shots at Brigham Young and multiple marriages.

1927

The Heart of Maryland.
Warner Brothers. Director, Lloyd Bacon. Cast: Dolores Costello, Jason Robards, Sr., Warner Richmond, Helene Costello, Carroll Nye, Charles E. Bull (as Abraham Lincoln), Walter Rogers (as General Grant), James Welch (as General Lee), Myrna Loy, Harry Northrup, Francis Ford (as Jefferson Davis),

Paul Kruger, Nick Cogley, Madge Hunt, Erville Alderson, S. D. Wilcox. A parade of historical personages enlivened this third version of the old Belasco warhorse, but the real attraction was dewy-eyed Dolores Costello, one of the screen's most beautiful women.

Uncle Tom's Cabin.
Universal. Director, Harry Pollard. Cast: James B. Lowe (Uncle Tom), George Siegmann (Simon Legree), Margarita Fischer (Eliza), Mona Ray (Topsy), Virginia Grey (Eva), Arthur Edmund Carewe, Eulalie Jensen, Jack Mower, Vivian Oakland, Lucien Littlefield, John Roche, Francis Ford, Nelson McDowell, Gertrude Astor, J. Gordon Russell, Rolfe Sedan. The emphasis was on the love affair of two slaves, George and Eliza Harris, in this elaborate version of the Stowe novel. It was revived a year after its original release with sound effects, a musical score, and the voice of Aunt Ophelia (Aileen Manning) endlessly calling for Topsy. In the 1950s, some enterprising promoters bought the rights, added a narration, and gave it a roadshow treatment, but the film was too old-fashioned to interest modern audiences.

1928

The Little Shepherd of Kingdom Come.
First National. Director, Alfred Santell. Cast: Richard Barthelmess, Molly O'Day, Doris Dawson, Gustav von Seyffertitz, David Torrence, Martha Mattox, Nelson McDowell, Victor Potel, Mark Hamilton, Gardner James, Walter Lewis, Claude Gillingwater, William Bertram, Walter Rogers (as General Grant). Richard Barthelmess was at the height of his popularity when he appeared in this remake of the Fox novel.

Court-Martial.
Columbia. Director, George B. Seitz. Cast: Jack Holt, Betty Compson, Doris Hill, Frank Lackteen, Pat Harmon, George Cowl, Frank Austin (as Abraham Lincoln). This bit of historical fiction made Belle Starr more of a patriotic Confederate guerrilla and less of a common outlaw, and showed her nobly sacrificing her life to save her lover, a Union Army officer, from a firing squad.

1929

Morgan's Last Raid.
Metro-Goldwyn-Mayer. Director, Nick Grinde. Cast: Tim McCoy, Dorothy Sebastian, Allan Garcia, Wheeler Oakman, Hank Mann, Montague Shaw. Tim McCoy was a member of Morgan's marauders.

1930

Abraham Lincoln.
United Artists. Director, D. W. Griffith. Cast: Walter Huston (Abraham Lincoln), Una Merkel (Ann Rutledge), Ian Keith (John Wilkes Booth), Kay Hammond (Mary Todd Lincoln), Hobart Bosworth (General Lee), Frank Campeau (General Sheridan), Fred Warren (General Grant), E. Alyn Warren, Henry B. Walthall, Ralph Lewis, Jason Robards, Sr., Helen Ware, Russell Simpson, Edgar Deering, James Eagle, Oscar Apfel, Hank Bell, Carl Stockdale. Griffith's first talking picture was a commendable if flawed study of Lincoln.

Only the Brave.
Paramount. Director, Frank Tuttle. Cast: Gary Cooper, Mary Brian, Phillips Holmes, Virginia Bruce, Morgan Farley, James Neill, Guy Oliver (as Ulysses S. Grant), John Elliott (as Robert E. Lee), E. H. Calvert, Freeman Wood, William LeMaire.

1931

Secret Service.
RKO Radio. Director, J. Walter Ruben. Cast: Richard Dix, Shirley Grey, William Post, Jr., Gavin Gordon, Fred Warren (as General Grant), Nance O'Neill, Florence Lake, Virginia Sale.

1934

Carolina.
Fox. Director, Henry King. Cast: Janet Gaynor, Lionel Barrymore, Robert Young, Richard Cromwell, Henrietta Crosman, Stepin Fetchit, Mona Barrie, Russell Simpson, Alden Chase. Barrymore was a Confederate veteran living in the past who disowns his son for marrying a Northern girl.

Operator 13.
Metro-Goldwyn-Mayer. Director, Richard Boleslawski. Cast: Marion Davies, Gary Cooper, Jean Parker, Ted Healy, The Four Mills Brothers, Katherine Alexander, Russell Hardie, Douglas Dumbrille, Willard Robertson, Francis McDonald, Hattie McDaniel, Marjorie Gateson, Walter Long, Wheeler Oakman, Don Douglas, Buddy Roosevelt, Wilfred Lucas, Richard Tucker, Sidney Toler, Fuzzy Knight, Robert McWade, Wade Boteler, James Marcus, DeWitt Jennings, Sterling Holloway, Douglas Fowley, Fred Warren (as General Grant), John Elliott (as General Lee), James Morton, Frank McGlynn, Jr. William Randolph Hearst may not have intended it as such, but *Operator 13* came out as a charming spoof of Civil War

spy stories, thanks largely to Marion Davies's tongue-in-cheek performance.

1935

The Littlest Rebel.
20th Century-Fox. Director, David L. Butler. Cast: Shirley Temple, John Boles, Jack Holt, Karen Morley, Bill Robinson, Guinn Williams, Frank McGlynn, Sr. (as Abraham Lincoln), Willie Best, Bessie Lyle, Hannah Washington. Shirley conned Old Abe out of a piece of apple pie and a pardon for her Confederate father.

So Red the Rose.
Paramount. Director, King Vidor. Cast: Margaret Sullavan, Randolph Scott, Walter Connolly, Janet Beecher, Elizabeth Patterson, Dickie Moore, Robert Cummings, Daniel Haynes, Clarence Muse, Johnny Downs, Harry Ellerbe, Charles Starrett. An offensive film that preserves all the clichés of the black slave and Southern aristocracy.

1936

The Prisoner of Shark Island.
20th Century-Fox. Director, John Ford. Cast: Warner Baxter (as Dr. Samuel A. Mudd), Gloria Stuart, Arthur Byron, Claude Gillingwater, O. P. Heggie, Harry Carey, Francis Ford, Douglas Wood, John Carradine, Frank McGlynn, Sr. (as Abraham Lincoln), Francis McDonald (as John Wilkes Booth), John McGuire, Ernest Whitman, Fred Kohler, Jr., Frank Shannon, J. M. Kerrigan, Maurice Murphy, Joyce Kay, Jack Pennick. The story of the Maryland surgeon who was sent to the Dry Tortugas for treating John Wilkes Booth after the assassination of Abraham Lincoln.

Hearts in Bondage.
Republic. Director, Lew Ayres. Cast: James Dunn, David Manners, Mae Clarke, Charlotte Henry, Henry B. Walthall, Irving Pichel, George Hayes, J. M. Kerrigan, George Irving, Ben Alexander, Oscar Apfel, Russell Hicks, Douglas Wood, Lane Chandler, Smiley Burnette, Fritz Leiber, Warner Richmond, Bodil Rosing, Erville Alderson. A drama of the *Monitor* and the *Merrimac.*

General Spanky.
Metro-Goldwyn-Mayer-Roach. Directors, Fred Newmeyer and Gordon M. Douglas. Cast: Spanky McFarland, Phillips Holmes, Ralph Morgan, Irving Pichel, Carl Switzer, Robert Middlemass, Louise Beavers, Rosina Lawrence, James Burtis, Willie Best. A spoof of Civil War spy stories done in the relaxed style of *Our Gang.*

1938

Of Human Hearts.
Metro-Goldwyn-Mayer. Director, Clarence Brown. Cast: Walter Huston, James Stewart, Beulah Bondi, Gene Reynolds, John Carradine (as Abraham Lincoln), Ann Rutherford, Guy Kibbee, Charles Coburn, Leatrice Joy, Charley Grapewin, Gene Lockhart, Sterling Holloway, Minor Watson, Robert McWade, Arthur Aylesworth.

1939

Young Mr. Lincoln.
20th Century-Fox. Director, John Ford. Cast: Henry Fonda, Alice Brady, Marjorie Weaver, Arleen Whelan, Eddie Collins, Pauline Moore, Richard Cromwell, Ward Bond, Spencer Charters, Donald Meek, Milburn Stone (as Stephen A. Douglas), Robert Lowery, Fred Kohler, Jr., Russell Simpson, Kay Linaker, Jack Pennick, Judith Dickens, Cliff Clark. Not about the Civil War period of Lincoln's life, but a fine film by John Ford with an understanding performance by Henry Fonda.

Gone With the Wind.
Metro-Goldwn-Mayer-Selznick. Director, Victor Fleming (with additional sequences by Sam Wood, George Cukor, William Cameron Menzies). Producer, David O. Selznick. Story by Margaret Mitchell. Screenplay by Sidney Howard. Photography, Ernest Haller and Ray Rennahan. Production Design, William Cameron Menzies. Cast: Clark Gable (Rhett Butler), Vivien Leigh (Scarlett O'Hara), Olivia de Havilland (Melanie), Leslie Howard (Ashley Wilkes), Thomas Mitchell (Gerald O'Hara), Barbara O'Neill (Ellen O'Hara), Hattie McDaniel (Mammy), Carroll Nye (Frank Kennedy), Laura Hope Crews (Aunt Pittypat), Harry Davenport (Dr. Meade), Ona Munson (Belle Watling), Evelyn Keyes, Ann Rutherford, George Reeves, Oscar Polk, Eddie Anderson, Butterfly McQueen, Victor Jory, Isabel Jewell, Paul Hurst, Cammie King, Rand Brooks, Tom Tyler, Yakima Canutt, Eric Linden, William Bakewell, Fred Crane, Ward Bond, Howard Hickman, Jane Darwell, Cliff Edwards, Olin Howlin, Ernest Whitman, Robert Elliott, Mary Anderson, Jackie Moran, George Meeker.

1940

Abe Lincoln in Illinois.
RKO Radio. Director, John Cromwell. Cast: Raymond Massey, Ruth Gordon, Gene Lockhart, Mary Howard, Dorothy Tree, Harvey Stephens, Minor Watson, Alan Baxter, Howard Da Silva, Maurice

FILMOGRAPHIES

221

Murphy, Louis Jean Heydt, Andy Clyde, Roger Imhoff, Leona Roberts, Elizabeth Risdon, Syd Saylor. Another fine drama of Lincoln's pre-Washington days.

Dark Command.
Republic. Director, Raoul Walsh. Cast: John Wayne, Walter Pidgeon, Claire Trevor, Roy Rogers, George Hayes, Porter Hall, Marjorie Main, Raymond Walburn, Joseph Sawyer, Helen Mackellar, J. Farrell MacDonald, Trevor Bardette. A fictionalized account of Quantrill's raid on Lawrence, Kansas.

The Man from Dakota.
Metro-Goldwyn-Mayer. Director, Leslie Fenton. Cast: Wallace Beery, Dolores Del Rio, John Howard, Donald Meek, Robert Barratt, Addison Richards, Frederick Burton, John Wray, William Haade.

Santa Fe Trail.
Warner Brothers. Director, Michael Curtiz. Cast: Errol Flynn (J. E. B. Stuart), Olivia de Havilland, Raymond Massey (John Brown), Ronald Reagan (George Armstrong Custer), Alan Hale, William Lundigan, Van Heflin, Gene Reynolds, Henry O'Neill, Guinn Williams, Alan Baxter, John Litel, Moroni Olsen (Robert E. Lee), David Bruce (Phil Sheridan), Hobart Cavanaugh, Charles D. Brown, Joseph Sawyer, Ward Bond, Russell Simpson, Charles Middleton, Erville Alderson (Jefferson Davis), Wilfred Lucas. Errol Flynn's portrayal of General J. E .B. Stuart in his early days bore no relationship to the real Stuart in this drama of Harper's Ferry.

Virginia City.
Warner Brothers. Director, Michael Curtiz. Cast: Errol Flynn, Randolph Scott, Miriam Hopkins, Humphrey Bogart, Frank McHugh, Alan Hale, Guinn Williams, John Litel, Douglas Dumbrille, Moroni Olsen, Russell Hicks, Thurston Hall, Ward Bond, George Reeves, Dickie Jones, Victor Killian, Charles Middleton, Monte Montague, Paul Fix, Charles Halton. The best of the Civil War out West adventures.

1941

Belle Starr.
20th Century-Fox. Director Irving Cummings. Cast: Gene Tierney, Randolph Scott, Dana Andrews, John Shepperd, Elizabeth Patterson, Chill Wills, Louise Beavers, Howard Hickman, James Flavin, Charles Middleton. Another fictionalized account of the woman outlaw as a Confederate raider, but more true than Columbia's *Court-Martial* of 1928.

1948

A Southern Yankee.
Metro-Goldwyn-Mayer. Director, Edward Sedgwick. Cast: Red Skelton, Arlene Dahl, Brian Donlevy, John Ireland, George Coulouris. Buster Keaton contributed many of the gags to this Civil War comedy.

Tap Roots.
Universal-International. Director, George Marshall. Cast: Susan Hayward, Van Heflin, Boris Karloff, Julie London, Whitfield Connor, Ward Bond, Richard Long, Arthur Shields, Ruby Dandridge, Russell Simpson.

1951

The Red Badge of Courage.
Metro-Goldwyn-Mayer. Director, John Huston. Cast: Audie Murphy, Bill Mauldin, John Dierkes, Royal Dano, Arthur Hunnicutt, Tim Durant, Douglas Dick, Robert Easton Burke. In 1974, Richard Thomas of television's "The Waltons" series starred in a made-for-tv feature of *The Red Badge of Courage.* It was a creditable effort directed by Lee Philips.

The Tall Target.
Metro-Goldwn-Mayer. Director, Anthony Mann. Cast: Dick Powell, Paula Raymond, Adolphe Menjou, Ruby Dee, Marshall Thompson, Richard Rober, Florence Bates, Will Geer, Leslie Kimmell (as Abraham Lincoln). An unsuccessful attempt to assassinate Lincoln on the train carrying him to his first inauguration was the theme of this film.

Red Mountain.
Paramount. Director, William Dieterle. Cast: Alan Ladd, Lizabeth Scott, Arthur Kennedy, John Ireland, Jeff Corey, James Bell, Francis McDonald, Carleton Young, Neville Brand, Walter Sande, Iron Eyes Cody, Jay Silverheels, Whit Bissell, Dan White. A fictional story of Quantrill out West.

Drums in the Deep South.
RKO Radio-King Brothers. Director, William Cameron Menzies. Cast: James Craig, Barbara Payton, Guy Madison, Barton MacLane, Craig Stevens, Tom Fadden, Robert Osterloh, Taylor Holmes, Robert Easton, Lewis Martin, Louis Jean Heydt, Dan White.

1953

The Vanquished.
Paramount-Pine-Thomas. Director, Edward Ludwig. Cast: John Payne, Jan Sterling, Coleen Gray, Lyle

Bettger, Willard Parker, Roy Gordon, John Dierkes, Charles Evans, Ellen Corby, Ernestine Barrier, Russell Gaige, Leslie Kimmell, Voltaire Perkins. A Confederate hero fights a carpetbagger villain out West.

1954

The Raid.
20th Century-Fox. Director, Hugo Fregonese. Cast: Van Heflin, Anne Bancroft, Richard Boone, Lee Marvin, Tommy Rettig, Peter Graves, Douglas Spencer, Paul Cavanagh, James Best, John Dierkes, Will Wright, Claude Akins, Harry Hines. Brisk direction made this low-budget film a better-than-average Civil War thriller.

1955

Prince of Players.
20th Century-Fox. Director, Philip Dunne. Cast: Richard Burton, Raymond Massey, Maggie McNamara, John Derek, Charles Bickford, Elizabeth Sellers, Eva Le Gallienne, Ian Keith, Christopher Cook, Sarah Padden, Ruth Clifford, Lane Chandler, Melinda Markey, George Melford. A biography of Edwin Booth, this film showed the emotional effects of the assassination of Lincoln by John Wilkes Booth on the theatrical family.

Seven Angry Men.
Allied Artists. Director, Charles Marquis Warren. Cast: Raymond Massey, Debra Paget, Jeffrey Hunter, Larry Pennell, Leo Gordon, Dennis Weaver, James Best, Guy Williams, Robert Osterloh, Robert Simon, Jack Lomas, James Edwards. Another account of the John Brown story.

1956

Friendly Persuasion.
Allied Artists. Director, William Wyler. Cast: Gary Cooper, Dorothy McGuire, Anthony Perkins, Marjorie Main, Richard Eyer, Phyllis Love, Robert Middleton, Walter Catlett, Theodore Newton, Mary Carr, Russell Simpson, Charles Halton. A Quaker family finds its deep-seated beliefs torn when the Civil War comes to southern Indiana.

Great Locomotive Chase.
Buena Vista-Disney. Director, Francis D. Lyon. Cast: Fess Parker, Jeffrey Hunter, Jeff York, Kenneth Tobey, John Lupton, Don Megowan, Eddie Firestone, Harry Carey, Jr., Stan Jones, Morgan Woodward, Lennie Geer. The Andrews's raid got a more straightforward telling in this Disney film, but it lacked the charm and comedy of Buston Keaton's The General.

1957

Band of Angels.
Warner Brothers. Director, Raoul Walsh. Cast: Clark Gable, Yvonne de Carlo, Sidney Poitier, Efrem Zimbalist, Jr., Patric Knowles, Rex Reason, Andrea King, Ray Teal, Carole Drake, Noreen Corcoran, William Forrest, Torin Thatcher. A strong contender for the worst motion picture about the antebellum South and the Civil War ever made.

Raintree County.
Metro-Goldwyn-Mayer. Director, Edward Dmytryk. Cast: Elizabeth Taylor, Montgomery Clift, Eva Marie Saint, Nigel Patrick, Lee Marvin, Rod Taylor, Agnes Moorhead, Walter Abel, Jarma Lewis, Tom Drake, Rhys Williams, DeForest Kelley, Russell Collins. M-G-M's $5 million film of the novel by Ross Lockridge, Jr. made even the Civil War a bore.

1958

The Proud Rebel.
Buena Vista-Goldwyn. Director, Michael Curtiz. Cast: Alan Ladd, Olivia de Havilland, Dean Jagger, David Ladd, Cecil Kellaway, Henry Hull, John Carradine, James Westerfield, Dean Stanton, Thomas Pittman.

Quantrill's Raiders.
Allied Artists. Director, Edward Bernds. Cast: Steve Cochran, Diane Brewster, Leo Gordon, Gale Robbins, Will Wright, Kim Charney, Robert Foulk, Glenn Strange, Lane Chandler, Guy Prescott, Dan White, Myron Healey. The raid on Lawrence again.

1959

The Horse Soldiers.
United Artists. Director, John Ford. Cast: John Wayne, William Holden, Constance Towers, Anna Lee, Althea Gibson, Hoot Gibson, Russell Simpson, Stan Jones, Carleton Young, Basil Ruysdael, Ken Curtis, O. Z. Whitehead, Jack Pennick, Fred Graham, William Forrest, Willis Bouchey. One of the best action films about the Civil War describing the famous Grierson raid to cut the Confederate supply lines to Vicksburg.

1961

The Little Shepherd of Kingdom Come.
20th Century-Fox. Director, Andrew V. McLaglen. Cast: Jimmie Rodgers, Luanna Patten, Chill Wills, Robert Dix, George Kennedy, Shirley O'Hara, Neil

Hamilton, Lois January, Ken Miller. A third remake of the John Fox, Jr. novel, this time with country singer Jimmie Rodgers in the lead.

1962

How the West Was Won.
Metro-Goldwyn-Mayer. Civil War sequence directed by John Ford; other sequences directed by Henry Hathaway and George Marshall. Cast, Civil War sequences: John Wayne, George Peppard, Henry Morgan, Russ Tamblyn. Other sequences: Debbie Reynolds, Carroll Baker, Henry Fonda, Lee J. Cobb, Raymond Massey (as Abraham Lincoln), Andy Devine, Carolyn Jones, Karl Malden, Gregory Peck, Robert Preston, James Stewart, Eli Wallach, Richard Widmark, Brigid Bazlen, Walter Brennan, David Brian, Agnes Moorehead, Thelma Ritter, Mickey Shaughnessy, Lee Van Cleef, Jay C. Flippen, Joseph Sawyer. John Wayne was General William T. Sherman in a brief episode at the Battle of Shiloh, with Henry Morgan as General Ulysses S. Grant.

1964

Advance to the Rear.
Metro-Goldwyn-Mayer. Director, George Marshall. Cast: Glenn Ford, Melvyn Douglas, Joan Blondell, Stella Stevens, Jim Backus, Andrew Prine, Jesse Pearson, Alan Hale, Jr., James Griffith, Michael Pate. A screwball Civil War comedy enlivened by Joan Blondell as the madam of a frontier brothel.

1965

Shenandoah.
Universal. Director, Andrew V. McLaglen. Cast: James Stewart, Doug McClure, Glenn Corbett, Patrick Wayne, Rosemary Forsyth, Phillip Alford, Katherine Ross, Charles Robinson, Paul Fix, Denver Pyle, Harry Carey, Jr., George Kennedy, Tim McIntire, Tom Simcox. A sensitive story about a Virginia family that tried to remain neutral in the Civil War.

1966

Alvarez Kelly.
Columbia. Director, Edward Dmytryk. Cast: William Holden, Richard Widmark, Janice Rule, Patrick O'Neal, Victoria Shaw, Arthur Franz, Richard Rust, Don Barry, Harry Carey, Jr., Roger C. Carmel. Widmark was a one-eyed Confederate sadist in this melodrama of the Civil War in Richmond.

THE FILMS OF ALLA NAZIMOVA

War Brides.
Selznick-Brenon. 1916. Charles Bryant, Richard Barthelmess, Gertrude Berkeley, Robert Whitworth, Nila Mac, Theodora Warfield, William Bailey, Ned Burton, Charles Hutchison. Director, Herbert Brenon.

Revelation.
Metro. 1918. Charles Bryant, Frank Currier, Bigelow Cooper, Syn M. DeConde, Eugene Borden. Director, George D. Baker.

Toys of Fate.
Metro. 1918. Irving Cummings, Charles Bryant, Frank Currier, Edward Connelly, Dodson Mitchell, Nila Mac. Director, George D. Baker.

Eye For Eye.
Metro. 1918. Charles Bryant, Charles K. French, Sally Crute, Donald Gallaher, E. L. Fernandez, Miriam Battista, Hardee Kirkland. Director, Albert Capellani.

A Woman of France.
1918. A five-minute propaganda film made to promote the sale of Liberty Bonds.

Out of the Fog.
Metro. 1919. Charles Bryant, Henry Harmon, Tom Blake, T. Morse Koupal, Nancy Palmer, George W. Davis. Director, Albert Capellani.

The Red Lantern.
Metro. 1919. Darrell Foss, Noah Beery, Winter Hall, Edward Connelly, Frank Currier, Virginia Ross. Director, Albert Capellani.

The Brat.
Metro. 1919. Charles Bryant, Darrell Foss, Bonnie Hill, Frank Currier, Amy Van Ness. Director, Herbert Blaché.

Stronger Than Death.
Metro. 1920. Charles Bryant, Henry Harmon, Charles K. French, William Orlamond, Herbert Prior. Directors, Herbert Blaché and Charles Bryant.

The Heart of a Child.
Metro. 1920. Charles Bryant, Claire DuBrey, Ray Thompson, Victor Potel, Nell Newman. Director, Ray C. Smallwood.

Madame Peacock.
Metro. 1920. George Probert, Rex Cherryman, William Orlamond, Albert Cody. Director, Ray C. Smallwood.

Billions.
Metro. 1920. Charles Bryant, Bonnie Hill, Victor Potel, Emmett King, William Irving. Director, Ray C. Smallwood.

Camille.
Metro. 1921. Rudolph Valentino, Rex Cherryman, Arthur Hoyt, Patsy Ruth Miller, Zeffie Tilbury, Edward Connelly, William Orlamond. Director, Ray C. Smallwood.

A Doll's House.
Allied Producers and Distributors-United Artists. 1922. Alan Hale, Philippe De Lacy, Nigel De Brulier, Wedgewood Nowell, Florence Fisher, Elinor Oliver. Director, Charles Bryant.

Salome.
Allied Producers and Distributors-United Artists. 1923. Nigel De Brulier, Rose Dione, Mitchell Lewis, Earl Schneck, Frederic Peters. Director, Charles Bryant.

Madonna of the Streets.
First National. 1924. Milton Sills, Claude Gillingwater, Wallace Beery, Tom Kennedy, Harold Goodwin, Vivian Oakland, Courtenay Foote, Herbert Prior. Director, Edwin Carewe.

The Redeeming Sin.
Vitagraph. 1925. Lou Tellegen, Carl Miller, Otis Harlan, Rose Tapley, William Dunn. Director, J. Stuart Blackton.

My Son.
First National. 1925. Jack Pickford, Constance Bennett, Ian Keith, Hobart Bosworth, Charles Murray, Dot Farley, Mary Akin. Director, Edwin Carewe.

Escape.
Metro-Goldwyn-Mayer. 1940. Robert Taylor, Norma Shearer, Conrad Veidt, Albert Basserman, Bonita Granville, Philip Dorn, Helmut Dantine, Blanche Yurka, Edgar Barrier. Director, Mervyn LeRoy.

Blood and Sand.
20th Century-Fox. 1941. Tyrone Power, Linda Darnell, Rita Hayworth, Anthony Quinn, Laird Cregar, Lynn Bari, J. Carroll Naish, John Carradine, George Reeves. Director, Rouben Mamoulian.

In Our Time.
Warner Brothers. 1944. Ida Lupino, Paul Henreid, Mary Boland, Nancy Coleman, Victor Francen, Michael Chekov, Faye Emerson, Ivan Lebedeff. Director, Vincent Sherman.

The Bridge of San Luis Rey.
Bogeaus-United Artists. 1944. Francis Lederer, Lynn Bari, Donald Woods, Akim Tamiroff, Blanche Yurka, Louis Calhern, Abner Biberman, Emma Dunn. Director, Rowland V. Lee.

Since You Went Away.
Selznick-United Artists. 1944. Claudette Colbert, Jennifer Jones, Shirley Temple, Monty Woolley, Robert Walker, Agnes Moorhead, Lionel Barrymore, Craig Stevens, Keenan Wynn, Hattie McDaniel, Guy Madison, Albert Basserman, Florence Bates, Lloyd Corrigan. Director, John Cromwell.

THE FILMS OF LOUIS WOLHEIM

Louis Wolheim was an extra and bit player in numerous films made by Theodore and Leopold Wharton at Ithaca, New York, in 1914–15 for release by Pathé, Essanay, and other companies. He was also an extra in films for various companies made in New York and Fort Lee, New Jersey, in 1916. His films as a feature player follow:

The Brand of Cowardice.
Metro-Rolfe. 1916. Lionel Barrymore, Grace Valentine, Marcia West, Robert Cummings, John Davidson, Frank Montgomery. Director, John W. Noble.

The Sunbeam.
Metro-Rolfe. 1916. Mabel Taliaferro, Raymond McKee, Gerald Griffin, David Thompson, Warner Anderson, Lillian Schafner, Dan Bertona. Director, Edwin Carewe.

The End of the Tour.
Metro-Rolfe. 1917. Lionel Barrymore, Ethel Dayton, Walter Hiers, Frank Currier. Director, George D. Baker.

The Millionaire's Double.
Metro-Rolfe. 1917. Lionel Barrymore, Evelyn Brent, Harry Northrup, John Smiley, Jack Raymond, H. H. Patee. Director, Harry Davenport.

The Eternal Mother.
Metro-Rolfe. 1917. Ethel Barrymore, Frank Mills, Maxine Elliott Hicks, J. W. Johnston, Charles W. Sutton. Director, Frank Reicher.

The Avenging Trail.
Metro-Yorke. 1918. Harold Lockwood, Sally Crute, Walter P. Lewis, Joseph Dailey, William Clifford. Director, Francis Ford.

The House of Hate.
Pathé. 1918. Pearl White, Antonio Moreno, Floyd Buckley, Peggy Shanor, John Webb Dillon, Paul Clerget, Joseph H. Gilmour. Director, George B. Seitz. A twenty-episode serial.

Peg O' the Pirates.
Fox. 1918. Peggy Hyland, Carleton May, Sidney Mason, James Davis, Frank Evans, Eric Mayne, Alex Carroll. Director, Oscar A. C. Lund.

A Pair of Cupids.
Metro. 1918. Francis X. Bushman, Beverly Bayne, Charles Sutton, Edgar Norton, Jessie Stevens. Director, Charles J. Brabin.

The Carter Case.
Oliver Films. 1919. Herbert Rawlinson, Marguerite Marsh, Ethel Grey Terry, Kempton Green, William Pike, Gene Baker, Leslie Stowe, Frank Wunderlee, Don Hall. Director, Donald MacKenzie.

The Belle of the Season.
Metro. 1919. Emmy Wehlen, S. Rankin Drew. Director, S. Rankin Drew. (Actually filmed in late 1917, release was withheld for more than a year.)

The Darkest Hour.
Vitagraph. 1919. Harry T. Morey, Jean Paige. Director, Paul Scardon.

A Manhattan Knight.
Fox. 1920. George Walsh, Virginia Hammond, John Hopkins, Warren Cook, William H. Budd, William T. Hayes. Director, George A. Beranger.

Dr. Jekyll and Mr. Hyde.
Famous Players-Lasky. 1920. John Barrymore, Martha Mansfield, Nita Naldi. Director, John S. Robertson.

Number 17.
Fox. 1920. George Walsh, Mildred Reardon, Charles Mussett, Lillian Beck, Harold Thomas, Spencer Charters, Jack Newton. Director, George A. Beranger.

Experience.
Famous Players-Lasky. 1921. Richard Barthelmess, Marjorie Daw, Lilyan Tashman, Nita Naldi, Kate Bruce, John Miltern, Sybil Carmen, E. J. Radcliffe, Leslie King, Edna Wheaton, Robert Schnable. Director, George Fitzmaurice.

Orphans of the Storm.
United Artists. 1921. Lillian Gish, Dorothy Gish, Monte Blue, Joseph Schildkraut, Creighton Hale, Leslie King, Frank Losee, Morgan Wallace, Lucille LaVerne, Sheldon Lewis, Frank Puglia, Kate Bruce, Sidney Herbert. Director, D. W. Griffith.

Determination.
Lee-Bradford Corporation. 1922. Maurice Costello, Corinne Uzzell, Irene Tams, Walter Ringham, Alpheus Lincoln, Bernard Randall, Byron Russell, Nina Herbert. Director, Joseph Levering.

Sherlock Holmes.
Goldwyn. 1922. John Barrymore, Carol Dempster, William Powell, Roland Young, Reginald Denny, Gustav von Seyffertitz, Hedda Hopper, David Torrence, Lumsden Hare, Anders Randolf, Margaret Kemp, Percy Knight, John Willard. Director, Albert Parker.

The Face in the Fog.
Goldwyn. 1922. Lionel Barrymore, Seena Owen, Lowell Sherman, George Nash, Mary MacLaren, Gustav von Seyffertitz, Marie Burke, Joseph Smiley, Martin Faust. Director, Alan Crosland.

Love's Old Sweet Song.
Lund-Norca. 1922. Helen Lowell, Donald Gallaher, Margaret Brown, Helen Weir, Ernest Hilliard. Director, Oscar A. C. Lund.

The Enemies of Women.
Goldwyn. 1923. Lionel Barrymore, Alma Rubens, William Collier, Jr., Pedro DeCordoba, Gladys Hulette, Gareth Hughes, William H. Thompson, Paul Panzer, Ivan Linlow, Betty Bouton. Director, Alan Crosland. Wolheim's scenes were deleted.

The Go-Getter.
Paramount. 1923. T. Roy Barnes, Seena Owen, Frank Currier, Tom Lewis, William Norris, Fred Huntley, Jane Jennings, William J. Sorrelle, John Carr, Dorothy Walters. Director, Edward H. Griffith.

The Last Moment.
Goldwyn. 1923. Henry Hull, Doris Kenyon, Louis Calhern, William Nally, Mickey Bennett, Harry Allen, Donald Hall. Director, J. Parker Read.

Little Old New York.
Goldwyn. 1923. Marion Davies, Harrison Ford, Mahlon Hamilton, Courtenay Foote, Sam Hardy, Charles Judels, J. M. Kerrigan, George Barraud, Stephen Carr, Harry Watson, Spencer Charters, Gypsy O'Brien, Marie Burke. Director, Sidney Olcott.

Unseeing Eyes.
Goldwyn. 1923. Lionel Barrymore, Seena Owen, Walter Miller, Gustav von Seyffertitz, Charles Beyer, Paul Panzer, Frances Red Eagle, Helen Lindroth, Louis Deer. Director, Edward H. Griffith.

The Uninvited Guest.
Metro-Goldwyn. 1924. Maurice 'Lefty" Flynn, Jean Tolley, Mary MacLaren, William N. Bailey. Director, Ralph Ince.

America.
United Artists. 1924. Carol Dempster, Neil Hamilton, Lionel Barrymore, Charles Emmett Mack, Lucille LaVerne, Frank McGlynn, Jr., Arthur Donaldson, Lee

Beggs, Frank Walsh, John Dunton, Sydney Deane, Harry Semels, Riley Hatch. Director, D. W. Griffith.

The Story Without a Name.
Paramount. 1924. Antonio Moreno, Agnes Ayres, Tyrone Power, Sr., Dagmar Godowsky, Maurice Costello, Jack L. Bohn, Ivan Linlow, Frank Currier. Director, Irvin V. Willat.

Lover's Island.
Associated Exhibitors. 1926. Hope Hampton, James Kirkwood, Ivan Linlow, Flora Finch, Jack Raymond, Flora LeBreton. Director, Henri Diamant-Berger.

Two Arabian Knights.
United Artists. 1927. William Boyd, Mary Astor, Michael Vavitch, Ian Keith, Boris Karloff, DeWitt Jennings, Michael Visaroff. Director, Lewis Milestone.

Sorrell and Son.
United Artists. 1927. H. B. Warner, Alice Joyce, Nils Asther, Mary Nolan, Anna Q. Nilsson, Carmel Myers, Norman Trevor, Mickey McBan, Paul McAllister, Lionel Belmore. Director, Herbert Brenon.

Tempest.
United Artists. 1928. John Barrymore, Camilla Horn, George Fawcett, Ullrich Haupt, Boris De Fas, Michael Visaroff, Lena Malena, Albert Conti. Director, Sam Taylor.

The Racket.
Paramount-Caddo. 1928. Thomas Meighan, Marie Prevost, George E. Stone, John Darrow, Lee Moran, Lucien Prival, Sam DeGrasse, G. Pat Collins, James Marcus, Burr McIntosh, Henry Sedley. Director, Lewis Milestone.

The Awakening.
United Artists. 1928. Vilma Banky, Walter Byron, Lola d'Avril, George Davis, William Orlamond, Carl von Hartmann, Virginia Jolley, Anne Warrington, Babe London. Director, Victor Fleming.

The Shady Lady.
Pathé. 1928. Robert Armstrong, Phyllis Haver, Russell Gleason. Director, Edward H. Griffith.

Wolf Song.
Paramount. 1929. Gary Cooper, Lupe Velez, Russ Colombo, Michael Vavitch, Constantine Romanoff, Ann Brody, Augustina Lopez, George Rigas. Director, Victor Fleming.

Square Shoulders.
Pathé. 1929. Junior Coghlan, Anita Louise, Philippe de Lacy, Johnny Morris, Montague Shaw, Kewpie Morgan, Clarence Geldert, Erich von Stroheim, Jr., Charles F. Riesner, Jr. Director, E. Mason Hopper.

Frozen Justice.
Fox. 1929. Lenore Ulric, Robert Frazer, Ullrich Haupt, Alice Lake, Gertrude Astor, Laska Winter, El Brendel, Warren Hymer, Tom Patricola, Charles Judels, Landers Stevens, Adele Windsor, Jack Ackroyd. Director, Allan Dwan.

Condemned.
United Artists. 1929. Ronald Colman, Ann Harding, Dudley Digges, Billy Elmer, Albert Kingsley, William Vaughn. Director, Wesley Ruggles.

The Ship from Shanghai.
Metro-Goldwyn-Mayer. 1930. Conrad Nagel, Kay Johnson, Carmel Myers, Holmes Herbert, Zeffie Tilbury, Ivan Linlow, Jack McDonald. Director, Charles J. Brabin.

All Quiet on the Western Front.
Universal. 1930. Lew Ayres, Slim Summerville, Russell Gleason, John Wray, William Bakewell, Scott Kolk, Raymond Griffith, Beryl Mercer, Harold Goodwin, Yola d'Avril, Ben Alexander, Owen Davis, Jr., Poupee Andriot. Director, Lewis Milestone.

Danger Lights.
RKO Radio. 1930. Jean Arthur, Robert Armstrong, Robert Edeson, Frank Sheridan, James Farley, Alan Roscoe, William B. Burt. Director, George B. Seitz.

The Silver Horde.
RKO Radio. 1930. Evelyn Brent, Jean Arthur, Blanche Sweet, Joel McCrea, Purnell Pratt, Gavin Gordon, Raymond Hatton, Ivan Linlow, William B. Davidson. Director, George Archainbaud.

The Sin Ship.
RKO Radio. 1931. Mary Astor, Ian Keith, Hugh Herbert, Alan Roscoe, Russell Power, Bert Stanley. Director, Louis Wolheim.

Gentleman's Fate.
Metro-Goldwyn-Mayer. 1931. John Gilbert, Leila Hyams, Anita Page, Marie Prevost, John Miljan, George Cooper, Ralph Ince, Frank Reicher, Paul Porcasi. Director, Mervyn LeRoy.

Selected Bibliography

Balshofer, Fred J., and Miller, Arthur C. *One Reel a Week*. Berkeley and Los Angeles, California: University of California Press, 1967.

Blesh, Rudi. *Keaton*. New York: The Macmillan Company, 1966.

Griffith, D. W. *The Man Who Invented Hollywood*. Edited and annotated by James Hart. Louisville, Kentucky: Touchstone Publishing Company, 1972.

Griffith, Linda Arvidson. *When the Movies Were Young*. New York: E. P. Dutton & Company, 1925.

Graham, Sheilah. *The Garden of Allah*. New York: Crown Publishers, Inc., 1970.

Henderson, Robert M. *D. W. Griffith: The Years at Biograph*. New York: Farrar, Straus and Giroux, 1970.

Irwin, Will. *The House That Shadows Built*. Garden City, New York: Doubleday, Doran & Company, Inc., 1928.

Langer, Lawrence. *The Magic Curtain*. New York: E. P. Dutton & Company, 1951.

Macgowan, Kenneth. *Behind the Screen*. New York: Delacorte Press, 1965.

Munden, Kenneth W., executive editor. *The American Film Institute Catalog-Feature Films, 1921–1930*. New York and London: R. R. Bowker Company, 1971.

Niver, Kemp R. *Motion Pictures From the Library of Congress Paper Print Collection, 1894–1912*. Berkeley and Los Angeles, California: University of California Press, 1967.

———. *The First Twenty Years*. Los Angeles: The Locare Group, 1962.

Ramsaye, Terry. *A Million and One Nights*. New York: Simon and Schuster, 1926.

Rosenberg, Bernard, and Silverstein, Harry. *The Real Tinsel*. New York: The Macmillan Company, 1970.

Ross, Lillian. *Picture*. New York: Rinehart and Company, 1952.

Sadoul, Georges. *Les Pionniers du Cinema*. Paris: Les Editions Denoel, 1947.

Sayler, Oliver M. *The Russian Theatre*. Boston: Little, Brown & Company, 1920.

Shulman, Irving. *Valentino*. New York: Trident Press, 1967.

Siegel, Joel E. *Val Lewton: The Reality of Terror*. New York: The Viking Press, 1973.

Spears, Jack. *Hollywood: The Golden Era*. South Brunswick, New Jersey, and New York: A. S. Barnes & Company, 1971.

Spehr, Paul C., and Staff of the Motion Picture Section, Library of Congress. *The Civil War in Motion Pictures*. A bibliography of films produced in the United States since 1897. Washington, D.C.: Library of Congress, 1961.

Wagenknecht, Edward. *The Movies in the Age of Innocence*. Norman, Oklahoma: University of Oklahoma Press, 1962.

Index of Names

Index of Films